Human Resource Management
and Digitalization

T0384159

Edited by
Franca Cantoni - Gianluigi Mangia

Human Resource Management and Digitalization

First published 2019
by Routledge
2 Park Square, Milton Park, Abingdon, Oxon OX14 4RN

and by Routledge
52 Vanderbilt Avenue, New York, NY 10017

First issued in paperback 2020

Routledge is an imprint of the Taylor & Francis Group, an informa business

and by G. Giappichelli Editore
Via Po 21, Torino – Italia

British Library Cataloguing-in-Publication Data
A catalogue record for this book is available from the British Library

Library of Congress Cataloging-in-Publication Data
A catalogue record for this book has been requested

ISBN 13: 978-0-367-58309-5 (pbk)
ISBN 13: 978-1-138-31335-4 (hbk)

Typeset in Simoncini Garamond
by G. Giappichelli Editore, Turin, Italy

The manuscript has been subjected to the double blind peer review process prior to publication.

CONTENTS

Part IV

COMPETENCIES AND ROLES

LIST OF ILLUSTRATIONS

Figures

Tables

FOREWORD

THE HUMAN SIDE OF DIGITALIZATION

The volume addresses the central point of the current debate on the relationship between *innovation 4.0* and *human resource management*. The interesting contributions respond effectively to the question in the title and clearly show the need to build virtuous complementarity between Human Resource Management and Technological Innovation.

At the present stage, both at the theoretical and operational management levels, we are discovering how full exploitation of new technologies is strongly interdependent with *organizational change*, the *quality of work* and *innovation of HR systems*.

In this volume different theoretical approaches are adopted, and a rich anthology of experiences and practices are collected coherently with the increase in complexity in the relationship between digital technologies and people. As the socio-material approach (Cecez-Kecmanovic et al., 2014) suggests, social and technical aspects are nowadays even more deeply intertwined than before, "the social and the material are inherently inseparable" stated Orlikowski and Scott in 2008 (p. 456). This far truer with digital technologies that are investing almost all the aspects of our private and working life.

The content of the book addresses the crucial aspects of the current trends. The introductory general section deepens the organizational implications of Internet of Things and *smart manufacturing*.

It underlines in a very appropriate way the necessity of relaunching the entrepreneurial spirit not only in start-ups and new ventures, but also within existing and well-established companies. Corporate entrepreneurship emerges as a key strategy for disseminating innovation, coupled with appropriate human capital training and development policies. The organizational change requires a radical transformation of HR departments that need to review their basic processes, taking into account how workers will interact with smarter machines.

The innovation of HR models is central to both access to new technologies and to evaluate how they are used and exploited.

The volume deals with the specific practices that must be developed by combining a growing autonomy of people with the growing need for collaboration between them. The empirical evidence presented and discussed shows that it is still unclear if one goes to greater standardization and work routinization rather than to greater autonomy and discretion of people involved. The emerging workplaces demand more and more versatility. On one side, people at work will be requested to have the ability to compile and analyse big data, to be able to effectively communicate what the data means, and to apply it to everyday business decisions. On the other, they will be requested to become proficient in using new collaboration approaches and tools (Colbert, Yee, & George 2016).

The contributions offer specific arguments on learning processes, new roles, new skills and competences required.

It emerges that the relationship between individual learning and organizational learning becomes more complex in the context of innovation 4.0 and this requires a deep transformation of business training. This becomes even more crucial if one considers that the labour market is showing shortages of new skills and competences and that the Italian university system shows significant delays in this regard.

The digital transformation of HR processes can lead to a greater weakness of its role - to the extent that selection, training and control are only based on big data - rather than to develop a new centrality of HR department if people managers take on the risk of giving meaning to such data.

The book is not aimed at providing all the answers, but it has the merit of raising the right questions to the attention of practitioners and scientific community.

The main node to be addressed at the organizational level regards the relationship between individual autonomy and managerial control. In addition, coexistence between young digital native workers and older workers is becoming a challenging issue within organizations, when younger employees are promoted into supervisory positions in which they then manage older subordinates (Kunze & Menges, 2017). A third issue, as far as the quality of work and HR processes are concerned, is the problem of polarization of competencies between high profiles - expected to be strengthened - and low profiles - which will tend to be marginalized – is well depicted. This opens a problem of fairness and requires a serious reflection about the risk of raise of wage inequalities.

On the background remains the unsolved paradox of innovation 4.0: on one side the organizational need to return to shared spaces and time and, on the other side, the increase of digitization and diffusion of smart working that risk to weaken and de-power this trend.

Cecez-Kecmanovic, D., Galliers, R. D., Henfridsson, O., Newell, S., & Vidgen, R. (2014). The sociomateriality of information systems: current status, future directions. *Mis Quarterly*, 38(3), 809-830.
Colbert, A., Yee, N., & George, G. (2016). The digital workforce and the workplace of the future. *Academy of Management Journal*, 59(3), 731-739.

Kunze, F., & Menges, J. I. (2017). Younger supervisors, older subordinates: An organizational-level study of age differences, emotions, and performance. *Journal of Organizational Behavior*, 38(4), 461-486.

Orlikowski, W. J., Scott, S. V. (2008) Sociomateriality: Challenging the Separation of Technology, Work and Organization, *The Academy of Managem*

Sergio Albertini
University of Brescia, Italy

Paolo Gubitta
University of Padova, Italy

Part I
OVERVIEW

Chapter 1

UNLOCKING THE IOT POTENTIAL IN MANUFACTURING: AN ORGANIZATIONAL ANALYSIS AND RESEARCH AGENDA [1]

Cristiano Ghiringhelli-Francesco Virili

SUMMARY: 1.1. Introduction. – 1.2. Background. – 1.3. Exploring the potential of IoT: from data to action, via decisions. – 1.4. Unlocking the potential of IoT: the organizational perspective. – 1.5. A suggested research agenda. – References.

1.1. Introduction

The basic concept underpinning the Internet of Things (IoT) is the possibility of connecting objects to the Internet, typically by means of a small and inexpensive "smart label". The transition from a world of objects to a world of smart objects connected, identified, and monitored in real time paves the way for radical innovations in the field of manufacturing: a development known as Smart Manufacturing (also referred to as Industry 4.0, Factory 4.0, Smart Enterprise, Industrial IoT). Over the past five years, Smart Manufacturing has gained significant momentum in terms of market diffusion, levels of investment, and productivity gains, as reported by a body of analytical studies (McKinsey & Co, 2015; GE & Accenture, 2014; DHL & Cisco, 2015; PWC, 2014).

Market diffusion. For example, one study indicates that the deployment of IoT by businesses has grown by 333% since 2012, reporting that 65% of companies sampled deployed IoT technologies in 2014 (compared to 15% in 2012) (Forrester Research, 2014). A survey of 235 German industrial companies conducted by the market research institution TNS Emnid found that *"while today only one fifth of the industrial companies have digitized their key processes along the value chain, in five years' time, 85% of companies will have implemented Industry 4.0 solutions in all important business divisions"* (PWC, 2014:7)

---

[1] A previous version of this research was presented at ItAIS 2016, the annual conference of the Italian chapter of the Association for Information Systems, Verona, October 7-8, 2016.

Investment levels. Furthermore, investments in Industry 4.0 solutions are forecast to account for over 50% of planned capital investment over the next five years (PWC, 2014). German industry will thus invest a total of €40 billion in Industry 4.0 every year by 2020. Applying the same investment level to the European industrial sector, the annual investments will be as high as €140 billion per annum" (PWC, 2014:7). In Italy, "Industria 4.0 National Plan 2017-2020" – recently promoted by the Italian Government – provides for a wide array of initiatives aimed at promoting investment in innovation and competitiveness according to the Industry 4.0 approach.

Productivity gains. Again, IoT is predicted to generate productivity gains of over 18% over the next five years, with estimated additional revenues averaging between 2% and 3% per annum (PWC, 2014). However, it should be frankly acknowledged that the long-term impact of IoT is currently difficult to estimate. Early ongoing projects show that the potential of IoT for manufacturing may only be unlocked by adopting new, and still largely unexplored, organizational solutions at a range of levels, including new organizational structures, systems, processes, and relationships. Innovative people management and HR development approaches are likely to be key success factors in Smart Manufacturing initiatives, and this generates novel research requirements in the field of organizational studies.

The aim of this chapter is to examine these requirements, contributing to the development of an organizational research agenda. More specifically, we first provide a brief macro overview of IoT innovations, emphasizing the factors underpinning their development as well as currently unresolved problem areas. Second, we outline the potential of IoT to enhance manufacturing via new business models and production paradigms. Third, we discuss the critical challenges associated with implementing IoT models, in terms of the organizational traits, work organization, workforce characteristics, change management, and organizational relationships required for their potential to be fully realised. Finally, we describe promising lines of enquiry and theoretical frameworks for future research programmes, with a view to defining an organizational research agenda with the power to assess emerging opportunities for smart manufacturing and analyse the related organizational issues.

1.2. Background

IoT definition. The IoT has been defined as *"a global infrastructure for the information society, enabling advanced services by interconnecting (physical and virtual) things based on existing and evolving interoperable information and communication technologies (ICT)*" (Recommendation ITU-T Y.2060, 2012:2). A key aspect of IoT is that it adds an "Any THING" dimension of communication to ICT. This expands opportunities for things and systems to be controlled remotely, but more importantly enables direct – thing-thing, human-thing, human-human (non-computer-mediated), thing-computer and computer-computer – interaction while continuing to exploit the existing network infrastructure (fig. 1).

Figure 1. The new dimension introduced in the IoT (Recommendation ITU-T Y.2060, 2012).

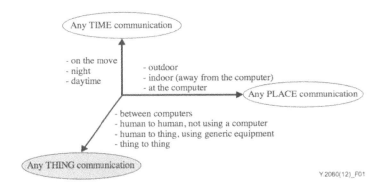

All these forms of interactions are driven by data and, at the same time, also produce data that may be processed by advanced systems (using, for example, algorithms) designed to support (or substitute – (Rifkin, 2014)) sophisticated human decision-making processes. Such "cyber-physical systems" – i.e., engineered systems that are built from, and depend on, the seamless integration of computational algorithms and physical components (National Science Foundation, 2016) – include smart firms, smart homes, and even smart cities, and offer enhanced efficiency, efficacy, accuracy, flexibility and economic benefits.

A macro-economic overview of IoT. It has been observed that the IoT re-configures the communication-energy-logistics circle in such a way that productivity is dramatically increased and marginal costs reduced. Consequently, IoT has the potential to boost a hybrid economy based on both the capitalistic and "Global Collaborative Commons" paradigms (Rifkin, 2014). In particular, Rifkin states that IoT could reconfigure the Communication-Energy-Logistic circle in such a way that the productivity dramatically grows and, at the same time, marginal costs fall down to near zero, in perspective making goods and services priceless, nearly free, and abundant.

Shortly, no longer subject to market forces. The new hybrid economy boosted by IoT is seen by Rifkin as based partially on the rules of the capitalistic paradigm (exchange value, financial capital, ownership, consumerist approach, competition), and partially on the new rules of the Global Collaborative Commons (sharing value, social capital, access, sustainability, cooperation) (Rifkin, 2014).

The recent growth in the IoT, privacy issues and further barriers. Even if the term "IoT" has been introduced in the 1995 by Kevin Ashton, a cofounder of the Massachusetts Institute of Technology Auto-ID Center (that created a global standard system for RFID), the IoT has only expanded significantly in the past five years (Rifkin, 2014; Lee & Lee, 2015). Up to 2010, many barriers hindered the growth of IoT, including the cost of sensors (such as tags and chips), gyroscopes and accelerometers, and the limited address space allowed by the IPv4 Internet protocol. However, as the cost of these components has decreased and the IPv4 Internet protocol has been substituted by IPv6, the IoT has seen major expansion. However, a highly critical aspect of the spread of IoT is privacy (Weber, 2010; Sicari et al., 2015).

Research has examined the complex challenges posed by personal security, technical security, and data protection issues, as well as by the current legal and standardization guidelines, all of which continue to slow down the broader diffusion of IoT (Rifkin, 2014; Lee & Lee, 2015; Weber, 2010; Sicari et al., 2015). Policy makers are now developing a common security framework (see AIOTI, launched by the European Commission in 2015).

Finally, two further aspects are currently working against IoT in manufacturing: first, a growing but still limited awareness, both in Italy and elsewhere (Staufen, 2015); second, a limited understanding of the organizational issues raised by IoT.

With regard the first issue, the awareness and/or knowledge of the IoT approach differs among countries. In a general view, it is higher in the German area (where the Industry 4.0 label has been introduced and developed), high in USA (where the same approach is known as Smart Manufacturing) and very low in Italy, as confirmed by a recent research which found that almost 70% of the Italian companies surveyed haven't started yet initiatives in the Industry 4.0. Only 20% have experienced Industry 4.0 (Staufen, 2015). Not surprisingly, in Italy the departments perceived as most involved are operations and logistics but – more than in Germany – sales are seen as a key application field. Moreover, very high organizational impacts are expected by Italian companies from Industry 4.0: approximately the 70% of companies surveyed expect benefits in areas such as business model, R&D, human resources qualities, improving overall organizational performance (above all quality of service).

In general, these data confirm that, at the moment, in Italy the Industry 4.0 approach is still a relatively new phenomenon, and this may still represent a serious barrier to its diffusion and experimentation. The Italian "Industria 4.0 National Plan" paves the way towards a wider adoption of the Industry 4.0 model by the Italian companies supporting the digitalization of industrial processes, the improvement in workers' productivity, as well as the development of new skills, new products and new processes (Minister of Economic Development, 2007).

1.3. Exploring the potential of IoT: from data to action, via decisions

IoT technologies help to develop "agile decision-making processes" for descriptive, diagnostic, prescriptive and predictive purposes at three different levels: 1) at the operational level, with a view to running and managing formal procedures; 2) at the continuous improvement level, in terms of designing formal procedures to enhance efficiency, productivity, flexibility, and adaptation; 3) at the organizational development level, with the aim of fostering organizational learning and the development of new business models and markets. The case of DHL provides one of the clearest available examples of these diverse functions of IoT.

An illustrative case study. In Europe as well as in the United States, logistics has been one of the first industries to start experiments on IoT for operations. In this field, the experience of DHL represents a very well-defined case study showing how the organizational structure, systems and processes have to be redesigned in order to unlock the potential embedded in the IoT technologies. DHL has conducted wide-scale experimentation in applying the IoT to its logistics operations. As result, DHL's most sophisticated operating sites currently apply IoT systems in all three main areas of the logistics value chain: Warehousing, Freight Transportation, and Last-Mile Delivery Operations (DHL & Cisco, 2015). This allows to appreciate, in particular, the cycle descriptive-diagnostic-prescriptive-predictive organizational decision-making process above introduced.

DHL Warehousing Operations and IoT: operation automation and optimization. With regard to Warehousing Operations, DHL has developed an IoT-enabled smart-inventory management system based on pallet or item-level tagging. This involves the use of devices such as RFID, wireless readers that receive, aggregate and send data (gathered from each pallet as it arrives through inbound gateways) to the WMS for processing, as well as cameras attached to warehouse gateways that can also be used for damage detection (by scanning pallets for imperfections). Each movement of a pallet generates a tag transmission report that is sent to the WMS and, in the case of misplacement or compromised temperature / humidity conditions, an automatic alert enables the warehouse manager to take corrective action. During the outbound delivery phase, pallets are scanned as they pass through an outbound gateway to ensure that the correct items are being shipped (in the optimal order of delivery), and stock levels are automatically updated in the WMS. In addition, warehouse vehicles (forklifts) and equipment are connected, with a view to preventing collisions among them or with warehouse staff (in the next section, we discuss the organizational effects of the "augmented workforce"), monitoring their movements, position and operating conditions, and predicting maintenance needs.

Freight Transportation Operations and IoT: better tracking, SC risk management, capacity optimization and predictive maintenance. The opportunity to tag individual goods and items (not just the whole container) opens up new possibilities for Freight Transportation Operations also. Connected sensors on board trucks, and multi-sensor tags on individual goods, transmit data concerning items' location/condition, generating an alert if a package is opened (possible theft). By tagging each good, logistics providers not only maintain real-time and highly precise (metre by metre, second by second) visibility of the movement and condition of goods at the item level, guaranteeing a higher level of transport visibility and security (and reducing theft and acting against the organized crime that affects ports and rest areas). Moreover, IoT data integration is of value in handling natural disasters, conflict, economic uncertainty, and market volatility. For example, referring to the DHL Resilience360 project for supply chain risk management, DHL declares that "in the future, Resilience360 could integrate all the data transmitted from assets and respond when a truck carrying urgent cargo is about to break down or when a warehouse has been flooded from a storm. It could also move a shipment from air freight to road freight to compensate for an airline strike" (DHL & Cisco, 2015:21). Sensors can monitor how often a truck, container or ULD is in use or idle and transmit this data to a central dashboard for optimal utilization analysis designed to identify spare capacity along fixed routes and solutions for consolidating and optimizing routes. Finally, an electronically-connected fleet can also enable predictive asset lifecycle management (see MoDe project): this involves the transmission of data (via a wireless network) from a maintenance platform to a central unit in the truck, and then back to the maintenance platform for analysis. This means that the driver and/or maintenance crew may be alerted of potential problems in advance.

Last-Mile Delivery operations and IoT: optimization of daily collection routes, enhanced tracking, temperature sensing and return trip optimization. DHL has made major changes to its Last-Mile Delivery operations thanks to IoT technologies. These are the operations that take place during the final leg of the delivery journey, which is strongly labour dependent and characterized by high consumer expectations. In light of these features, IoT technologies can enable the logistics provider to develop a cost-effective solution. For example, DHL delivery operators can optimize their daily collection routes by skipping empty mailboxes (thanks to sensors placed in individual boxes). In the interest of offering a flexible delivery address service, tagged parcels provide recipients with more detailed information about when their parcel is expected to arrive, giving them the opportunity to specify the delivery address at the last minute. In addition (although currently only in Germany), temperature-controlled smart lockers can replace traditional mailboxes and ensure "first-time every-time" delivery of parcels, groceries, and other environmentally sensitive goods. A similar scenario will apply to "smart home" products, which consumers are beginning to adopt. Finally, DHL is testing new business models for monetizing and optimizing the return trip, possibly by using IoT to connect delivery staff with surrounding vehicles and individuals.

The case reported gives a clear example of how the development of an organizational capability, in terms of flexibility and responsiveness in decision-making, actual as well as predictive, is a key point introduced by IoT.

While the first two levels (Warehousing Operations and Freight Transportation Operations) mostly refer to intra-organizational decision-making processes, the third level (Last-Mile Delivery operations) is mainly focused on inter-organizational relationships and new business model development.

IoT potential: improved productivity and quality, new production systems, value chain management, and new business models. As outlined above, the IoT approach enables agile decision-making processes by sustaining: operational tasks (in the case of DHL: the optimization of fleet and asset management; the real-time updating of inventory level data; and the real-time monitoring of a shipment's location-condition-security); continuous improvement (in the case of DHL: the elimination of time-consuming manual activities; optimized inventory and asset management, preventing costly out-of-stock scenarios; optimized energy consumption); and organizational development (in the case of DHL: temperature-controlled smart lockers enabled by e-commerce and developments in the smart home sector). From a broader perspective, such agile decision-making processes can potentially produce substantial added value for organizations at multiple levels.

Improved productivity and quality. The marked improvements in productivity and quality discussed in the DHL case study are just an illustration of a wide range of potential IoT-based innovations that may be implemented at any point along the value chain. In product development, for example, IoT technologies can help to achieve low-cost variability, evergreen design, new user interfaces and augmented reality, ongoing quality management, connected service, and system interoperability. In marketing and sales, they can support new ways of segmenting and customizing, and new customer relationships. In terms of after-sale service, they can enable the provision of remote service, preventive service and augmented-reality-supported service, and the gathering of valuable data from product users (Porter & Heppelmann, 2015).

New production paradigms. IoT innovation in production gives rise to five main developments (Porter & Heppelmann, 2015). The first of these is the smart factory concept. A smart factory is a flexible network of cyber-physical systems that automatically supervise production processes and adapt their own functioning in real-time, in response to operating conditions. The connectivity and data-processing capacity of networked machines allow production processes to be radically optimized, minimizing downtime, costs and waste, and maximizing productivity, efficiency and security. The second outcome is simplified components: "the physical complexity of products often diminishes as functionality moves from mechanical parts to software" (Porter & Heppelmann, 2015:104). In the automotive industry, for example, the Volkswagen Group is moving towards the introduction of the virtual cockpit, in which car data may be viewed on a high-tech display. The third development concerns reconfigured assembly processes: the use of standardized platforms secures economies of scale and lowers inventory. The fourth benefit is continuous product operations: smart and connected products include a cloud-based technology stack, which is a component that the manufacturer can improve throughout the life cycle of the product. Finally, a fifth spin-off of IoT technologies may be labelled "the new lean" (Porter & Heppelmann, 2015; Staufen, 2015): potentially, the data transmitted by connected products can facilitate the rationalization of product use and activities across the value chain, by reducing or eliminating waste, pre-empting the need for service prior to a failure, revealing that maintenance may be deferred, and reducing downtime.

Significant changes in the value chain management. New data resources and new opportunities for Data Analytics introduced by IoT technologies allow for a wide range of opportunities capable of generating significant changes in the whole value chain. In the product development area, for example, in terms of low cost variability, evergreen design, new user interfaces and augmented reality, ongoing quality management, connected services, systems interoperability. In the marketing and sales area in terms of new ways to segment and customize, new customer relationships, new business models focused on systems (instead of discrete products). In the after-sale field, in terms of remote service, preventive service and augmented reality supported service and collection of data from users.

New business models. IoT innovation can prompt the adoption of radically new business models and frameworks (Dijkman et al., 2015). For example, according to one report (McKinsey & Co, 2015), it appears that four new types of business model are emerging in the field of manufacturing: a) platforms (on which products, services, and information may be exchanged via predefined communication streams), b) "as-a-service" business models (in which technology and automation providers move from selling machinery to a pay-by-usage model), c) Industrial Property Rights-based business models (introducing modes of recurring revenue generation in addition to – or instead of – a one-off asset sale) and d) data-driven business models (that introduce new ways of collecting and using data either for direct monetization – such as Google's search engine, or the crowdsourcing of data whereby companies obtain services, ideas, or content via the contributions of a large group of people or online community – or for indirect monetization – using the insights obtained via IoT technologies to identify and target specific customer needs and characteristics).

1.4. Unlocking the potential of IoT: the organizational perspective

Inside the corporation: organizational systems, processes and structure. We believe that, in the IoT approach, a key source of competitive advantage is the organization's ability to fully exploit the potential value of the data generated during its operations. This requires conducting effective data analysis and using it to inform the decision-making processes governing organizational action and the management of uncertainty (Simon, 1957; Thompson, 1967). Data gathered, produced and shared by the machines, components, devices and products involved in organizational operations are only potentially useful. They remain meaningless if they are not appropriately selected, understood and processed. In other words, IoT technologies introduce the potential to enhance both current and predictive decision-making processes (Bosch IoT Lab White Paper, 2014), but this opportunity will only be realized if the company develops the specific organizational capability to use it to drive and regulate its operations. The experience of

IoT pioneers proves that the greatest challenges associated with the IoT approach are, first and foremost, organizational.

Systems and processes. The radical enhancing of production systems described above may only be attained if organizational decision-making processes are appropriately redesigned and well integrated with internal operations. In the case of DHL, for example, Warehousing, Freight Transportation and Last-Mile Operation – which comprise the entire life-cycle of the company's delivery service – have been closely integrated with one another: hence, the sharing of data among the three functions allows mutual regulation to take place. In other words, IoT requires a holistic enterprise management approach that breaks down traditional modes of organization and organizational silos. In manufacturing, the need for a global approach is particularly strong: here, for example, the IoT paradigm demands full integration among production systems and Enterprise Resource Planning (ERP) systems, Product Data Management (PDM) Systems, Product Lifecycle Management (PLM) systems, Supply Chain Management and Customer Relationship Management (CRM) systems. According to some analyses, the integration of systems that are usually managed independently of one another can facilitate gains in efficiency of up to 26% (McKinsey & Co, 2015).

Organizational Structures. Nonetheless, this type of integration does not require replacing current systems with totally new systems. Rather, it implies redesigning organizational structure and operating systems in line with the holistic management perspective invoked above. The Candy corporation provides an interesting case study in the implementation of this crucial approach. Candy is known for its SimplyFi program, a wide range of smart home appliances that can communicate with the user via Internet (http://candysimplyfi.com). However, more saliently to our purposes in this paper, Candy has recently also changed its internal structure, introducing a new functional unit (labelled "Connect Unit") with the task of coordinating the entire IoT program. This unit collates and analyses marketing, IT, and Customer Relationship Management issues with a view to strengthening and coordinating R&D IoT programs. Similarly, the Bosch Group has created a specific unit (named "Bosch Software Innovations") charged with developing services for smart products by involving both internal product-based business units and customers (Bosch IoT Lab White Paper, 2014). More generally, it seems that at least three new types of organizational unit are emerging. First, Unified Data Organization Units. Porter observes that many companies are creating dedicated data groups with the function of consolidating data collection, aggregation and analytics. Such groups are responsible for making data and related insights available across functions and business units, and typically they are led by a C-level executive (the Chief Data Officer – CDO) who reports to the CEO (sometimes to the CFO or CIO). Ford Motor Company provides an example: it recently appointed a chief data and analytics officer to develop and implement an enterprise-wide data analysis strategy. Second, DEV-OPS Units, whose role is to manage and optimize the ongoing performance of connected products after they have left the factory. This type of unit brings together software-engineering experts from the traditional product-development organization (the "dev") with staff members from IT, manufacturing, and service who are responsible for product operation (the "ops"). Third, Customer Success Management Units are responsible for managing customer experience and ensuring that customers get the most from the product.

In conclusion, giving that each smart product can tell companies a lot about the customer experience, the product itself becomes a sensor that gauges the value customers are receiving. Importantly, Porter specifies that this new unit does not necessarily replace sales or service units, but assumes primary responsibility for customer relationships after the sale: consequently, it does not operate as a self-contained silo, but collaborates on an ongoing basis with marketing, sales, and service.

Inside the corporation: HR and people management. – New work organization. In an IoT-enabled work environment, it is likely that most of the people in an organization will use non-traditional interfaces to interact with networks of things in advanced ways. In the DHL case study, for example, significant changes have taken place in the role and the activities of logistics staff: the workers' actions are embedded in the IoT system, with warehouse staff connected to the Internet of things via scanners, smart devices and wearables that receive and send data in real-time. Similarly, Caterpillar have developed a suite of tools including cameras for human-operated vehicles, which monitor driver fatigue by tracking key indicators such as pupil size and blink frequency. Wearables, in particular, are likely to became the main way of interacting during operations: the smart glasses, for example, introduce the opportunity of interacting in a natural way within a work environment built on data-driven and collaborative workflows, meaningful integration of data and tools and hands/eyes-free interactions.

Roles, competence and skills and the augmented employee concept. As work organization and environment are transformed by the drivers described above, roles, competencies and skills will be required to change dramatically. In terms of competencies, for example, companies need to differentially adapt the capabilities and skills base of their employees across a wide range of functions. At the shop-floor staff level, basic process and IT systems know-how are required to ensure the connection between the digital and physical sides of the operation. At a more general level, in-depth overall understanding of corporate processes, systems, and data is prerequisite to developing new business models and operational improvements based on cross-functional information. Furthermore, companies need data and process experts who can operate at the interfaces between functions and systems and are able to work in close synergy with subject-specific experts, such as shop-floor managers, customer relationship managers, and supply chain managers. When developing new data-driven business models, such data experts are required to play a key coordinating role in new product design, given their broad overall knowledge of the production chain.

In short, as processes and business models become more agile and data-based, employees will require completely new skills and qualifications. At the moment, we know little about exactly what competences will be needed. Companies that have pioneered IoT technologies in manufacturing say less on this crucial issue than on other topics for which key insights have already emerged. Nonetheless, in line with our analysis so far, it is reasonable to posit that an effective IoT work environment will have three main traits: specifically, it is data-driven, exploits collaborative workflows and is based on hands/eyes-free interaction. These characteristics will likely lead to the development of the "augmented employee". This expression relies on a new employee profile that we need to explore and understand. "Today's products are designed so they can be assembled quickly by unskilled workers. 3D printing will introduce much more design freedom, allowing manufacturers to reduce their reliance on unskilled labour and also to create unique designs that could not be executed with traditional manufacturing", ABB Venture Capitals Managing Director Girish Nadkarni says (Deloitte, 2014:8). The role of humans will mainly concern data treatment and analysis, supervision and advanced decision-making. This will require a small number of highly skilled people focused on innovation and improvement; more generally, it will alter the workforce configuration required by the organization.

HR management innovations. From another perspective, the changes in the work environment and workforce profile just outlined, may only be obtained by transforming HR management accordingly. Bringing an IoT approach to bear on the HR function will include enhancing the performance management process and related compensation model, as well as agile working schemes, by drawing on data from IoT systems, while job design may take into account real workloads as measured via IoT data collection. In addition, HR Analytics solutions may be appropriately integrated with

IoT systems. Recruitment and Training & Development initiatives will need to take into account the new skills required by workers. Skills shortages will emerge in new areas (for example, in the availability of managers capable of leveraging Big Data analyses to make good decisions), and a new cultural mindset will be required to support collaborative data-driven work environments, enhanced leadership styles, agile working approaches, and virtual team collaboration. Nonetheless, the crucial issue at this point in time is that a Human Resources approach to the design and implementation of IoT systems has currently yet to be defined.

Outside the corporation: inter-organizational relationships and value networks. – New inter-organizational relationships. IoT introduces the opportunity to share and integrate data, not only within individual companies, but also across different organizations (Reaidy et al, 2015). This has key implications for both traditional and new business models. Closer integration among the companies in the value chain can generate a wide range of benefits, such as enhanced organizational flexibility, greater customer satisfaction, faster times to market, a more efficient division of labour, and higher rates of innovation and speed. The great complexity of the current competitive scenario and the intense innovation efforts that it demands justify the need for cooperation schemes among groups of companies with complementary know-how. In the automotive industry, for example, manufacturers have begun developing interdisciplinary partnerships with suppliers from other industries (such as component manufacturers, chemical companies and, recently, companies such as Apple and Google). In short, IoT technologies, by sustaining horizontal integration and the creation of value-added networks across the value chain, introduce opportunities not only to develop new business models, but also to enhance and/or upgrade traditional business models.

The role of SMEs. A further key development enabled by IoT technologies in terms of new inter-organizational relationships and business models is the opening created for SMEs to play a significant role in the newly emerging business scenario. Arguably, SMEs will enjoy increased opportunity to introduce their businesses into supply chains by leveraging IoT systems. On joining forces with larger value chains, they will no longer be mere suppliers within Smart Manufacturing scenarios, but will become stable partners in Open Innovation streams (Gershenhorn, 2016). SMEs have long been engaging with this challenge, but now have the opportunity to reinforce and accelerate the process of change (Faller & Feldmüller, 2015).

Organizational change management concerns. The IoT approach requires organizational change initiatives aimed at introducing a holistic enterprise management approach that can not only accomplish the integration of all internal processes, but also develop new relationships with external partners across the value chain. One of the most crucial challenges for organizational change management is the need to integrate staff with different work styles from highly diverse backgrounds and cultures (Porter & Heppelmann, 2015). A further challenge is the increase in complexity caused by the need to significantly revisit organizational structure, policies and norms. Finally, IoT will not only demand reconfiguration of the organization at the formal level, but also the appropriate culture, motivation, and level of engagement. These dimensions are a fundamental leverage in a work environment founded on advanced activity such as sense-making, interpretation, decision-making, flexibility and continuous improvement. Finally, seeing the lack of experience and competencies, traditional and new structures likely need to operate in parallel, and temporary solutions like hybrid or transitional structures will be required (Porter & Heppelmann, 2015).

1.5. A suggested research agenda

We have discussed some key IoT organizational challenges, including structures and systems, work organization, workforce qualities and change management strategies within Smart Manufacturing. The manufacturing sector is entering a new developmental stage with huge potential. However, this potential may only be fully harnessed by making significant changes at multiple levels of the organization in ways that are still largely unexplored. Thus, here below, we summarize the key areas of research and detailed research topics touched on in our analysis, also suggesting possible theoretical frameworks and a sample of bibliographical references.

The four promising research areas suggested here are spanning different disciplines: the IoT system area is related to the technical, computer science and engineering challenges of IoT development and evolution. The following three research areas are managerial and organizational, at different levels of analysis: interorganizational (area 2, organizational ecosystems) and intraorganizational with a focus on people and behaviours (area 4: HR and people management) or on organization redesign (area 3: structure, systems and processes).

Research area 1: Enabling technologies. In the ICT area, significant research challenges are emerging with the emergence and continuous evolution of the IoT system. An early systematic account is given in (Miorandi et al., 2012).

The research taxonomy proposed by the authors is based on the simple idea that in a smart objects world, 1) anything communicates; 2) anything is identified; 3) anything interacts. Each of these three basic aspects is related with a complex area of technical innovation and research, as depicted in the figure below.

Figure 2. Taxonomy of ICT research areas relevant to Internet-of-Things (Miorandi et al., 2012).

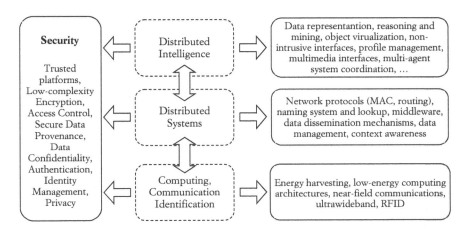

Anything communicates generates new needs in the research area depicted in the lower part of the picture, "Computing, Communication and Identification" technologies and their typical challenges related to the small size and low consumption needs of smart devices.

Anything is identified calls for research in the area of distributed network systems (middle part of the picture), with specific issues related to the enormous number of distinct but similar micro-devices actively operating in IoT networks.

Anything interacts raises even more advanced research challenges in the area of distributed intelligence (upper part of the picture), including new interfaces, new big data collection and analysis methods, new multi-agent coordination systems, and related issues with interesting intersection with the Artificial Intelligence research world, particularly in the areas of augmented and virtual work operators.

Security, depicted in the left part of the picture, cross-cuts and integrates the three ICT research areas illustrated above and urges for much needed and relevant research. The IoT system poses unprecedented security challenges: an enormous number of objects would produce detailed and potentially open confidential information. The controlled availability, monitoring and actual use of IoT data requires innovations in identification, confidentiality, authentication, and privacy technologies, standards and platforms that are urgently calling for new efforts in research and practice.

Research area 2: Organizational ecosystems. IoT innovations have a high potential of transformation or organizational relationships. We suggest here three major investigation areas, reflecting some of most important open issues in the business arena. Organizational and IS scholars may help to understand and shape IoT innovations at the interorganizational level by leveraging important conceptual tools: business models, value chain, and SME innovation network analyses.

The business model research area has developed a significant amount of conceptual analyses and frameworks, with an important impact in the business arena, particularly in the area of BM generation frameworks and tools, with international best sellers like (Osterwalder and Pigneur, 2013). It has been authoritatively recognized that BM transformation can originate organizational innovation at any level, raising complex issues (Chesbrough, 2010). The already rich organizational research agenda in the BM area (Zott et al., 2011), would therefore hopefully include future opportunities and challenges connected with IoT-enabled business models, like for example new services in the advanced logistics industry, illustrated earlier in this chapter.

The value chain transformation is a relevant instance of the wider phenomenon of IT-enabled interorganizational relationships. In their introduction to the special issue of Organization Science "Organizing for innovation in a digitized world" Yoo et al. (2012) show how distributed and combinatorial innovations are happening and diffusing through digital platforms. The IoT-enabled service innovations exemplified in this chapter typically show such characteristics. Value chains are classical loci of this type of digital innovation, which cannot be confined within a single organization. Organizational boundaries (re)definition is therefore a major area of analysis in this regard (Santos, and Eisenhardt, 2005), with specific applications and challenges in the vertical value chains (Jacobides, and Billinger 2006) an in the so called "netchains" (Lazzarini et al. 2001) integrating vertical supply chains and horizontal networks.

The role of SMEs in an IoT world could capture research attention for reasons indirectly related to the organizational boundaries redefinition. In an IoT world, more than in the past, business and process knowledge cannot be concentrated in a few large organizations, but tend to distribute among several actors including SMEs, according to a tendency already in act, discussed for example in (Chesbrough, 2006). Therefore, besides a growing importance of SMEs in open innovation models (Lee et al. 2010), we can envision new opportunities for SMEs in IoT systems, deserving a special place in our research agenda.

Research area 3: Organizational structure, systems, and processes redesign and change. Also core organizational design research areas would be affected by the emerging IoT revolution. The analysis above has shown how IoT-enabled organizations may have new functional units, new positions, and new management processes with a special attention to agility and to decentralized and real-time decision-making (see for example (Winby and Worley, 2014). Such complex changes would need not only a new attention to organizational redesign frameworks, practices and tools, but also a challenging and unprecedented need to face organizational change processes with hybrid sources of uncertainty and resistance to change, connected not only to the human factor, but also to complex connected behaviors of smart devices, components and machines. Managerial decision processes integrated and powered by big data analysis may be a key area of competitive pressure for successful IoT implementation, both within the organization (George et al., 2014), and along the whole supply chain (Sanders 2016). Well known change management and innovation management approaches like organizational ambidexterity (O'Reilly III and Tushman 2013) or dynamic capabilities (Teece and Pisano, 1994) may need a special rethinking in this context. A basic approach for investigation would be exploring such new phenomena with well known theoretical lens or empirical approaches, like for example recent studies on supply chain agility (e.g. Blome et al., 2013; DeGroote and Marx, 2013). Even more ambitious and exciting would be to draw on IoT world exploration new cues and original explanations for better understanding or even redefining our classical concepts. We could for example rethink and extend our original idea of organizational ambidexterity on the basis of IoT-enabled organizational change explorations.

Research area 4: HR and People management. Ironically (but not surprisingly), the advent of smart objects may more deeply affect humans than technical systems. An IoT-enabled organization of work may require profound transformations, including innovative job design, new personal competences and skills, transformed work relationships and therefore a deep rethinking of HRM policies and practices, including recruitment and selection, training and development, performance management, reward, career paths, etc. At a first level, typical studies on work design (e.g. Humphrey, 2007; Parker, 2014) and job characteristics (e.g. Hackman and Oldham, 2005) might be applied and revisited in smart factories and IoT-enabled organizations. At a second level, research in the world of HRM practices would certainly welcome analyses and interpretations of the radical transformation potentially associated with smart production systems. Besides case studies and qualitative explorations, surveys and empirical analyses may help to uncover the many unknown facets of the forthcoming IoT work organizations. An exemplary research piece in a different area might be the recent study of the mediating role of innovation in the relationship between HRM practices and organizational performance (Chowhan, 2016). A further dimension calling for research is the advent and growing importance of analytics and big data analysis in an IoT context, as discussed above in this chapter. The advent of analytics in HR has been recently studied only with regard to specific systems similar to specialized balanced scorecards (HR analytics: see e.g. Aral et al., 2012; Douthit and Mondore, 2014; Fink, 2010). The application of big data analytics to IoT-enabled work processes, monitored, controlled and adjusted in real time, is still an emerging topic with a high potential of implications and research in the immediate future.

Area	Key Research Topics	Disciplines/Theoretical Frameworks and Sample References
1- The IoT System: enabling technologies	• Security (low-complexity encryption, access control, secure data provenance, data confidentiality, identity management, privacy …) • Distributed intelligence (complex data handling, visualization, interfaces, multi-agent systems …) • Distributed systems (network protocols, naming systems, middleware, data dissemination, context awareness …) • Computing, Communication, Identification (low energy computing, energy harvesting, near-field communication, ultra-wide band, RFID, …)	Computer Science, Information Science, Systems Engineering IoT research (Miorandi et al, 2012)
2- Organizational Ecosystems	• New business models (BM); transformation of traditional business models • Transformation of the value chain (vertical and horizontal) • The role of SMEs in the enhanced value chain and new business models	• Business Model research issues (Zott et al, 2011); BM generation frameworks (Osterwalder & Pigneur, 2013); BM Innovation (Chesbrough, 2010). • Interorganizational relationships; organizational networks; theory of the firm, IT-enabled organizational relationships (Yoo et al, 2012); dynamic firm boundaries in value chains (Jacobides & Billinger, 2006; Santos & Eisenhardt, 2005); netchains (Lazzarini et al., 2001) • Organizational research on SMEs; SMEs, innovation and organizational choices (Lee et al., 2010; Teece & Pisano, 1994; Chesbrough, 2006)
3- Organizational Structure, Systems and Processes	• Organizational structure changes (e.g., new functional units, impacts on traditional functional units, new C-Level roles, etc.) • Redesign and integration of internal processes (special focus on decision-making) • New approaches to integrating organizational systems • New lean management opportunities • 3D prints, wearables, smart devices/machines/components: roles and organizational impacts • Effective change management approaches	• Dynamic Capabilities and operations (Blome et al, 2013) • Impact of ICT on supply chain agility and firm performance (DeGroote & Marx, 2013; Sanders, 2016) • Transformation of management processes (Winby & Worley, 2014; George et al, 2014) • Ambidexterity approach (O'Reilly III & Tushman, 2013)

4- HR and People Management	• Work organization transformation and related effects on
	  * job design choices
	  * transformation of roles (new roles emerging, traditional roles modified/obsolete)
	  * competencies, capabilities and skills maps (for each organizational role)
	  * skill shortage issues and consequences in terms of recruitment and T&D initiatives
	  * main HR policies and practices (performance management, reward, career paths, etc.)
	• The "augmented worker" profile, traits and HR management
	• Links between IoT and HR Analytics approaches
		• Effects of innovation on the strategy/HRM relationship (Chowhan, 2016)
		• Job design framework and choices (Humphrey et al, 2007; Hackman & Oldham, 2005; Parker, 2014)
		• Business, human resource analytics, and information technology (Aral et al, 2012; Douthit & Mondore, 2014; Fink, 2010)

References

Aral, S., Bryjolfsson, E., Wu, L. (2012). Three-way complementarities: performance pay, human resource analytics, and information technology. *Management Science*, 58 (5), 913-931.

Blome, C., Schoenherr, T., and Rexhausen, D. (2013). Antecedents and enablers of supply chain agility and its effect on performance: a dynamic capabilities perspective. *International Journal of Production Research*, 51, 1295-1318.

Bosch IoT Lab White Paper (2014). Business Models and the Internet of Things (www.iot-lab.ch).

Chesbrough, H. (2010). Business model innovation: opportunities and barriers. *Long Range Planning*, 43(2), 354-363.

Chesbrough, H. (2006). Open Business Models: How to Thrive in the New Innovation Landscape, Harvard Business Press, Boston, MA.

Chowhan, J. (2016). Unpacking the black box: understanding the relationship between strategy, HRM practices, innovation and organizational performance. *Human Resource Management Journal* 26, 112-133.

DeGroote, S.E., and Marx, T.G. (2013). The impact of IT on supply chain agility and firm performance: An empirical investigation. *International Journal of Information Management* 33, 909-916.

Deloitte, (2014). Industry 4.0. Challenges and solutions for the digital transformation and use of exponential technologies.

DHL & Cisco (2015). IoT in Logistics. A collaborative report by DHL and Cisco on implications and use cases for the logistics industry (http://www.dpdhl.com)

Dijkman, R.M., Sprenkels, B., Peeters, T., Janssen, A., (2015). Business models for the Internet of Things. *International Journal of Information Management*, 35, 672-678.

Douthit, S., Mondore, S. (2014). Creating a business-focused HR function with analytics and integrated talent management. *People and Strategy*, 36 (4), 16-21.

Faller, C., Feldmüller, D. (2015). Industry 4.0 Learning Factory for regional SMEs, *Procedia CIRP*, 32, 88-91.

Fink, A. (2010). New trends in human capital research and analytics. *People and Strategy*, 33 (2), 15-21.

Forrester Research (2014). Internet-Of-Things Solution Deployment Gains Momentum Among Firms Globally.

GE and Accenture (2014). Industrial Internet Insights report for 2015.

George, G., Haas, M., Pentland, A. (2014). Big data and management. *Academy of Management Journal*, 57 (2), 321–326.

Gershenhorn, A., 2016, Entrepreneurs without Borders, UPS Inc. (www.ups.com)

Hackman, J.R., Oldham, G.R. (2005). How job characteristics theory happened. The Oxford Handbook of Management Theory: The process of Theory Development, 151-170.

Humphrey, S.E., Nahrgang, J.D., Morgeson, F.P. (2007). Integrating motivational, social, and contextual work design features: A meta-analytic summary and theoretical extension of the work design literature. *Journal of Applied Psychology*, 92(5), 1332.

Jacobides, M.G., Billinger, S. (2006). Designing the boundaries of the firm: From "make, buy, or ally" to the dynamic benefits of vertical architecture. *Organization Science*, 17(2), 249-261.

Lazzarini, S., Chaddad, F., & Cook, M. (2001). Integrating supply chain and network analyses: the study of netchains. *Journal on Chain and Network Science*, 1(1), 7-22.

Lee, I., Lee, K. (2015). The Internet of Things (IoT): Applications, investments, and challenges for enterprises. *Business Horizons*, 58, 431-440.

Lee, S., Park, G., Yoon, B., & Park, J. (2010). Open innovation in SMEs – An intermediated network model. *Research Policy*, 39(2), 290-300.

McKinsey & Co (2015). Industry 4.0. How to navigate digitization of the manufacturing sector, McKinsey Digital.

Minister of Economic Development, 2007. INDUSTRIA 4.0" ITALY'S NATIONAL PLAN FOR INDUSTRY, http://www.sviluppoeconomico.gov.it/images/stories/documenti/INDUSTRIA-40-NATIONAL%20PLAN_EN-def.pdf.

Miorandi, D., Sicari, S., De Pellegrini, F., & Chlamtac, I. (2012). IoT: Vision, applications and research challenges. *Ad Hoc Networks*, 10, (7), 1497-1516.

National Science Foundation (2016). Cyber-Physical Systems (CPS), https://www.nsf.gov.

O'Reilly III, C.A., and Tushman, M.L. (2013). Organizational Ambidexterity: Past, Present, and Future. Academy of Management Perspectives *27*, 324-338.

Osterwalder, A., & Pigneur, Y. (2013). Business model generation: a handbook for visionaries, game changers, and challengers. John Wiley & Sons.

Parker, S.K. (2014). Beyond Motivation: Job and Work Design for Development, Health, Ambidexterity, and More. *Annual Review of Psychology* 65 (1), 661-691.

Porter, M.E, Heppelmann, J.E. (2015). How Smart, Connected Products Are Transforming Companies. *Harvard Business Review*, October, 96-114.

PWC – PricewaterhouseCoopers (2014). Industry 4.0 – Opportunities and Challenges of the Industrial Internet.

Reaidy, P.J., Gunasekaran, A., Spalanzani, A. (2015). Bottom-up approach based on Internet of Things for order fulfillment in a collaborative warehousing environment. *Int. J. Production Economics*, 159, 29-40.

Recommendation ITU-T Y.2060 (2012) (http://www.itu.int).

Rifkin, J. (2014), The Zero Marginal Cost Society: The IoT, the Collaborative Commons, and the Eclipse of Capitalism, Palgrave Macmillan, NY.

Sanders, N.R. (2016). How to Use Big Data to Drive Your Supply Chain. *California Management Review 58*, 26-48

Santos, F.M., & Eisenhardt, K. M. (2005). Organizational boundaries and theories of organization. *Organization Science*, 16(5), 491-508

Sicari, S., Rizzardi, A., Grieco, L., Coen-Porisini, A. (2015). Security, privacy and trust in Internet of Things: The road ahead, *Computer Networks*, 76, 146-164.

Simon, H.A. (1957). Administrative Behavior, Macmillan, New York.

Staufen (2015). Industria 4.0. Sulla strada della fabbrica del futuro. Qual è la situazione dell'Italia?

Teece, D., & Pisano, G. (1994). The dynamic capabilities of firms: an introduction. *Industrial and Corporate Change, 3*(3), 537-556.

Thompson, J. (1967). Organizations in Action, McGraw-Hill, New York.

Weber, R.H. (2010). Internet of Things. New security and privacy challenges. *Computer Law & Security Review*, 26 (1), 23-30.

Winby, S., and Worley, C.G. (2014). Management processes for agility, speed, and innovation. Organizational Dynamics *43*, 225-234.

Yoo, Y., Boland Jr, R. J., Lyytinen, K., & Majchrzak, A. (2012). Organizing for innovation in the digitized world. *Organization Science*, *23*(5), 1398-1408.

Zott, C., Amit, R., & Massa, L. (2011). The business model: recent developments and future research. *Journal of Management*, *37*(4), 1019-1042.

Chapter 2

THE CASE OF CORPORATE ENTREPRENEURSHIP WITHIN ITALIAN SMES

Federico Moretti-Stefano Denicolai-Aurelio Ravarini

2.1. Introduction

The term "entrepreneur" has a long story, both in academic literature and in common language. The term was first introduced in 1755 by French economist Richard Cantillon as a derivation of the verb *entreprendre,* as he used the term to describe a person who is willing to take non-negligible risks. The connection between entrepreneurial behavior and economic activities was highlighted by Schumpeter (1934), who argued that the entrepreneur continuously seeks for business opportunities, in order to introduce innovative factors. In this light, the entrepreneur differs from the manager, since the former aims at introducing s new combinations of production factors in the productive process, while the latter aims at simply managing and organizing the production factors efficiently on the basis of the techniques provided. Entrepreneurial innovation – according to Schumpeter – can appear in five ways: 1) the introduction of a new product or a new feature on an existing product; 2) the introduction of a new production process; 3) the creation of a new type of organization; 4) the creation of a new market; 5) the establishment of a new source of raw materials. The work of Schumpeter has been extended by various scholars in subsequent studies (including Kirzner et al 1973, Abernathy and Clark, 1985, Drucker, 1985).

For many years, scholars focused on defining who the entrepreneur is and what he/she does. However, the concept of entrepreneurship encompasses at least two other dimensions: 1) the presence of business opportunities, and 2) the presence of individuals who conduct entrepreneurial activities. As such, the focus should be on the entrepreneurial function, rather than on the characteristics of the entrepreneur as a person.

Entrepreneurship and innovation can be pursued by various groups of people and through different growth strategies (Hagen et al., 2014). Yet, this not exclude that – in certain business contexts, especially small firms – the entrepreneurial function may be conducted by a single person.

Entrepreneurship is usually related to: 1) the presence of an unexplored potential for innovation, which lies in the ability of identifying market opportunities (Shane & Venkataraman, 2000); and risk-taking behaviour, which derives from the development of new initiatives (Knight, 1921).

Stevenson and Jarillo (1990) helped in categorizing entrepreneurship, by sorting out the antecedents of entrepreneurship (why entrepreneurs act), the consequences of entrepreneurship (what happens when entrepreneurs act) and the management of entrepreneurial activities (how entrepreneurs act).

Given this background, we explore how these dynamics take place within small companies among employees which are not co-founder of the company. In other words, we are interested in people which put in practice an entrepreneurial mindset within medium-small organizations, though they are not 'entrepreneurs' (not yet), whilst they are 'just employees'. Mainstream literature studied 'entrepreneurship' in the context of big organizations. We argue that in the contemporary economy innovation strategies implemented by big and small companies are converging to similar patterns, thus highlighting the need for a better understanding of the corporate entrepreneurship phenomenon regardless from firm size implications.

Over the last twenty years, many researchers have demonstrated the effectiveness of Corporate Entrepreneurship (CE) as a mean for revitalizing companies and improving their long-term financial performance. In particular, the strength of this relationship tends to increase over time and again and CE turned out to be a particularly effective practice among companies in a "hostile environment" (Covin and Slevin, 1991).

Recent studies on CE found out that strategic renewal, innovation and corporate venturing positive influence overall, subjective and objective firm performance.

Since entrepreneurship stems from individual competencies, the Human Resource (HR) function plays a key role in the development of CE practices that encourage entrepreneurial behaviors. The Human Resource Management policies that contribute to the creation of an entrepreneurial working environment are recruitment and selection, job design, performance management, training and development and a system of retention and incentive mechanisms (Garzoni, 2010).

According to these considerations, the research question we address in this article is the following: What (Human Resource) Management practices have been implemented by medium-small entrepreneurship-driven companies?

The paper is organized as follows: in the following section, we review the literature on corporate entrepreneurship, specifying the dimensions of corporate entrepreneurship, a competence-based framework for analysis of corporate entrepreneurship, and on human resource management processes used to foster entrepreneurial behavior inside organizations. We then introduce the methodology used for the study in chapter 3 and introduce the selected case studies in chapter 4. In section 5, we review the results arising from the selected cases and we conclude in section 6 by discussing the implications for academics and professionals in the field.

2.2. Literature review

2.2.1. Dimensions of corporate entrepreneurship

The corporate dimension of entrepreneurship started gaining the attention of scholars about two decades ago. Academics took on corporate dimension in order to offer a more complete approach to the study of entrepreneurship. Since then, the concept of entrepreneurship occurring inside a pre-existing firm has been labelled in several ways, including: corporate entrepreneurship, internal corporate entrepreneurship (intrapreneurship), entrepreneurial management and strategic entrepreneurship. Although these concepts are often interchangeable (Hornsby et al, 2002), scholars tend to prefer the term "intrapreneurship" (short for intra-corporate entrepreneurship) rather than corporate entrepreneurship, since the former does not make any reference to the size of the firm, while the latter is often connected to large-sized corporations. Yet, intra-corporate entrepreneurship can be applied in small and large firms alike, irrespective of relative size, provided that such firms possess the resources used for entrepreneurial purposes.

Intrapreneurship is not the sole way of developing entrepreneurial behavior in pre-existing corporate environments. Chang (1998), as an example, argues that there are many opportunities to exploit innovative and entrepreneurial behavior to generate new knowledge outside of firms' boundaries, using the term "exopreneurship" to indicate the phenomenon. Exopreneurship process include organizations acquiring innovation from external agents, through relationships with joint ventures, external venture capital funds, subcontracting and the development of strategic alliances.

Summing up, while entrepreneurs innovate for themselves, intrapreneurs undertake innovation activities on behalf of an existing organization, while exopreneurs innovate as part of an external network.

Figure 1 illustrates the relationship between Corporate Entrepreneurship, Entrepreneurship, Intrapreneurship and Exopreneurship, adapted from Christensen (2004). The dotted line in the figure means that the company operates beyond its borders. This is the reason why in the first case the rectangle on the left is separated from the other two. As a matter of fact, one of the possible outcome of Entrepreneurship is a new independent venture. The rectangle on the right, which is half dotted, indicates that the company is pursuing innovation through external network.

Figure 1. The relationship between corporate entrepreneurship, entrepreneurship, intrapreneurship and exopreneurship.

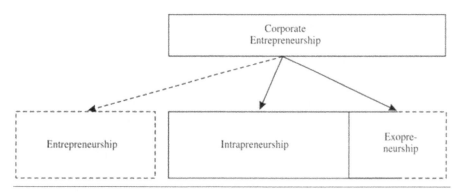

The three approaches to entrepreneurship have resulted in several definitions of corporate entrepreneurship over the last 20-30 years. According to Morris and Kuratko (2002) for example, corporate entrepreneurship is *"a term used to describe entrepreneurial organization inside established mid-sized and large organizations"*. Sathe's (1989) definition about corporate entrepreneurship is «*a process or organizational renewal*[1]». According to Zahra (1991), CE is *"a formal or informal activity aimed at creating new business in established firms through product and process innovations and market developments*[2]".

---

[1] Sathe, V., (1989) «Fostering entrepreneurship in a large diversified firm», *Organisational Dynamics*, Vol. 18, pp. 20-32.

[2] Zahra, S.A., (1991) «Predictors and financial outcomes of corporate entrepreneurship: an exploratory study», *Journal of Business Venturing*, Vol. 6, pp. 259-285.

2.2.2. A competence-based framework

Corporate entrepreneurship involves a set of various activities, such as innovation in products and processes, the development of internal and external corporate ventures and the development of new business models, which require an array of roles, behaviors, and individual competencies. Hayton and Kelley (2006) define individual competencies, distinguishing them from various individual difference constructs.

They argue that – given the unique requirements of corporate entrepreneurship – a competency-based approach is better suited to assess organizational human capital needs, compared to more traditional job-analytic methods, such as the task-based approach or work-based approach.

2.2.2.1. Individual factors for entrepreneurial development

Amongst all the elements needed to build a successful entrepreneurial organization, the individual role of the champion/intrapreneur is – perhaps – the most critical. Without the presence of a leadership which encompass a strategic vision and the perseverance showed by individuals inside organizations, it is hard to imagine concrete results. What are the individual characteristics of the intrapreneurs? How to recognize them and transform individual competencies in strategic capabilities of the whole organization?

A first possible answer to this question has been given by Pinchot III (1985) in the definition of the intrapreneurs' characteristics. In this light, intrapreneurs share some characteristics with entrepreneurial behaviors and attitudes which are typical for managers, for example in terms of motivation and problem-solving attitude.

While scholars mostly focused on characteristics of entrepreneurs, we argue that the extant literature has so far overlooked intrapreneurs as the focus of analysis. In a similar fashion to Pinchot III (2005), Morris, Kuratko & Covin (2008) argue that Intrapreneurs share at least six psychological traits with entrepreneurs: 1) *Motivation*, in terms of outcomes or in accepted challenges, rather than in power, money, status or desire of acceptance; 2) *Ability of managing events* (*locus of control*). Entrepreneurs are firmly convinced that by combining their personal commitment with enough time and resources, they can change their job, markets, and industries in which they operate. In short, they trust in their own ability to shape the surrounding environment; 3) *Weighted risk-taking propensity*, balanced between risk-averting or risk-taking behavior. A "weighted" risk implies they still face some degree of likelihood of failure, but the individual had considered and estimated the likelihood and the importance of the main risk factors, and he tried to manage or reduce some of these risk factors. 4) *High toler-*

ance of ambiguity, meaning the capacity of timely assessing facts and relations, without necessarily frame them into existing schemes; 5) *Auto-motivation and autonomy in task accomplishment,* that imply the capability of taking decisions and define objectives autonomously; and 6) *Tenacity and perseverance,* together with the ability of managing stress and working under pressure.

These characteristics are valid for both the entrepreneur *tout court* and the intrapreneur. However, it is difficult to define the ideal "prototype" of the entrepreneur. As a matter of fact, the differences among these characteristics and their intensity are the outcome of social variables (family, educational context, values learned, the location of birth the potential opportunities precluded). This makes the identification of a unique model for cognitive-behavioral development extremely hard.

2.2.2.2. Organizational factors: four entrepreneurial competencies

A role represents a particular domain within the effectiveness of behaviors will be assessed. Several important roles have been associated with the success of corporate entrepreneurship. Key roles identified in the literature include: the technical innovator (Block & MacMillan, 1993; Maidique, 1980), the innovation champion (e.g., Maidique, 1980; Schon, 1963; Shane, 1994), the executive champion or sponsor (Maidique, 1980; Rothwell et al., 1974), and the knowledge broker (Hargadon, 1998, 2002; Hargadon & Sutton, 2000).

In small firms, the four competencies may be collocated within a single individual. As firms increase in size, the corporate entrepreneurship competencies will become dispersed vertically and horizontally across individual employees and functions.

The four entrepreneurial competences are the following: 1) Innovating: the innovator role requires an ability to identify new market, organizational or technological opportunities ad combine new or existing resources in unique and creative ways (Shane and Venkataman, 2000); 2) Brokering: the primary role of the broker is to access new sources of information and knowledge, transferring this knowledge and combining different sources, both existing and new (Hargadon, 2002); 3) Championing: "champions" are the member of the organization who inspire other members with their vision of the innovative potential, contributing therefore to sustain innovation (Howell and Higgins, 1990); and 4) Sponsoring: sponsoring is a fundamental in order to boost CE in complex organization, where entrepreneurs not always can realize their initiatives and they are not sufficiently supported by internal sponsors (Day, 1994).

In complex organizations, the four categories of competencies may not co-exist in the same person. However, they represent – at the corporate level – the capability of the company as a whole of running innovative projects. In this way, *innovators* (who identify opportunities) may differ from *brokers* (who create conditions for the knowledge transfer), from *champions* (who identify which innovations deserve support) and from *sponsors* (who provide the needed resources).

From Hayton and Kelley (2006), we list the main individual competences that qualify the four categories of entrepreneurial competences at the corporate level: 1) innovating; 2) brokering; 3) championing; and 4) sponsoring.

In complex organizations, innovation develops in teams with high-specialized individuals, who have collective multidisciplinary vision. Creativity is the core capability in terms of innovation, together with tenacity and openness experience. Brokering focuses more on organizational aspects, such as knowledge transfer and on supporting access to resources. The influence and networking skills are therefore crucial, while credibility and conscientiousness are required to spread innovative knowledge inside the organization. Champions often times have a more multidisciplinary profile rather than specialized knowledge. They leverage on their analogic reasoning, influencing and developing emotional intelligence skills to create a "sense of urgency" needed to start the change. Also in this case, credibility and trust that those people inspire is a key factor, together with risk tolerance, that technicians in large-sized companies often lack. Sponsors, compared to champions, use their leadership to procure useful resources (e.g. human, financial) to realize transformational projects. In all the four categories, passion is a common factor which is useful to identify innovations, to transfer knowledge across the organization, and to select and support innovative projects (Denicolai et al., 2015).

2.2.3. Human Resource Management (HRM)

2.2.3.1. HRM architecture

The competencies-based framework is the basis for building a HR architecture that foster entrepreneurship. This framework rises some interesting questions for the HR architecture, with respect to the following activities: staffing, training and career development and performance management.

Hayton and Kelly (2006) argue that "the knowledge of where competent behaviors are most likely to arise will aid in locating where assessment and development activities should be targeted". Hence, the four entrepreneurial competencies (innovation, brokering, championing and sponsoring) are associated with some organizational positions. Sponsoring competence, for instance, is most likely to be observed at higher hierarchical levels in organizations with greater control over necessary resources (Maidique, 1980). Consequently, innovation competence is more likely to occur at lower levels and the need for brokering competence is most likely to arise in formal linking positions such as task-force membership (Hargadon, 1998, 2002). Championing and brokering competencies, indeed, are most likely to arise in the middle layers of organizations (Howell & Higgins, 1990; Kuratko, Ireland, Covin & Hornsby, 2005).

From a performance management perspective, it is important to highlight the fact that personality characteristics are not an appropriate basis for performance evaluation, as the inclusion of such measures tends to lead to bias, dissatisfaction, and ineffective feedback (Tziner & Kopelman, 2002; Wiersma & Latham, 1986). Therefore, in order to design an effective performance appraisal system, the focus should be on specific behaviors inferred from the description of the relevant competency. In this way, these appraisal mechanisms will be more valid, reliable, and acceptable to both raters and ratees (Tziner & Kopelman, 2002; Wiersma & Latham, 1986).

2.2.3.2. HRM practices

According to the competence-based framework, entrepreneurship emerges from individual behaviors. It is common knowledge that especially in big companies, individual behaviors are heavily influenced by the presence (or lack) of incentives. For the purposes of corporate entrepreneurship, the Human Resource function (HR) plays a key role. What distinguishes Human Resource Management (HRM) from traditional human resource functions is the higher involvement in the strategic corporate choices. Specifically: 1) in the superior attention given to the external environment by the employees working in the HR function; 2) in the development of long-term oriented activities; and 3) in the identification of the modalities through which developing individual competencies that are consistent with corporate vision.

How to create a working environment conducive to entrepreneurial development? One of the most important aspect is the recruiting and selection process. Intrapreneurs cannot be nominated or simply assigned to projects: they should propose themselves in a voluntary way and bring their own vision of what they want to do (Chambeau and Shay, 1984).

In Table we list the HRM policies a company should adapt to foster entrepreneurial behavior within the organization. The table is adapted from Morris, Kuratko and Covin (2008).

Selection operates ex-ante in the creation of a strategic working context, where every person that join the organization is involved in entrepreneurial projects from the beginning. Recruitment practices should be pointed to the hiring of creative people that are innovation-driven, can work in an autonomous way, and are risk-taker.

Job design is also central in the definition of a context conducive to entrepreneurship: less structured tasks make the interaction with other organization's members – in the realization of multidisciplinary projects – easier. Moreover, a higher level of autonomy and outcome orientation favor the development of individual behavior which is more coherent with the evolution of the environment (internal and external) where individuals operate.

In terms of performance evaluation, a balance between individual and collective outcomes is required. In communicating their performance expectations, companies should focus more on outcomes (rather than on processes), with a medium- or long-term orientation. They should reason in terms of overall effectiveness rather than on efficiency. This process of job design is often not easy to be realized for medium and big companies, since it is the opposite compared to traditional schemes based on managerial efficiency and short-term outcomes.

Table 1. HRM Policy and Entrepreneurial Behavior.

HRM POLICY	PRACTICES THAT FOSTER ENTREPRENEURSHIP
RECRUITMENT	Candidates search from both internal and external sources Variety in careers' path Selecting criteria more general and less formalized Open recruitment and selection procedures
JOB DESIGN	Long term orientation in the planning Wide task definition Less structured duties and tasks Outcome orientation in job description Search for a high involvement of employees in duties and tasks definition
PERFORMANCE EVALUATION	Employees' involvement Balance orientation individual-team Emphasis more on effectiveness than efficiency Outcome orientation (no process orientation) Use of subjective criteria that consider innovative potential Emphasis on medium-long term performance Failure tolerance
TRAINING AND DEVELOPMENT	Long term career orientation Wide training (not only technical) Training defined on individual basis (no systematic training) Employee's participation in decision-making process Emphasis on managerial competencies Continuous training (also at top-level)

BONUS AND INCENTIVES	Emphasis on medium-long term performance
	Decentralized to department or division level
	Customized
	Emphasis on individual performance and collective efforts
	Bonus and incentives based on merit
	Relevant bonuses from the financial point of view

2.2.3.3. Incentive mechanisms

Perhaps the most important way to stimulate innovation is the use of bonus and incentives. These practices can assume several forms, from money bonuses to status acknowledgement or career promotion.

To understand the role of incentives, the focus is on individual motivation. Motivation is driven by three factors (Porter and Lawler, 1968): 1) the relationship between individual effort and the performance management system; 2) the relationship between corporate performance and the achievement of corporate recognitions; and 3) the capacity of the firm to offer valuable bonus and recognitions.

In general terms, entrepreneurial behaviors expected from a supervisor include idea generation, support of the ideas of other employees and creativity in resource searching to realize own ideas. If these behaviors are not relevant to the performance management system, it is less likely that entrepreneurial employees will act entrepreneurially, since they are not expected to do so. Moreover, without a clear relationship between expected outcomes and expected recognitions, individual motivation will be even lower.

The principles useful to realize incentive programs that encourage entrepreneurship (Kanter, 1994) are the following: 1) Emphasize success more than failure. Managers tend not to identify positive aspects if they constantly look for negative ones; 2) Recognize and reward in public occasions. If it is not done in public, the recognition has less value and it reduces the positive impact for which it has been designed; 3) Recognize correct behaviors in a clear and personal way. Avoid excessive or superficial recognitions; 4) Customize recognitions. Define several ways to recognize and regards the realization of corporate behavior that are on the desired direction; 5) Recognize contributes throughout all the duration of a project. Rewards contributions right after that a result has been achieved; 6) Avoid the perception according to which a reward has been given casually or paternalistically; 7) Explain clearly why rewards have been given and make sure that employees understand those reasons; 8) Work on reinforcing the reward effect through meetings, newsletters in annual reports and in other occasions; and 9) Recognize the reward, meaning to recognize who gave major contribution.

2.2.3.4. Organizational culture conducive to entrepreneurial development

Without a managerial culture that supports entrepreneurship and its manifestations and permeates the organizational context, it is hard to implement the HRM practices before descripted. At the opposite, in presence of a highly entrepreneurial organizational culture the operational mechanisms give support and reinforce the values at the basis of the culture itself. The focus of this section is on *shared beliefs* regarding rewards, risks, opportunities and rules from one side, control systems and learning mechanisms on the other (Sathe, 2003) – see Table .

One of the main driver to foster CE, as reported before, is the role of incentives for the entrepreneurial support. Yet, the presence of excessive financial incentives may cause the opposite effect. It creates the perception of inequality inside a group and may lead to push away those people who contributed to the success of a new initiative, once they receive high monetary bonus.

Monetary bonuses are normally associated with compensation for personal risk taken by the intrapreneur. In order to avoid this, the company should shift from monetary incentives to other type of incentives, such as social recognitions and corporate recognitions.

Table 2. Shared beliefs on bonus, risks and opportunity search.

Factor	Impact on new business creation
High monetary bonus incentive people to purse new entrepreneurial initiatives	Negative
Personal risk perception reduction increases the possibility to create new initiatives	Positive
Opportunity taboos presence	Negative
Divisional managers are free to carry forward their own business beliefs	Positive
Rule-bending	Positive
Ethically wrong behaviors have been punished	Positive
Failure tolerance	Positive

Literature review highlights a research gap. While extant studies have highlighted the results arising from different HR management practices in fostering corporate entrepreneurship in different organizations, all of them seem to focus on large, international companies from Europe (Germany, Spain, Netherlands, Turkey) and Asia (Japan, China, South Korea, India).

We argue that studies need to include the examination of the same practices in the context of SMEs.

We seek to fill this gap by studying such dynamics in the context of Italian SMEs, specifically through two companies operating in the digital sector. Our aim is to respond to the following research question: *What Human Resource Management practices have been implemented by entrepreneurship driven companies?*

2.3. Research design

In the light of the proposed literature review, we propose a case study analysis. We selected two cases of Italian-based medium-small companies operating in the digital industry. Both companies are located in northern Italy, in the Lombardy region. In both cases, we interviewed entrepreneurs to sort out whether they implemented Human Resources Management practices to foster entrepreneurial behavior inside the organization.

We use Wolcott and Lippitz (2007) framework to categorize organizational approach to corporate entrepreneurship (see Figure 2). This framework proposes a matrix classification of such approaches, according to two dimensions: *organizational ownership* and *resource authority*. The first dimension, organizational ownership describe how responsibilities and accountability for new business creation are distributed, whether in a designated group of people, or diffused across the organization. The second dimension, resource authority, defines whether firms use dedicated funds for intrapreneurial ideas, or whether ad hoc resources are devoted on a case by case analysis.

The combination of the two dimensions generate a matrix with four dominant models: *the opportunist* (diffused ownership and ad hoc resource allocation), *the enabler* (diffused ownership and dedicated resources), *the advocate* (focused ownership and ad hoc resource allocation) and *the producer* (focused ownership and dedicated resources).

Figure 2. Four models matrix.

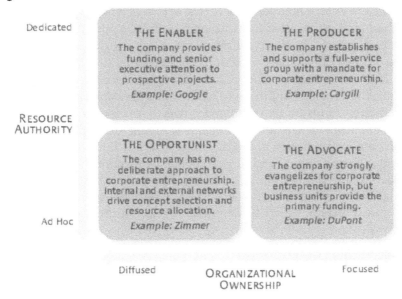

Dedicated

THE ENABLER

The company provides
funding and senior
executive attention to
prospective projects.

Example: Google

THE PRODUCER

The company establishes
and supports a full-service
group with a mandate for
corporate entrepreneurship.

Example: Cargill

RESOURCE
AUTHORITY

THE OPPORTUNIST

The company has no
deliberate approach to
corporate entrepreneurship.
Internal and external networks
drive concept selection and
resource allocation.

Example: Zimmer

THE ADVOCATE

The company strongly
evangelizes for corporate
entrepreneurship, but
business units provide the
primary funding.

Example: DuPont

Ad Hoc

Diffused   ORGANIZATIONAL   Focused
                  OWNERSHIP

The *Enabler* model requires that employees across the company will be willing to work on new projects if they are given an adequate support. Companies belonging to this model can count on dedicated resources. However, they do not have any formal organizational ownership. Usually, companies manage corporate entrepreneurship by defining clear criteria for selecting which opportunities to pursue, then providing application guidelines for funding, then apply transparent decision-making choices, together with active support from senior management (Wolcott and Lippitz, 2007). Perhaps the most famous company example for the enabler model is Google. Even though nowadays the company has evolved from its corporate entrepreneurial approach, it still allows employees were allowed to spend 20% of their time to promote their ideas to colleagues, assemble teams, explore concepts and build prototypes. Yet, allocating resources for CE is a necessary but not sufficient condition to succeed. Personnel development and executive engagement are also critical. (Wolcott and Lippitz, 2007).

The Advocate model offers alternative mechanisms to manage CE. According to this model, companies assign organizational ownership for the creation of new businesses, while intentionally providing modest budgets to the core group. Companies belonging to the advocate model acts as evangelists and innovation experts, facilitating corporate entrepreneurship in conjunction with business units. (Wolcott and Lippitz, 2007). A company example is Du Pont, a multinational chemical company. In 1999, Du Pont's CEO Chad Holliday realized that the company need a push to growth, that despite high returns in the prior six years, has been declining. A small grouped focused on company growth has been created that it turned out it contributed to the improvement of Du Pont performance.

Finally, the Producer approach to CE involves the deployment of significant dedicated funds or active influence over business-unit funding. The goals are to encourage latent entrepreneurs from one side, and to stimulate cross-division collaboration from the other. Cargill Inc. the $75 billion global agriculture products and service company based in Wayzata, Minnesota (USA) followed this approach. The company indeed has established its Emerging Business Accelerator to evaluate new business opportunities.

In the next section, we briefly describe the selected case studies.

2.4. Case studies description

2.4.1. FacilityLive

FacilityLive is an Italian high-tech SME based in Pavia, London and Brussels, which develops a next generation technology for the organization, management and search of information. It is a software platform driven by a next generation search engine, with patents granted in 44 countries worldwide (including Europe, USA, Canada, Japan, Korea, Russia, Israel, South Africa and Australia).

The FacilityLive project was born in 2001, when the two founders, Gianpiero Lotito and Mariuccia Teroni, decided to devote themselves to the study of a new method for the organization and accessing of information. The first code was written in 2008 and this allowed the software platform to be a technologically advanced and leading-edge product in terms of innovation. In 2009 the platform was shown in Silicon Valley to six majors who endorsed the project, and it was presented to the British press, which welcomed the product and its extraordinary user experience with enthusiasm. In 2011, with the birth of the FacilityLive Start Up, the company started product commercialization.

Nowadays, the company employs around 100 people in its offices in Pavia (Italy), London (United Kingdom) and Brussels (Belgium).

2.4.2. 7Pixel

7Pixel group is a web-company founded in 2002 by the CEO, Nicola Lamberti. Over the years 7Pixel helped more than 13 million users in searching for their ideal products. The company employs four different platforms: TrovaPrezzi and Shoppydoo are two price comparison platforms which allow users to search for the most convenient product, among 12 million offers and 24 product groups. Drezzy is a price comparison platform that allows the user to search the desired product between 1.300.000 products belonging to the fashion world. MissHobby is a marketplace where creatives and handmade passionate can buy the desired product, choosing among a wide range of handmade and vintage products.

Today, the company employs 140 people, and generates a turnover of about euro 45 Million. The headquarter is in Giussago (Pavia, Italy). 7Pixel has two other branches, located in Varese (Varese, Italy) and Madrid (Spain).

The 7Pixel group was established in 2002 with the technologic expertise of the associate founders with the mission of creating a complete service in terms of consultancy, project and realization of search engines in the rising e-commerce sector. One year later the company launched TrovaPrezzi, the search engine specialized in price comparison, where users can consult a wide offer of products such between electrical appliance, mobile, IT, electrical and many categories more.

2.5. Findings

2.5.1. FacilityLive

2.5.1.1. Intrapreneurship

In terms of intrapreneurship, FacilityLive's CEO and founder Gianpiero Lotito states that the entrepreneurial mind-set of the people working in the company is the core source for success.

> "An entrepreneurial mindset is needed to navigate the turbulence and opportunity of the 21st century economy. Startups live in a dynamic and disruptive environment that is changing continuously. Therefore, an entrepreneurial mind set is a pre-requirement for every start upper and FacilityLive is not an exception. On the contrary, people without this entrepreneurial approach couldn't suit with startups' values".

2.5.1.2. Risk propensity and failure tolerance

"1% inspiration, 99% perspiration" (Thomas Edison).

With this quote Lotito replied to the question about the company's failure tolerance. He suggested that the management of failure is a formative experience especially for startup and SMEs. As a matter of fact, the *learn-*

ing by doing, together with a medium-high risk propensity represent the philosophy of FacilityLive. Making mistakes is allowed, but it is important to identified them as quickly as possible, and therefore react.

In order to face the issue of failure tolerance, FacilityLive adopted the *Agile Development* manifesto (REF), that presents a set of principles for software development, where requirements and solutions evolve through collaboration among self-organizing, cross-functional teams. It promotes adaptive planning, evolutionary development, early delivery, and continuous improvement, and it encourages rapid and flexible response to change. Agile itself has never defined any specific methodologies to achieve this, but many have grown up as a result and have been recognized as being "Agile".

2.5.1.3. HRM practices

2.5.1.3.1. *Recruitment and selection* – From a recruiting and selection perspective, FacilityLive has built a strong eco-system which efficiently connects the company with the University of Pavia. FacilityLive's headquarter is based at the "Polo Tecnologico" in Pavia, a business incubator where many other startup projects are created, developed and accelerated.

FacilityLive is contributing in building a European eco-system for startups. This scenario is motivating several Italians and European young talents that choose to stay in Europe rather than going overseas to look for better job opportunities, containing in this way this phenomenon famous as *brain leakage*.

2.5.1.3.2. *Retention mechanisms* – In many digital company cases, including FacilityLive, the first retention mechanism offered is a high entry-level salary. Moreover, according to the CEO, continuous change in job positions implies a speculative approach to work. In this light, FacilityLive adopted a retention mechanism based on Microsoft model: employees are incentivized to stay in the company thanks to the possibility to purchase part of equity shares. This retention mechanism has a stronger compared to other monetary bonuses which are usually linked to the accomplishment of specific goals and objectives. This approach, according to Lotito, is risky, since employees may decide to leave the company as soon they receive a bonus payment.

2.5.1.3.3. *Four models framework* – Again, by using Wolcott and Lippitz (2007) framework, we analyze the two dimensions on how companies approach corporate entrepreneurship.

FacilityLive has a diffused organizational ownership. This means that there the responsibility for developing entrepreneurial initiatives is diffused across the company, rather than focused on a designated group or groups of people. From a resource authority perspective, instead, there are no funds dedicated to Corporate Entrepreneurship.

Moreover, this company presents an innovative structure that allows every employee to access resources in a lean manner which shortened the authoritative procedures. The organizational structure, once flat, is now more pyramidal, and has a "dynamic" hierarchy where ad-hoc cross-functional teams, called *squad,* that are challenged to manage ideas from employees. The goal is to bring people with different expertise together to solve a specific problem or to explore a potential solution, or sometimes to manage a project. However, projects tend to have a more formal structure, timelines and a definite end point.

The philosophy of FacilityLive is that sharing ideas outside the borders of the company is important to pursue innovation and development. Intellectual property is legally protected by patents obtained in 44 countries. The know-how instead, is shared and the risk of leakage is controlled by the abovementioned retention mechanisms. Thus, the possibilities of buying company equity shares represent an additional value for employees.

In summary, within FacilityLive every employee has an entrepreneurial mind-set. Entrepreneurship is fostered thanks to a dynamic organizational structure that allows the creation of cross-cultural teams.

From a Human Resource Management perspective, Entrepreneurship is fostered through the use of monetary (high salary entrance, equities' purchasing) and non-monetary incentives (the sense of belonging to the company). Those incentives represent also effective retention mechanisms, that yet do not include any other monetary bonus based on goals achievement.

Following the framework proposed by Wolcott and Lippitz (2007), FacilityLive can be placed in the *opportunist* model (see Figure). The organizational responsibility for entrepreneurial initiatives is distributed across the company while, in a resource authority perspective, entrepreneurial projects are financed *ad hoc*, and not trough a dedicated fund for intrapreneurial initiatives.

Figure 3. Four Models Matrix – FacilityLive.

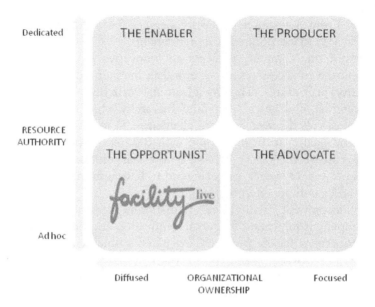

2.5.2. 7Pixel

2.5.2.1. Intrapreneurship

The CEO Nicola Lamberti believes Drezzy platform is a clear example of Corporate Entrepreneurship within the 7Pixel group. Specifically, Drezzy was developed from an idea of two PhD students of the University of Varese, who first designed and implemented a prototype of the platform for price comparison.

Yet, the challenge at 7Pixel is to diffuse the entrepreneurial attitude across the company. To do so, the company has recently adopted the Holacracy organizational. The impact on employees was relevant, although not all of them reacted in the same way. Some employees suffered from this change, while employees with an entrepreneurial mindset, showed a positive reaction, recognizing that the new model could enhance their potential and favor diffused intrapreneurship.

The dynamic environment helped the company to rethink and reshape their internal processes and structures, abandoning the traditional top-down hierarchy in favor of a decentralized management model. This new model for managing organizations removes power from top management and distributes it across clear roles, which can then be executed autonomously, without the need of a micromanaging boss. The work is actually more structured than in a conventional company: there is a clear set of rules and processes for how to split work within a team, defining team member's roles.

In most companies, each person has exactly one job description that is often imprecise, outdated, and irrelevant to their day-to-day work. In Holacracy, people have multiple roles, often within a team, and those role descriptions are constantly updated by the team itself. This structure allows people a lot more freedom to express their creative talents, and the company can take advantage of those skills in a way it could not before. These roles are not directly tied to the people filling them, since when an employee is filling a role, he/she is able to energize the work with a level of clarity and awareness most traditional employees do not have. Finally, roles can be constantly updated without office politics.

The agility that Holacracy provides comes directly from truly distributed authority. In traditional organizations, managers loosely delegate authority. Any initiative outside the norm typically requires the boss' approval, explicitly or implicitly. In Holacracy, authority is truly distributed and decisions are made locally by the individual closest to the front line.

In traditional companies, the organizational chart is usually modified every few years. These cyclical "reorgs" are an attempt to keep the company updated with the changing environment. In Holacracy, the organizational structure is updated every month in every circle (i.e. what roles are doing and owning what work or decisions).

2.5.2.2. HRM practices

7Pixel provides multiple incentives to keep their employees, mostly focusing on co-operation and on sense of belonging, rather of money incentives. A unique corporate-culture designed around the employee's needs is the most effective and efficient type of incentive.

First, the company does not provide bonuses related to goal achievements, since they risk creating an internal competition that may discourage co-operation.

Additionally, several services contribute to retention. As an example, the company organizes a summer camp for the sons of employees inside the headquarters.

Money incentives are presents, but they are customized on needs of each individual, as if she was a family member. As an example, 7Pixel offers a monthly bonus of 200 euros per baby, to partially cover the nursery school's fees, which are very expensive.

2.5.2.2.1. Risk propensity and failure tolerance

As the CEO reported, *"decisions are the average of the thinking of many people"* at 7Pixel. This is the reason why the company has a medium profile in terms of risk propensity and failure tolerance.

2.5.2.2.2. Performance evaluation

The CEO stated that 7Pixel currently lacks a clear performance evaluation management process, although the company is working on the improvement of this function. The HR department is currently implementing in the Holacracy model a project that deals with objectives definition and a continuous performance evaluation.

2.5.2.2.3. Training and development

7Pixel has implemented a training plan that includes a budget dedicated to every employee, that is split in 3 categories: 1) "Individual" budget: 50% of the total budget is managed by the employee, with the constraint that a percentage of it has to be culture related. For instance, if an employee would like to take a language course, he/she can use this budget to pay for it; 2) "Team" budget: 25% of the total budget is managed by the team leader ("Lead link") who will invest this money in improving the soft skills of the employees working in his team ("circles"); and 3) "Corporate" budget: the last 25% of the budget is managed by HR department to foster the soft skills of the employee in a company perspective.

For a company that works in the IT industry, it is crucial to keep updated under the individual, as well as the company perspective. The risk of being stick to just one programming language in some cases may bring to the company failure. If, for example, a company had worked for 30 years using Cobol language, the sudden change of programming language in IT industry may require to the company a transformational change that is costly in terms of time and efforts. Therefore, 7Pixel implemented a practice to prevent this dependence from one programming language. 7 Pixel's coders – about 40 people – are indeed allowed to invest 1 hour per day in a self-managed study-group, where they can split work between them and then meet to share that knowledge.

This allowed the company to evolve from a technological point of view, switching from one programming language to others. In addition, the company developed the capability of managing the co-existence of different code languages upon different layers. This practice has two advantages: on one hand, the company is constantly updated with new state-of-the-art technology; on the other hand, coders can increase their skills and competencies that may be appreciated even in other working contexts.

2.5.2.2.4. Four models framework

The CEO highlighted the importance of having an Entrepreneurship diffused across the company, through which all employees work full time as entrepreneurs inside their role. If entrepreneurship was bounded to a limited amount of time, the risk is that employees would operate for the remaining time following the traditional model. In this regard, the philosophy of 7Pixel is that everyone has to act entrepreneurially inside their role, irrespective of the magnitude of responsibilities.

Summing up, 7Pixel's strategy to foster Corporate Entrepreneurship pushes on individual entrepreneurship inside a specific role. This strategy has been implemented thanks to Holacracy, a new way of running organizations that removes power from a management hierarchy and distributes it across clear roles, which can then be executed autonomously, without a micromanaging boss.

From a Human Resource Management perspective, 7Pixel focuses on the conditions that help to create a friendly working environment. The company offers several additional services which represent a more effective retention mechanism than traditional bonuses, designed on goal achievement. Monetary incentives are still present, but they are customized around the employees' needs.

Entrepreneurship is also fostered through a training plan that includes a budget that can be invested to improve employees' soft skills. Furthermore, coders spend one hour per day in a self-organized study group sessions which allow them to be always updated with the new state-of-the art technology.

Figure 4. Four Models Matrix – 7Pixel.

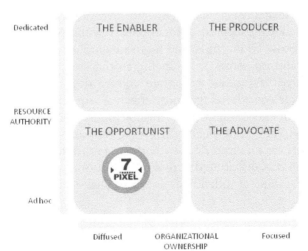

Following the framework proposed by Wolcott and Lippitz (2007), 7Pixel follows "the opportunist" model (see Figure 5). Projects are financed *ad hoc* and the organizational responsibility is diffused across the company.

2.6. Discussion and conclusions

Despite the several labels and perspectives used by scholars to refer to Corporate Entrepreneurship (CE), three are the CE outcomes generally accepted by the academic world, and they are the result of the evolution of the CE concept: Corporate Entrepreneurship, also known as Intrapreneurship or Intracorporate Entrepreneurship is realized when members of an organization stimulate strategic renewal and innovation in an existing company, or when they create new independent ventures.

Several findings emerge from the two case studies. Within FacilityLive, entrepreneurship is a pre-requirement and it is boosted through both monetary and non-monetary incentive mechanisms. Entrepreneurship is diffused across the company, and entrepreneurial projects, financed *ad hoc*, are efficiently managed thanks to a dynamic hierarchy that allow the creation cross-functional teams. This evidence shows how even innovative SMEs relies on hierarchy and procedures, which do not inhibit proactivity and entrepreneurial attitude of employees. However, hierarchical structures and routines are present *but different* compared to traditional big companies, and rooted on very different corporate culture.

Within 7Pixel group, an organizational model recently adopted by the company pushes on the individual entrepreneurship. This model removes power from a management hierarchy and distributes it across clear roles, which can then be executed autonomously, without the need of a micromanaging boss. To incentive and motivate employees, 7Pixel focuses on co-operation and on sense of belonging to the company, rather than on money incentives. A unique corporate culture designed around the employee's needs is considered the most effective and efficient type of incentive. From both the organizational responsibility and resource authority points of view, 7Pixel and FacilityLive have the same approach: entrepreneurial projects are financed *ad hoc* – without a fund dedicated to CE – and entrepreneurship is distributed across organization, rather than be limited to a group or groups of individuals as what usually happens in big organizations.

The comparison between the 7Pixel approach to Corporate Entrepreneurship and the model adopted – until few years ago – by Google, provides some interesting insights and managerial implications. Google allowed their engineers to employ 20% of their working time on personal projects, that of course, at some point, had to turn out to be consistent with Google's vision. This approach raises two issues. The first one regards the creation of an effective performance management system, able to evaluate these "personal" projects and to measure their outcomes. Secondly, the choice of setting a fix amount of working time on entrepreneurial projects represents a double-edged sword: in this way entrepreneurship risks to be bounded to the amount of time dedicated. Google's engineers, therefore, were operating entrepreneurially just for 20% of their working time, while for the remaining 80% they were still operating according to the traditional guidelines.

7Pixel approach to Corporate Entrepreneurship instead, has a more holistic view of entrepreneurship. In fact, the organizational model recently adopted by 7Pixel aims at fostering an individual entrepreneurship, diffused at every level of the company. This is possible thanks to a distributed authority – that replaced delegated authority – and to dynamics roles – that replaced static job description. At 7Pixel therefore, every employee is the entrepreneur within his role. This interesting insight represents a new way of approaching Corporate Entrepreneurship that could be used as reference by those companies that are looking for *best practices* to become more innovative and entrepreneurship oriented.

This study also offers strong theoretical contributions to the research. First of all, to our knowledge, it is the first study to focus on corporate entrepreneurship in the context of small and medium innovative organizations, and specifically on digital companies. In addition, the focus on Human Resource Management practices that foster entrepreneurial behaviors represents a novelty in the field. In addition, we argue the topic is relevant for professionals in the field as well, since it offers a blueprint on which HR practices should be adopted by companies trying to develop entrepreneurial behavior inside the organization.

References

Abernathy W.F., Clark K., (1985). «Innovation: mapping the winds of creative destruction», *Research policy*, Vol. 14, No. 1, pp. 3-22.

Block, Z., MacMillan, I., (1993). *Corporate venturing*, MA: Harvard Business School Press, Cambridge.

Chambeau F., Shay E.M., (1984). «Harnessing entrepreneurial energy within the corporation», *Management Review*, pp. 17-20.

Chang, J., (1998). «Model of corporate entrepreneurship: intrapreneurship and entrepreneurship», *Borneo Review*, Vol. 9, No. 2, pp. 187-213.

Christensen, K., (2004). «A classification of the CE umbrella: Labels and perspective», *Internal Journal of Management and Enterprise Development*, Vol. 1, No. 4, pp. 301-315.

Covin, J.G., Slevin, D.P., (1991). «A conceptual model of entrepreneurship as firm behaviour», *Entrepreneurship Theory and Practice*, Vol. 16, pp. 7-24.

Day, D.L., (1994) «Raising radicals», *Organization Science*, Vol. 5, N. 2, pp. 148-172, 1994.

Denicolai, S., Ramusino, E.C. and Sotti, F. (2015). The impact of intangibles on firm growth. *Technology Analysis & Strategic Management*, 27, 219-236.

Drucker P.F., (1985). «The discipline of innovation», *Harvard Business Review*, vol. 63, No. 3, pp. 67-72.

Garzoni A., (2010). *Corporate Entrepreneurship. Stimolare l'imprenditorialità all'interno delle aziende complesse*, Egea, Milano.

Hagen, B., Denicolai, S. and Zucchella, A. (2014). International entrepreneurship at the crossroads between innovation and internationalization. Journal of International Entrepreneurship, 12, 111-114.

Hargadon, A.B., (2002). «Brokering knowledge: Linking learning and innovation», *Research in Organizational Behavior*, Vol. 24, pp. 41-85.

Hargadon, A.B., (1998). «Firms as knowledge brokers: lessons in pursuing continuous innovation», *California Management Review*, Vol. 40, No. 3, pp. 209-227.

Hargadon, A., Sutton, R.I., (2000). «Building an innovation factory», *Harvard Business Review*, Vol. 78, No. 3, pp. 157-166.

Hayton, J.C., Kelley, D. J., (2006). «A Competency-Based Framework for Promoting CE», *Human Resource Management*, 45(3), pp. 407-427.

Hornsby, J.S., Kuratko, D.F., Zahra, S.A., (2002). «Middle managers' perception of the internal environment for corporate entrepreneurship: Assessing a measurement scale», *Journal of Business Venturing*, Vol. 17, No. 3, pp. 253-273.

Howell J.M., Higgins C.A., (1990). «The champions of technological innovation», in Administrative Science Quarterly, Vol. 35, pp. 317-341.

Kanter R., (1994). *Innovative Reward System for the changing Workplace*, McGraw-Hill, New York.

Kirzner I.M., (1973). *Competition and entrepreneurship*, The University Press, Chicago.

Knight F., (1921). *Risk, uncertainty and profit*, Augustus Kelley, New York.

Kuratko, D., Ireland, R.D., Covin, J.G., & Hornsby, J.S. (2005). «A model of middle level managers' entrepreneurial behavior». *Entrepreneurship Theory and Practice*, 29, 699-716.

Maidique, M.A., (1980). «Entrepreneurs, champions, and technological innovation», *Sloan Management Review*, Vol. 21, N. 2, pp. 59-76.

Morris, M.H., Kuratko, D.F., Covin J.G., (2008). *Corporate entrepreneurship & innovation*, Thomson South Western, Mason.

Morris M.H., Kuratko, D.F., (2002). *Corporate Entrepreneurship*, Harcourt College Publishers, Orlando, Florida.

Pinchot III, G., (1985). *Intrapreneuring. Why you don't have to leave the corporation to become an entrepreneur*, Harper & Row, New York.

Porter L.W., Lawler E.I., (1968). *Managerial attitudes and performance*, Irwin, Homewood, Illinois.

Rothwell, R., Freeman, C., Horlsey, A., Jervis, V.T.P., Robertson, A.B., Townsend, J., (1974). «SAPPHO updated - Project SAPPHO phase II», *Research Policy*, Vol. 3, No. 258-291.

Sathe V., (2003). *Corporate Entrepreneurship. Top managers and new business creation*, Cambridge University Press, Cambridge.

Sathe, V., (1989). «Fostering entrepreneurship in a large diversified firm», *Organisational Dynamics*, Vol. 18, pp. 20-32.

Schon, D.A., (1963). «Champions for radical new inventions», *Harvard Business Review*, Vol. 41, No. 2, pp. 77-86.

Schumpeter, J.A., (1934). *The Theory of Economic Development*, Harvard University Press, Cambridge.

Shane, S., (1994). «Cultural values and the championing process», *Entrepreneurship: Theory and Practice*, Vol. 18, No. 1, pp. 25-41.

Shane S., Venkataraman S., (2000). «The promise of entrepreneurship as field of research», *Academy of Management Review*, Vol. 25, No. 1, pp. 217-226.

Stevenson, H.H., Jarillo, J.C., (1977). «A paradigm of entrepreneurship: entrepreneurial internal environment for corporate entrepreneurship: assessing a measurement scale», *Journal of Business Venturing*, Vol. 17, No. 3, pp. 253-273.

Tziner, A., & Kopelman, R.E. (2002). «Is there a preferred performance rating format? A non-psychometric perspective». *Applied Psychology*, Vol. 51, pp. 479-503.

Wiersma, V.C., & Latham, G.P. (1986). «The practicality of behavioral observation scales, behavioral expectation scales and trait scales». *Personnel Psychology,* Vol. 39, pp. 619-628.

Wolcott L.C., Lippitz M.J., (2007). «Four Models for Corporate Entrepreneurship», *MIT Sloan Management Review,* Vol. 49, No. 1.

Zahra, S.A., (1991). «Predictors and financial outcomes of corporate entrepreneurship: an exploratory study», *Journal of Business Venturing*, Vol. 6, pp. 259-285.

Chapter 3
HRM 4.0: THE DIGITAL TRANSFORMATION OF THE HR DEPARTMENT

Rita Bissola-Barbara Imperatori

SUMMARY: 3.1. Introduction. – 3.2. Work and industry 4.0. – 3.2.1. New spaces and time. – 3.2.2. New stakeholders. – 3.2.3. Big data analytics. – 3.3. HRM department and industry 4.0: the HR competences. – 3.3.1. New HR role: an old tale or a new chance? – 3.4. HRM department, organization and industry 4.0: the design thinking approach. – 3.5. Conclusion. – References.

3.1. Introduction

A deep and lasting change is currently affecting economies worldwide and even greater turbulence will manifest in the near future. After the Internet revolution that brought about e-commerce in the early 2000s, digitalization enabled by the Internet of Things (IoT) and other technologies have recently led the business sector into the smart era, which is quickly striding forwards in the wake of Industry 4.0: the so-called 4th Industrial Revolution after the 1st generated by mechanization, the 2nd characterized by the intensive use of electricity, and the 3rd defined by the introduction of the Internet and digitization (Lasi, Fettke, Kemper, Feld, and Hoffman, 2014).

Industry 4.0 or Smart Industry is considered the fourth industrial revolution as it is predicted to profoundly change work and consequently the field of Human Resource Management (HRM). Smart industries are defined as "industries that have a high degree of flexibility in production, in terms of product needs (specifications, quality, design), volume (what is needed), timing (when it is needed), resource efficiency and cost (what is required), being able to (fine)tune to customer needs and make use of the entire supply chain for value creation. It is enabled by a network-centric approach, making use of the value of information, driven by ICT and the latest available proven manufacturing techniques" (Habraken and Bondarouk, 2017, p. 240).

Three components essentially enable transforming today's industrial production into Industry 4.0 factories: complex technological solutions to support job tasks, technologies that allow converting physical objects into digital things by adding (or through) components (e.g., sensors and Radio-Frequency Identification – RFID), so that they become data collection technologies, and advanced connectivity ensuring real-time data acquisition and enabling numerous smart objects (digital things) to continuously communicate (Habraken and Bondarouk, 2017; Lasi et al., 2014; Lee, Bagheri, and Kao, 2015; Strohmeier, 2017).

The IoT is the critical infrastructure that enables the current paradigm shift in industrial production. IoT refers to the possibility of connecting numerous physical objects (things) to the Internet so that they can interact and exchange data, thus turning into smart things. Smart objects embed electronics that enable them to sense, communicate, interact, and integrate seamlessly with each other, with humans, and with the environment (Piazza, 2017; Strohmeier, 2017). The resulting combination of smart objects can in this way enable unprecedented autonomous context-aware behaviours, thus allowing machines to become more flexible and make decisions independently (Habraken and Bondarouk, 2017; Strohmeier, 2017).

The association of IoT with other recent technologies, such as augmented reality, artificial intelligence, cloud computing, 3D printers, advanced robotics, as well as autonomous and near-autonomous vehicles, further amplifies the disruptive potential of this on-going paradigm shift described as bringing about opposite, foretold, and profound economic and social changes (Lee et al., 2015; van Kruining, 2017).

The functionalities of these bundles of technologies provide an extremely broad range of applications to different domains, amongst which those in business are of primary importance (Lasi et al., 2014; Strohmeier, 2017). Beyond applications in logistics, transportation, and retailing, manufacturing constitutes one of the main business application domains. Smart production equipment guides activities in smart manufacturing environments. Self-organizing networked machines detect and configure the production components, workers are thus supported by machines, for example, in the assembly of new products. In particular, smart shelves and smart work pieces can directly communicate with the digital devices workers use to provide them with information on where to find specific components (Piazza, 2017). The smart production scenario envisages modular and efficient manufacturing systems that allow products to control their own manufacturing process with the personalization of single products, while maintaining the same cost level of mass production (Lasi et al., 2014). When products are embedded with sensors or tagged with RFID and smart shelves are part of the IoT applications, items can be tracked in real time and enable warehouses to be digitally managed. Such an item tracking system can easily be extended to other organizations as the label passes through on its way to the end market, thereby achieving real time and universal monitoring of goods throughout the overall supply chain (Lee et al., 2015; Piazza, 2017).

In view of the growing adoption of IoT and other high-tech solutions in several business domains, the general expectation is that employees will increasingly use and interact with smart technologies when performing their job activities, and these new work processes will thereby also affect HRM (Bremer, 2015; Piazza, 2017).

The aim of the present contribution is to shed light on the main effects of the ongoing 4th industrial revolution on HRM department activities. In particular, changes in the nature and organization of work, together with the growing availability of data (Big Data) are deemed two main phenomena driving changes in HRM. Some conditions relate to the HR Department's ability to transform and hence win the never-ending challenge of retaining a strategic function in the 4.0 era. Moreover, the introduction of the design thinking approach as part of the organizational culture and therefore as the HR Department's mission is deemed a competence that should inform work and collaboration in 4.0 organizations. Some theoretical as well as managerial implications of the proposal are presented in the last part of this chapter.

3.2. Work and industry 4.0

Digitization is referred to as disruptive innovation that opens up new business and social opportunities, while at the same time challenging the consolidated way of conceiving 'work'. These challenges require both people and organizations to change. Workers should develop new competencies and capabilities, from technological expertise to essential social, emotional, and creative skills (Colbert, Yee, and George, 2016), while organizations should redesign their structures, processes, and culture to lead the new work (Kane, Palmer, Phillips, Kiron, and Buckley, 2016).

Industry 4.0 is changing the nature of human work; what workers used to do is increasingly being done by machines and will be accompanied by changing tasks that require full integration with those of machines.

Research suggests a job polarization (Brynjolfsson and McAfee, 2014) and predicts that jobs where humans have advantages over machines will be preserved, while jobs where computers and robotics have advantages will decrease (Levy and Murnane, 2014). As a consequence, in the near future, machines will perform not only routine activities and human tasks will be characterized by growing autonomy and empowerment at decreasing costs (Holland and Bardoel, 2016).

What is more, human work is not only changing because of different content, but is about working differently: new spaces, new time, new stakeholders, and the availability of new data are reshuffling the new 4.0 way of working and managing work.

3.2.1. New spaces and time

Digitization offers new ways of working by eliminating physical and time barriers. The 4.0 revolution is changing the *time and space* dimensions of work, extending new flexible organizational opportunities to the whole workforce, including blue-collar workers: smart working, agile working, new virtual production – also across the globe – are only a few new job design examples. As a consequence, traditional 9-to-5 five days a week jobs are likely to decline, and more varied and flexible forms (as for work time and space) will arise.

While smart and agile working is deemed to be about working more flexibly across time and space, the shift is not simply about where and when work occurs, but encompasses a new mindset that must shift from 'work as presence' to 'work as results'.

This shift is made possible by four organizational requirements. First, smart organization entails new digital competences from the workforce as a whole to remotely interact with machines, with colleagues and supervisors in a collective context. Second, it requires new behavioural competences both for employees and supervisors. As for supervisors, it entails an empowering leadership style based on clear goal setting and continuous feedback to help workers assume their own responsibilities and exploit the great amount of information available. As for workers, the new agile and flexible industry 4.0 requires the ability to self-manage activities and communicate, collaborate, and interact in a virtual space. Third, organizational processes and people practices have to be consistent with the new way of working and should align the behaviours of supervisors and workers towards the new digital culture. For instance, performance must be clearly defined and measured as work results, compensation and career paths must be organized consistently with flexible work; the ways of interaction, the time and space for collaborations have to be openly set; organizational spaces (i.e., office and plants) must be specifically redesigned for the new work processes.

There is evidence that these changes could have a positive impact on both people and organizations, enabling a better work-life balance for a wider cohort of workers. Furthermore, digitization also enables organizations to provide clear goals and real-time feedback, sustaining the continuous development and engagement of workers (Sonnentag, Binnewies, and Mojza, 2008). From the organization's perspective, agile working offers a more efficient way of designing work, reducing absenteeism, enhancing work productivity, and enabling costs savings in relation to buildings and general expenses.

On the other hand, both research and practice suggest some potential risks and downsides of the 4.0 work space and time revolution. From the employee perspective, these changes lead to a growing sense of job insecurity and technological angst. They seem to influence the quality of social interactions towards a higher degree of personal isolation and closeness (Turkle, 2011). Moreover, continuous learning and the difficult to separate the work and non-work domain could cause work-life balance conflicts, stress, and burnout, especially for those who are not digital natives (Butts, Becker, and Boswell, 2015). Moreover, there is evidence that these radical changes could negatively affect individual creativity and critical thinking, forcing employees to focus on narrow work activities mainly driven by the pace and rhythm of machines (Jackson, Dawson, and Wilson, 2001).

3.2.2. New stakeholders

The 4.0 revolution is changing the role of the ecosystem of stakeholders, including traditional employees and managers, but also new workers, such as freelancers, non-traditional and contingent workforces, vendors and customers. The new ways of producing and delivering goods and services involves stakeholders more actively and enlarges the number of actors who directly participate in the business activities (Sokol, 2015; Bondarouk and Brewster, 2016; Kane et al., 2016). These changes are producing at least two main and relevant effects that have affected the new way of working in the 4.0 domain.

The first effect is the shift from 'employment' to 'work'. The traditional internal full-time worker, such as employees, middle and top managers, more frequently collaborate across space and with other people 'outside of employment', such as freelancers, independent professionals, and contractors, thanks also to digital platforms in dynamic value-creation networks (Lasi et al., 2014).

Many organizations outsource digitally mediated work as a way of transcending some of the constraints of their local labour markets, such as software development by freelancers on a cloud platform. Furthermore, at times, work is performed even by volunteers, such as the creative work of gamers (Sokol, 2015).

As a consequence, traditional internal full-time employees, the predominant way of working and living in the 20th century, seems to be progressively substituted by a wide variety of non-employment and more precarious work arrangements. New and diverse people offer their work to organizations on a project-basis, and moreover, need to collaborate with each other. Modern forms of association, such as digital freelancers' unions and updated labour market regulations, will increasingly emerge to complement the new organizational models (Klotz, 2016).

The second effect is the shift from 'organization' to 'open community'. Traditional external stakeholders in the industry 4.0 context, such as customers and suppliers, but also competitors, are enabled to collaborate in a boundary-less and open community, where traditional hierarchical organization-based coordination and control mechanisms will be replaced by social control and technology complementarity. As a consequence, the traditional internal vs. external stakeholder distinction would seem to no longer fit, changing over time and across space.

There is evidence that these changes could have a positive impact on organizations and people. They produce a higher degree of organizational innovation and enable more agile organization forms and lower organizational costs (Bissola, Imperatori, and Biffi, 2017). There is also evidence that more flexible and entrepreneurial working conditions could positively affect job engagement and intrinsic motivation, supporting individual creativity and job satisfaction (Rich, Lepine, and Crawford, 2010; Zhang and Bartol, 2010). The new digitalization enables internal and external stakeholders to share knowledge and collaborate across organizational boundaries, also increasing their competences and experiences.

On the other hand, detractors of the 4.0 revolution predict that smart machines will replace human work and that this will not only occur for routine activities, hence causing unprecedented job losses and consequently dramatic unemployment. Full-time employment will be substituted by a wide variety of more precarious work arrangements, forcing organizations to redefine and continuously change the architecture of their management practices to better cope with the increasing diversity of the workforce and negatively affecting job security and employee self-esteem (Markoulli, Lee, Byington, and Felps, 2017).

3.2.3. Big data analytics

The ongoing 4th industrial revolution is not just transforming work, but is profoundly affecting employee management within organizations. One of the direct consequences of adopting advanced robotics and having smart objects in 4.0 factories is that they can provide real time data. Some also provide continuous feedback on the task performance of employees, thus opening up new avenues in employee performance management systems (Khanna, 2016). This is just one example of the transformation potential that digitization is bringing to the HR department, which will benefit from the great amount of data on people (both internal to the enterprise, but also external) that smart objects together with other technologies, such as data warehouses, business intelligence, and cloud computing, but also potentially social media are able to provide (LaValle, Lesser, Shockley, Hopkins, and Krushwitz, 2011). The seamless integration of real time employee data, inbuilt analytical capabilities, and referencing big data enable Digital HR solutions to provide meaningful insights (Khanna, 2016). The information obtained is called Big Data Analytics (Marler, Cronemberger, and Tao, 2017) defined as the "integration of relevant HR data from different sources, the performing of organizational and workforce analysis on this captured data and ultimately the gleaning of insights from the findings to shape decisions for better organizational performance" (Kapoor and Kabra, 2014).

HR big data analytics extensively overcome the concept of HR metrics that primarily focus on cost reduction and the process improvement of HR service outcomes. They encompass three levels: descriptive, predictive, and prescriptive, and include a vast array of solutions starting from simple HR metrics, workforce forecasting models and investment analysis to arrive at predictive models and "what-if scenarios" (Marler et al., 2017). Three aspects describe HR analytics and contribute to their better understanding: they are not just metrics related to HRM efficiency and effectiveness, they imply the integration of data both from inside and outside the organization, they allow providing meaningful insights and even predicting future events that may have a critical impact on the business, thus linking HR decisions to organizational performance (Marler et al., 2017).

In particular, the ability to link HR decisions to better performance and competitive advantage by providing HR output indicators, such as productivity, will enable HR leaders performing a role in strategic discussions with the business and become a fully-fledged strategic business partner (Khanna, 2016; Marler et al., 2017).

Despite the announced benefits that big data analytics could provide to the HR department, few organizations have made much progress in developing capabilities to adopt analytics as the basis for decision-making. The reasons are essentially two. On the one hand, HR professionals demonstrate reluctance towards analytical thinking, asserting that the core of their job and motivation are people and not data. On the other, HR analytic products sold on the market are complex to use when performing more than a simple strategic analysis, yet software houses do not offer adequate training to their customers (Angrave, Charlwood, Kirkpatrick, Lawrence, and Stuart, 2016).

To avoid losing the opportunities related to big data analytics, the HR department should therefore develop an analytical mindset and become used to building the analytical model that represents the causal factors underlying the problem under consideration, training in more ordinary activities related to data management and governance (Angrave et al., 2016).

The new work spaces, the unconventional job time, the new stakeholder relations as well as adopting big data analytics require new competences and new practices to enable the new digital ways of managing, organizing, performing, and leading work activities. The new and mixed stakeholder and employment relationships require new and aligned management practices to properly attract, select, and engage external as well as internal stakeholders, and to best match the demand and supply of skills and capabilities in the entire product lifecycle (Bissola and Imperatori, 2012). The growing reality of real time employee data can provide meaningful insights and enable data-driven decision-making. They require increasing the digital and analytical capabilities within organizations and of HRM professionals.

3.3. HRM department and industry 4.0: the HR competences

The depicted challenging 4.0 scenario represents a tremendous opportunity for the HRM domain, providing stimuli to develop positive social change and adopt new digital systems and innovative organizational solutions. HRM professionals can help old and new business leaders, employees, and the new digital (and not yet digital) workforces shift to the 4.0 mindset. It can also change the controlling (i.e., measuring) function and prevent the potential 4.0 drawbacks, such as people discomfort and incompetence at the individual level, inertia and loss of control at the organizational level, and growing unemployment and social inequality at the societal level.

In facing this opportunity, the HRM department needs to change towards HRM 4.0, redesigning its role and redefining its value, and consequently developing new competences and practices. These changes represent a new world for HRM professionals that can potentially open up new career opportunities and transform the impact that HRM has on people, businesses, and society at large (Strohmeier and Parry, 2014; Bondarouk and Brewster, 2016).

All this also leads to changes in HR management and offers new opportunities provided that:

- the HRM department evolves its identity and its skills towards ICT (hybridization), becoming a "more evidence-based" department by gaining strength and learning to use big data to argue, support, and demonstrate the validity and value of its proposals and actions;
- the HRM department aims to evolve and develop the mindset and competences of workers so as to prepare them for the "smart revolution";

- the HRM department prevents the dark side of industry 4.0 (measuring, keeping the 4.0 industry impact under control on worker welfare and wellbeing, and organizational sustainability), becoming a facilitator for institutions and guarantor of the socio system.

3.3.1. New HR role: an old tale or a new chance?

In 1997, Dave Urlich proposed a multi-role model for the HR department, adopting a wider variety of roles from more administrative to more strategic ones. The debate on which and, more interestingly, how HR professionals could enact a more powerful and recognized role within organizations from the business perspective is an old issue for both HR practitioners and scholars (Ulrich, 1997). More recently, Ulrich and Dulebohn (2015) depicted a new HR role related to a new (i.e., the fourth) development wave. The initial wave concerned HR administrative work, where HR professionals focused on work terms and conditions with the aim of complying with the labour norms. The second wave concerned designing and implementing innovative, effective, and specific HR practices, such as staffing, compensation, training, career management, and so forth, with the aim of properly managing employee performances across their professional cycle. The third wave related to strategic HR work, namely, the alignment between HR practices and the organization's strategy with the aim of becoming a business partner legitimized by top and line managers. Finally, the more modern fourth wave should be about driving business value and connecting HR practices to the external organizational context and stakeholders, with the aim of serving the end market (customers and investors) as well as the internal market (employees and managers).

Relying on a wide survey, Urlich and colleagues found that HR professionals have to combine six domains of competence to successfully drive and produce business value (Urlich, Younger, Brockbank, and Urlich, 2011):

- *Capability builder*: the ability to align the individual competences with the company's culture and strategy.
- *Change champion*: the ability to activate and sustain organizational change.
- *Technology proponent*: the ability to use technology to deliver HR administrative systems more efficiently and help people use technology to stay connected.
- *Innovator and integrator*: the ability to develop talent, drive performance, and build leadership brands.
- *Strategic positioner*: the ability to interact with the organization, using business language, co-creating an organizational strategy agenda, aligning organizational actions to meet customer needs, and deeply

knowing the general business conditions (e.g., social, technological, economic, political, environmental, and demographic trends).

- *Credible activist*: the ability to engender trust by building relationships, growing in business acumen, and shaping HR professional credibility and image.

Digital transformation and the industry 4.0 revolution both challenge all these six domains and offer more opportunities for HR professional to better perform their multifaceted role (see Table 1).

- Research confirms that smart technology enables a closer alignment among people and between people and the organization, allowing more direct and transparent communications. On the other hand, it requires new digital competences and behaviours of both HR professionals and the new workforce (Bissola and Imperatori, 2014; Lee et al., 2015).
- There is evidence that smart technology pushes towards radical organizational change, allowing new organizational solutions and continuous improvements, but also requiring facing personal resistance in an open context (Habraken and Bondarouk, 2017).
- Digitization enables HR professional to profoundly change people practices, such as new performance management tools, new mentoring and feedback processes, which rely on smart technology, but require a strong partnership with the ITC domain and related digital competences (Cappelli and Tavis, 2016).
- 4.0 technologies enable new, less costly and even more strategic e-HRM solutions, but require new HR practices and a new organizational mindset for employees as well as supervisors who need to be involved in the adoption, co-design, and implementation of the new practices (Bondarouk and Brewster, 2016).
- The distinction between internal and external stakeholders is less relevant in the 4.0 era. This means that HR professionals could exploit their competencies to better manage both internal and external workforces, from traditional employees to customers and volunteers who, at the same time, but in different ways, 'work' for and across the organization. Meanwhile, this change requires a new HR mindset, more open towards the external organizational environment (Bissola and Imperatori, 2012).
- The potential drawbacks of industry 4.0 require a more socially responsible HR department that should act as community guarantor. On the other hand, smart technology enables real-time data collection and analyses, offering the foundations for evidence-based people management and monitoring processes (Angrave et al., 2016).

Table 1. HR competency domain and digitization: opportunities and challenges.

OPPORTUNITIES for HRM 4.0	HR COMPETENCY DOMAINS	CHALLENGES for HRM 4.0
- direct and transparent communication and knowledge-sharing processes	CAPABILITY BUILDER	- new digital competences for HR professionals and the new workforce
- practicability of new organizational solutions and continuous improvements	CHANGE CHAMPION	- personal resistance in an open context and in conflictual instances
- improvement of new work solutions based on new technology (e.g., smart working, work platform)	TECHNOLOGY PROPONENT	- stronger partnerships with the ITC domain and development of related digital competences
- new e-HRM practices to better manage work relationships and co-creation processes	INNOVATOR AND INTEGRATOR	- new organizational mindset for employees as well as supervisors
- exploitation of HR practices for internal and external stakeholders who 'work' for and across the organization.	STRATEGIC POSITIONER	- new HR mindset and competences to cope with the external environment
- real-time data collection, offering the foundations for evidence-based people management and monitoring processes	CREDIBLE ACTIVIST	- new 4.0 work drawbacks, such as work-life imbalance, stress, work isolation, work insecurity

Despite the flourishing literature on the strategic role of the HR department and the new smart opportunities, the actual image of HR professionals would seem to be far from fully legitimized. There is evidence that the HR professional image is not always portrayed as strategic and relevant (e.g., Gibb, 2000; Hallier and Summers, 2011), and the debate on how to effectively interpret its multifaceted role is still ongoing (Ulrich, 2016).

The reasons behind a sloppy HR image can be various, from lack of competences to deeply-rooted negative stereotypes due to the economic crisis and labour plights (Hallier and Summers, 2011).These competences certainly entail some intrinsic tensions and suggest that HR professionals have to simultaneously pursue and face some apparently conflicting goals and issues: operational efficiency and strategic effectiveness; short term and long term orientation, past and future focus, outside and inside, organization and employee perspectives, social responsibility and shareholder return on investment. Moreover, it is also a riskier time for HR due to increased expectations. HR professionals today are under more scrutiny than ever to respond as their role takes on a higher profile (Ulrich and Dulebohn, 2015; Urlich, 2016).

A coherent and enabling method for the new organizational reality is that the HRM department promotes a design thinking culture throughout the organizations (inside and outside). This method enables collective innovation and open collaboration that advances through prototyping.

3.4. HRM department, organization and industry 4.0: the design thinking approach

The advanced digitization currently occurring within factories and affecting all enterprise activities will impact HRM department responsibilities and actions. Such a change will affect HRM in two different ways, both directly and indirectly. The combination of the recent Internet evolution and future-oriented technologies will offer new opportunities to the HR department to quantitatively compute its performance as well as predict its future outcome indicators and their antecedents, thus admitting HR managers to the strategy table. Moreover, some more routine activities traditionally pertaining to the HR department are in the process of being digitalized (e.g., detecting presence, some training activities), while others have been charged to employees and line managers (e.g., updating personal data and career advancement), thus allowing the HR department to focus on more strategic and value added activities (Khanna, 2016).

As for the indirect effect, digitization is changing the nature of work, disentangling it from time and space constraints. As an organizational unit in charge of designing and managing work, the HR department will undergo a profound change in the principles and practices to effectively manage work and employees in the 4.0 enterprise (Lee et al., 2015).

The stakes in the 4th industrial revolution are high. It is not just a matter of enhancing analytic and IT competences within the HR department and the rest of the enterprise: to win the challenge of leading the workforce and the whole organization through the paradigm shift brought about by the 4.0 industrial revolution, in this phase, the HR department is particularly urged to play the role of change champion (Ulrich et al., 2011). Therefore, the HR department's focus should be on the organizational culture.

Successful 4.0 enterprises are open, they act as networks that have extremely permeable organizational boundaries, they rely on a highly educated, technologically advanced, engaged workforce expected to actively interact with autonomous, context-aware machines, even able to make decision independently. In such a context, the human contribution cannot but be flexible, responsive, qualified, and innovative. Collaboration will be essential and continuous in 4.0 organizations. Even more important and new is that collective effort will require collaboration among individuals, but also between individuals and machines.

A valuable approach that can inform the culture of organizations transiting to the 4.0 era is the design thinking approach. Design thinking provides a useful method to deal with the overall complexity, uncertainty, and ill-defined problems that characterize business realities in this period of profound change (Glen, Suciu, and Baughn, 2014). This is also consistent with the need for integrative and holistic thinking to deal with the increased complexity embedded in the paradigm shift that is redefining the world of HR and organizations more widely (Gilbert, 2012; Karakas, 2011).

The essential ingredients of the design thinking approach include exploration and reflective iteration, a human-centred approach, observation, visualization and prototyping (Brown, 2008, 2009; Glen et al., 2014). Design thinking draws on the creative processes associated with design and is a recognized methodology enabling innovation (Leavy, 2010; Nielsen and Stovang, 2015). Designers confront problems by becoming directly involved, learning about the problem and trying out various solutions. In this paradigm, understanding the problem and its solution is a co-evolving process that includes iterations as a means of clarifying the issues (Beckman and Barry, 2007). Low or high fidelity prototypes together with sketches and flowcharts are ways of advancing understanding of the problem to be solved. Working on a tangible object allows collective action and the integration of useful but very different contributions for a deep understanding of the problem, developing new knowledge and collaborating around innovation (Dunne and Martin, 2006). The ideas are thus translated into observable objects that enable collaborating in the development of broad ideas, visualizing the designers' thoughts and thereby overcoming the challenge of expressing these through words, which in turn leads to co-creation through criticism, feedback, and further developments (Goel, 1995; Schön and Wiggins, 1992). The iteration process of simultaneously proposing alternatives and progressing in understanding the problem ends when the solution is considered good enough to meet the beneficiary's expectations (Nielsen and Stovang, 2015; Kimbell, 2011).

In the design thinking perspective, the innovation process is therefore

grounded in in-depth knowledge of the context within which the need arises and where the solution will be applied (Beckman and Barry, 2007). Designers immerse themselves to consider the point of view of the subject of
study so that they can understand user needs (Kimbell, 2011). Therefore,
ethnography and focus groups are considered a particularly effective method of collecting information on the user context and needs, as well as on
the environment itself in which the solution is to be applied (Beckman and
Barry, 2007).

As the organizational environment becomes more and more complex,
solutions can only derive from the contribution of a plurality of diverse
competences that become embedded in the organization. Our proposal is
therefore a practice-based focus on the relation between creation and re-
flection-upon-the-creation, thereby enabling constantly improving solutions and re-creation. Reflection is at the core of design thinking that could
thus constitute the essence of a new approach to completely revise the design of the organizational structure and HR practices to enable the enterprise to face and value the opportunities the 4.0 revolution offers. In other
words, design thinking could essentially be the basis of a new approach to
organizational design and collective action that completely subverts the linear
approach of analytic reasoning that entails dissecting phenomena into their
component elements (Glen et al., 2014; Johansson-Skoeldberg, Wodilla, and
Cetinkaya, 2013). Conversely, it facilitates the integration of perspectives,
collaboration beyond organizational boundaries, the definition of new paradigms for job design, and unpredictable solutions for the interaction between
humans, advanced robotics, and cognitive computing. Through design thinking, "managers build a unique and unanalyzable capacity for problem solving
that improves through experience and practice rather than through theory
or techniques", thus a valuable approach to deal with unexplored environments and obtain unique and creative solutions to unprecedented organizational issues, such as the those that enterprises will need to face soon
(Johansson-Skoeldberg et al., 2013, p. 125).

3.5. Conclusion

Work is unquestionably changing. The digitization of factories that is leading to the convergence of the digital and the physical is transforming the
workplace, requiring employees to work next to robot workers (Habraken
and Bondarouk, 2017). This will occur not just in factories but progressively in offices. Robots, will appear more and more in humanoid form within
15-20 years, able to perform activities typically associated with knowledge
work, such as creative, decision making, and emotion-related management

tasks. In this way, they may become full-fledged employees and human office employees may end up considering them colleagues (Klotz, 2016).

Industry 4.0 and the transformation of knowledge work will also affect the tasks of the HR department where digitization may take over many tasks (Klotz, 2016; Piazza, 2017; Strohmeier, 2017). The HR department may hopefully be released from part of their tasks and gain time to perform its strategic role. This would mean time on the one side to ferry the human workforce towards developing new competences to get ready for the upcoming 4th industrial revolution and the introduction of humanoid robots in the workplace, and on the other, to re-think/re-conceive HR systems and managerial practices that may fit with the new terms of the employee-organization relationship, thus able to support workforce motivation given the transforming work environment.

Design thinking, an approach that integrates and maximizes the innovative potential of collaboration with divergent perspectives may be an extremely useful methodology to succeed in the 4.0 challenge. It could enable the HR department and its stakeholders, e.g., first line supervisors, middle and top managers, to become involved in the co-creation of renewed HR practices that meet the needs of the workforce in the new workplace (Bondarouk and Brewster, 2016). Similarly, if the HR department acts as change agent in spreading an organizational culture informed by the design thinking principles, it will help workers establish relationships with robot workers, learn how to work next to them, and complement their abilities.

Such awareness draws attention to the relevance of HRM studies and scholars to advance the debate on the social effects of the 4th industrial revolution. Theoretical as well as empirical evidence of the HRM perspective may shed light in particular on approaches and variables that could support the transition through the new organizational context and avoid internal organizational rifts that could result in difficult social conditions or even revolt.

Consistently with this possibility, HRM scholars on their side should theorize on revising the HR department roles in light of the smart revolution that is transforming business processes (Ulrich et al., 2011). This is not a matter of conceiving new roles, but rather studying and predicting how the existing roles of the HR department need to change in consideration of the new wave of digitalization. Similarly, the HR academic community should work on updating the characteristics and components in the field of strategic HRM.

The risk is that HR managers and professionals do not seize the opportunity of leading organizations in the digital era. There is evidence that HR mangers are discussing the implications of 4.0 digitalization, but little has been done up to now to advance the digital transformation of the HR department (Piazza, 2017; Strohmeier, 2017). There is even evidence that some HR professionals still consider the new world of computing, analytics, big data, and robots as a fad or just one of several managerial fashions that will pass just as all the previous ones (Marler et al., 2017).

It is our opinion that besides being dangerous for the whole enterprise, it would also mean losing the opportunity for the HR department to change its destiny from an ancillary organizational unit to becoming leader of the digital transformation. This new avenue could also be a great opportunity for the HR department to restore its professional credibility and image after the last economic crisis and the consequent labour plights.

References

Angrave, D., Charlwood, A., Kirkpatrick, I., Lawrence, M., Stuart, M. (2016). HR and analytics: why HR is set to fail the big data challenge. *Human Resource Management Journal*, 26(1), 1-11.

Beckman, S.L. Barry, M. (2007). Innovation as a learning process: embedding design thinking. *California Management Review*, 50(1), 25-56.

Bissola, R Imperatori, B. (2014). The unexpected side of relational e-HRM: Developing trust in the HR department. *Employee Relations*, 36(4), 376-397.

Bissola, R., Imperatori, B. (2012). Sustaining the stakeholder engagement in the social enterprise: The human resource architecture. Pp. 137-160. Jill Kickul, Sophie Bacq (Eds). *Patterns in social entrepreneurship research*. Northampton, MA, Edward Elgar.

Bissola, R., Imperatori, B., Biffi, A. (2017). A rhizomatic learning process to create collective knowledge in entrepreneurship education: Open innovation and collaboration beyond boundaries. *Management Learning*, 48(2), 206-226.

Bondarouk, T., Brewster, C. (2016). Conceptualising the future of HRM and technology research. *The International Journal of Human Resource Management*, 27(21), 2652-2671.

Bremer, S. A. (2015). *Simulated worlds: A computer model of national decision-making. Princeton*, NJ, Princeton University Press.

Brown, T. (2009). *Change by design: How design thinking transforms organizations and inspires innovation*. New York, NY, Harper Business.

Brown, T. (2008). Design thinking. *Harvard Business Review*, 86(6), 84-92.

Brynjolfsson, E., McAfee, A. (2014). *The second machine age: Work, progress, and prosperity in a time of brilliant technologies*. New York, NY, WW Norton & Company.

Butts, M. M., Becker, W.J., Boswell, W.R. (2015). Hot buttons and time sinks: The effects of electronic communication during nonwork time on emotions and work-nonwork conflict. *Academy of Management Journal*, 58(3), 763-788.

Cappelli, P., Tavis, A. (2016). The performance management revolution. *Harvard Business Review*, 94(10), 58-67.

Colbert, A., Yee, N., George, G. (2016). The digital workforce and the workplace of the future. *Academy of Management Journal*, 59(3), 731-739.

Dunne, D. Martin, R. (2006). Design thinking and how it will change management education: an interview and discussion. *Academy of Management Learning and Education*, 5(4), 512-523.

Edgell, S., Gottfried H., Granter E., eds. (2015). *The Sage handbook of the sociology of work and employment*. Thousand Oaks, CA, Sage Publications Ltd.

Gibb, S. (2000). Evaluating HRM effectiveness: the stereotype connection. *Employee Relations*, 22(1), 58-75.

Glen, R., Suciu, C., Baughn, C. (2014). The need for design thinking in Business Schools. *Academy of Management Learning & Education*, 13(4), 653-667.

Goel, V. (1995). *Sketches of thought*. Cambridge, MA, MIT Press.

Habraken, M., Bondarouk, T. (2017). Smart Industry Research in the Field of HRM: Resetting Job Design as an Example of Upcoming Challenges. In Tanya Bondarouk, Huub J.M. Ruël, Emma Parry (eds.) *Electronic HRM in the Smart Era*, pp. 221–259. Bingley, UK, Emerald Publishing Limited.

Hallier, J., Summers, J. (2011). Dilemmas and outcomes of professional identity construction among students of human resource management. *Human Resource Management Journal*, 21(2), 204-219.

Holland, P., Bardoel, A. (2016). The impact of technology on work in the twenty-first century: Exploring the smart and the dark side. *The International Journal of Human Resource Management*, 27(21), 2579–2581.

Gilbert, D.H. (2012), From chalk and talk to walking the walk: Facilitating dynamic learning contexts for entrepreneurship students in fast-tracking innovations. *Education + Training*, 54(2/3), 152-166.

Glen, R., Suciu, C., Baughn, C. (2014). The need for design thinking in Business Schools. *Academy of Management Learning & Education*, 13(4), 653-667.

Jackson, T., Dawson, R., Wilson, D. (2001). The cost of email interruption. *Journal of Systems and Information Technology*, 5(1), 81-92.

Johansson-Skoeldberg, U., Wodilla, J., Cetinkaya, M. (2013). Design thinking: Past, present and possible futures. *Creativity and Innovation Management*, 22(2), 121-146.

Kane, G.C., Palmer, A.N., Phillips, D., Kiron, N. Buckley, N. (2016). Aligning the Organization for Its Digital Future, *MIT Sloan Management Review and Deloitte University Press*, July 26, 1-27.

Kapoor, B., Kabra, Y. (2014). Current and future trends in human resources analytics adoption. *Journal of Cases on Information Technology* (JCIT), 16(1), 50-59.

Karakas, F. (2011), Positive management education: creating creative minds, passionate hearts, and kindred spirits. *Journal of Management Education*, 35(2), 198-226.

Khanna, S. (2016). The Nuances of Digital HR. *Human Capital*, May, 41-42.

Kimbell, L. (2011). Rethinking design thinking: Part I. *Design and Culture*, 3(3), 285-306.

Klotz, F. (2016). Are You Ready for Robot Colleagues? *MIT Sloan Management Review*, 58(1), 1-8.

Lasi, H., Fettke, P., Kemper, H.G., Feld, T., Hoffmann, M. (2014). Industry 4.0. *Business & Information Systems Engineering*, 6(4), 239-242.

LaValle, S., Lesser, E., Shockley, R., Hopkins, M. S., Kruschwitz, N. (2011). Big data, analytics and the path from insights to value. *MIT Sloan Management Review*, 52(2), 21-32.

Leavy, B. (2010). Design thinking – a new mental model of value innovation. *Strategy & Leadership*, 38(3), 5-14.

Lee, J., Bagheri, B., Kao, H. A. (2015). A cyber-physical systems architecture for industry 4.0-based manufacturing systems. *Manufacturing Letters*, 3, 18-23.

Levy, F., Murnane, R. J. (2012). *The new division of labor: How computers are creating the next job market*. Princeton, NJ. Princeton University Press.

Markoulli, M., Lee, C.I., Byington, E., Felps, W. A. (2017). Mapping Human Resource Management: Reviewing the field and charting future directions. *Human Resource Management Review*, 27(3), 367-396.

Marler, J.H., Cronemberger, F., Tao, C. (2017). HR Analytics: Here to Stay or Short Lived Management Fashion? Bondarouk, T., Ruël, H. J., Parry, E. (Eds.). *Electronic HRM in the Smart Era*. Pp. 59 - 85. Bingley, UK, Emerald Publishing Limited.

Nielsen, S.L., Stovang P. (2015). DesUni: university entrepreneurship education through design thinking. *Education + Training*, 57(8/9), 977-991.

Piazza, F. (2016). Internet of Things-Induced Changes to HRM – A Framework Integrating Innovation and HRM. Paper presented at the *6th International e-HRM Conference: From Digital to Smart Human Resource Management*. Enschede (The Nederlands), October, 27-28.

Rich, B.L., Lepine, J. A., and Crawford, E. R. (2010). Job engagement: Antecedents and effects on job performance. *Academy of Management Journal*, 53(3), 617-635.

Schön, D.A., Wiggins, G. (1992). Kinds of seeing in designing. *Creativity and Innovation Management*, 1(2), 68-74.

Sokol, M. (2015). The Future of Work. *People + Strategy*, 38(3), 8-10.

Sonnentag, S., Binnewies, C., and Mojza, E.J. (2008). "Did you have a nice evening?" A day-level study on recovery experiences, sleep, and affect. *Journal of Applied Psychology*, 93(3), 674.

Strohmeier, S. (2016). Smart HRM – A Delphi Study on the Application and Consequences of the Internet of Things in Human Resource Management. Paper presented at the *6th International e-HRM Conference: From Digital to Smart Human Resource Management*. Enschede (The Nederlands), October, 27-28.

Strohmeier, S. Parry, E. (2014). HRM in the digital age–digital changes and challenges of the HR profession. *Employee Relations*, 36(4), guest editorial.

Turkle, S. (2011). *Alone together: Why we expect more from technology and less from each other*. New York, NY, Basic books.

Ulrich, D. (2016). HR at a crossroads. *Asia Pacific Journal of Human Resources*, 54(2), 148-164

Ulrich, D. (1997). Measuring human resources: an overview of practice and a prescription for results. *Human Resource Management*, 36(3), 303-320.

Ulrich, D., Dulebohn, J. H. (2015). Are we there yet? What's next for HR? *Human Resource Management Review*, 25(2), 188-204.

Ulrich, D., Younger, J., Brockbank, W., & Ulrich, M. (2011). Competencies for HR Professionals Working Outside-In. *The RBL White Paper Series*. Retrieved online: https://faculty.mu.edu.sa/public/uploads/1360249894.7981human%20 resource169.pdf.

van Kruining, I. (2017). The dis-app-earance of HRM: Impact of Digitization on the HRM Profession. In Bondarouk, T., Ruël, H. J., Parry, E. (Eds.). *Electronic HRM in the Smart Era*. Pp. 311-337. Bingley, UK, Emerald Publishing Limited.

Zhang, X., Bartol, K.M. (2010). Linking empowering leadership and employee creativity: The influence of psychological empowerment, intrinsic motivation, and creative process engagement. *Academy of Management Journal*, 53(1), 107-128.

Part II
PRACTICES

Chapter 4

HOW TECHNOLOGY HAS REDEFINED HUMAN RESOURCE PRACTICES? UNDERSTANDING THE USE OF SMART WORKING

Stefano Forte-Pietro Previtali-Danila Scarozza

4.1. Introduction

As the next wave of technological change has started to emerge in the workplace, it is timely to explore the impact of information and communication technology (ICT) on work (Holland, Bardoel, 2016). As Morgan (2014) notes, there are many fascinating things happening in the world of technology that are impacting on work. Today, successful organisations are increasingly characterized by the ability to abandon now inappropriate working configurations (Birkinshaw et al., 2008) to support new organisational principles, new methods and tools through which work practices are accomplished (Hamel, 2012). The use of ICT provides an opportunity to be innovative in when we work, where we work and the way we work (Harvey, 2010). Specifically, there has been a noticeable diffusion among organisations of innovative ways of working and growing opportunities for their employees to perform work activities remotely, let them generally free to choose where (places) and when (time) carry out the assigned activities (spatial-temporal flexibility). This resulted in an increasing interest showed by both academics and practitioners towards different typologies of remote work arrangements, including telework, home-based telework, mobile work, virtual teams and, more recently, smart work (or smart working - SW).

Specifically, SW has the potential to offer a wide range of individuals an alternative to traditional work arrangements. SW succeeds in modifying traditional work conditions and their natural environment, searching different and (till now) not totally and uniquely defined solutions, essentially grounded on a greater discretion in work activities and on a larger responsibility towards results workers are requested to provide. These two elements together are indeed believed to favour better performances by workers and so to increase competitiveness (Haines, St-Onge, 2012; Wood et al., 2012) essential for enterprises' survival and development (Chiaro et al., 2015). This connection explains the increasing interest for SW by the business world and by the consultancy, that offer support for the realization of projects in the field (Clapperton, Vanhoutte, 2014; Iacono, 2013; Hartog et al., 2015).

Furthermore, over the last few years managers have started to acknowledge the potential advantages offered to both employees and organisations by SW. Howcroft and Taylor (2014) point out that society is seeing a new wave of revolutionary technology that provides the platform for significant change in the way people work. These changes are creating renewed interest in how work is conceptualized – what we describe as the 'smart-side' of technology.

Also in the Italian context – especially after the adoption of the Law n.81/2017 – Smart Working (SW) has emerged as a "new" way to define what is considered as an innovative approach to work organisation and human resource management.

In this frame this chapter proposes a conceptual models to better define SW. Furthermore, analysing the TIM Group case study the chapter aims to investigate the nature and the dynamics of SW in order: a) to offer a contribution to the debate on the workplaces' changes in response to increasingly sophisticated technology; b) to understand the effects of SW in terms of both work-life balance, individual performance and external benefits.

4.2. Conceptualizing smart working

Technologies have changed (through enabling and/or constraining) HRM practices by introducing for example, e-recruitment, e-training, e-competence management or e-work (Stone, Deadrick, Lukaszewski, & Johnson, 2015). These technologies have brought a new vocabulary to the HRM discourse as the conventional terminology is supplemented by new terms like electronic HRM (e-HRM), HRM data mining, HRM cloud computing, application of HRM (for mobile technologies) and HRM big data (Bondarouk, 2014). These technologies have altered the HRM organisational communications (Kiesler, Siegel, & McGuire, 1984), and enabled new means of employer branding (Martin & Cerdin, 2014). In particular, changes in HRM and technologies have modified the geographical boundaries of HRM practices, distances in and between organisations have become shortened. Due to diverse technological advancements, organisations can offer their employees new ways of working by eliminating physical and time barriers and relying on such organisational forms as HRM shared services, virtual teams or SW. In their turn, technology-enabled new organisational forms embrace new stakeholders in HRM processes. Applying smart working – for example – workers, first line supervisors, middle and top managers get directly involved in co-creation of HRM.

Starting from these premises and focusing on SW, this chapter was inspired by following questions (Figure 1): *i*) to what extent is the interface between organisational model for working and new technology contextually bound? *ii*) what are the combination of the different elements affecting the configuration of SW? *iii*) what are the outcomes of SW likely to be for smar-workers, organisations and society?

Figure 1. The conceptual Framework.

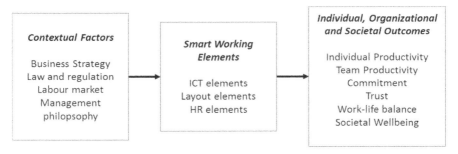

Source: our elaboration

The context

An important element for an effective SW implementation (not external to it, but part of the SW itself) is the context within which SW is adopetd. SW could be seen as a system consisting of people, technology, organisations, and management practices related to human resource management. According to the principle of equifinality (Von Bertalanffy, 1969) the same final state may be reached from different initial conditions and HRM antecedents, in different ways, through different mechanisms. In order to better understand the relevance of SW and its functioning within organisations, the context can be defined as the HRM context as the relevant external and internal conditions and elements. The external elements include societal values, the laws, the regulation the labour market and the business conditions within which the organisation has to work. There will be elements that are more directly under the organisation's control but that are limited by previous managerial decisions and history, including the workforce characteristics. There will also be elements that are directly related to the business but are outside the direct remit of HRM, such as the management philosophy and the business strategy.

Focusing on SW, probably location has a major effect on how SW is understood and implemented, what practices have legitimacy and what the effects of those practices are likely to be (Brewster & Mayrhofer, 2012). Countries have different SW regulations and practices because they are in different situations, have different cultures and different institutions. Specifically, governement and regulations play an important role for changing HRM practices and – consequently – SW (Jackson, Schuler, & Jiang, 2014; Rodriguez & Johnstone, 2015). In particular, regulations for the Italian context was one of the most important elements. The adoption of the Law n. 81/2017 defined SW as "a way to regulate the workers-organisation relationship, according to an agreement between the parties, also recurring to forms of organisation by stages, cycles and goals, without a defined timetable or place constraints working and the opportunity to use any technological tools to perform activities". Moreover, the Law (art. 18) stated that the main purpose of this new way to work is "both to increase competitiveness and to facilitate the balance of working and living times". The ratio of the Italian legislation is, on the one hand, to promote an improvement of the organisations' productivity and – on the other hand – to guarantee a better work life balance to workers involved in the SW adoption (Capobianco, 2017).

Also globalisation will apply to SW too, since universal 'good practice' will inevitably spread around the world (Cooke, 2003), but there is little evidence that countries are becoming more alike in the way they conceive of and manage SW (Gooderham & Nordhaug, 2011). National differences are explained by cultural differences (Aycan et al., 2000) and institutional differences. There may be debate about the balance between these explanations but together or independently culture and institutions will impact the SW/technology interface too.

The smart-working elements
The development and diffusion of ICT, can support organisations in developing a SW system (Ahuja et al., 2007). Previous literature has analysed how ICT has made work more portable and pervasive (Yoo et al., 2010), there is not yet a comprehensive understanding the elements on which organisations should focus in case they want to adopt a SW organisational model.

According to the analysis developed by Mann (2012), the three elements that can constitute a SW model are:

1. the *ICT element*: it is referred to the usage of ICT-based solutions. ICT solutions allow workers to share more easily files, information, data and ideas (Chudoba et al., 2005). In such a way, all employees can interact in real time in a flexible and effective way by contributing to a SW environment (software collaboration);

2. the *HR element*: this includes the innovations in the HR practices and in the organisational model (HR element). Changes in the HR practices can be introduced when a new organisational model is chosen, as SW is. Specifically, change management actions for managing the organisational models chosen can be applied by the organisations (Cameron and Green, 2012), such as training programmes, new communication plans, projects of cultural change, processes reorganisation or a re-desing of job role profiles;

3. the *layout element*: it is related to the reconfiguration of the workplace and of the office layout. According to some study, the strategy focused on the spatial reconfiguration of the office have an important role for the effectiveness of a SW system. The attention to the layout can increase individual and team productivity and can allow to workers to better their work-life balance. Therefore, particular office reconfigurations may lead to innovative ways of collaborating with others and thus simplifying the development of a SW model.

Table 1. Smart-working elements.

Elements	Dimension	Reference
ICT	Extent to which employees telework Use of ICT personal devices and/or external ICT services	Martínez-Sánchez et al. (2007)
HR	Extent to which employees can manage in a flexible way their working hours Change management actions implemented in the organisation and new HRM practices/tools developed	Coenen and Kok (2014)
Layout	Adoption of initiatives of redesigning of the physical workspace for creating environments more flexible and oriented to collaboration	Elsbach and Pratt (2007)

Source: adapted by Gastaldi et al. (2014)

Individual, Organisational and Societal Outcomes

SW has various impacts and consequences at different level: individual, organisational and societal. An understanding of these will help identify the values and motives that may support the promotion of this way of working.

At the *individual level* a potential benefit of SW is represented by the opportunity for individual workers to establish an arrangement that is very personal and conducive to a superior quality of domestic life. SW can offer opportunities for people to improve their worklife balance more so than under traditional work conditions (Duxbury & Higgins, 2002). As a result, smart workers are often more motivated and enjoy better job satisfaction than conventional workers (Spillman & Markham, 1997; Himmelsbach, 1998; James, 2004). The positive perception of an improved work/life balance is recognized as one of the most important outcome of SW adoption. Other studies, suggested that smart workers are more committed since they worked longer hours than traditional employees, often without additional payment or remuneration for these extra hours (Huws, Robinson, & Robinson, 1990; Michelson, 2000; Hill, Hawkins, Ferris, & Weitzman, 2001; Duxbury & Higgins, 2002a; Peters, Wetzels, & Tijdens, 2008). One of the more sufficient potential benefits is increasing worker productivity that accrues from the practice of SW (Ruth & Chaudhry, 2008). Organisations and businesses that have embraced telework have been able to increase output with the same number of staff, or reduce headcount and still provide the same level of service to their clients and customers.

Looking at the *organisational* level, SW must not be considered in isolation but rather placed in the overall context of existing and continuous business reorganisation and change management environments. SW has the potential to become an integral, rather than an optional, way of working. Studies have shown SW can increase organisational productivity (Baruch, 2000). SW can reduce absenteeism and increases resilience, especially with decreased stress and anxiety levels and more control over working times and location (Costa et al., 2004; Olsen & Dahl, 2010). Another organisational impact of telework is the improvement it offers for services to customers in a variety of ways. It can allow higher personalised responses to customer demands without the need for a conventional base or office. This flexibility can fit into the ethos of how a company or organisation operates and can lead to co-operative work across international boundaries and different time zones. SW implies also a rethiking of the control and supervision issues (Flynn, 1995; Baruch, 2000): the organisations need to trust unsupervised workers in a different manner. Moreover, the management of individual differences, and indeed similarities, between women and men and how they perceive their professional and domestic roles is an important issue when considering the adoption or development of SW. However, White et al. (2010) maintained gender differences associated with frequency of working from home is insignificant, indicating a slightly lower proportion of females working from home at least once a week.

Finally, *societal outcomes* can be regarded also as the long-term outcomes (Bondarouk & Brewster, 2016). Organisations need to create economic value but today they need to be also sustainable: since organisations derive their legitimacy from society, HRM decisions and practices will have long-term benefits for the society.

In literature, there was a lack of interest in and evidence about the effects of SW adoption both on the community within which the organisation operates and – more in general – on the society. Nevertheless, with the more recent development of notions such as sustainable HRM (Ehnert & Harry, 2011; Taylor, Osland, & Egri, 2012) and corporate social responsibility (Lindgreen & Swaen, 2010) this is beginning to change. From a societal poin of view, in fact, the magnitude of the impact of SW on environment, mobility and socioeconomic aspects is therefore relevant in order to determine whether a further encouragement of SW is useful and sustainable for the society as a whole (Tom van Lier et al., 2012). SW can be seen a way of offering environmental protection benefits by reducing, or eliminating, the commute to work leading to less fuel consumption and less C02 emissions, fewer traffic congestion problems and, savings in energy use in urban office spaces and buildings (Verbeke, Schulz, Greidanus, & Hambley, 2008; Nidumolu, Prahalad, & Rangaswami, 2009). Although these benefits are, to a certain extent, achievable with the correct understanding and strategies, the impact of SW on society continues to remain poorly understood (Glaister, 2008). SW also has the potential to bring about a more equitable distribution of economic activity throughout geographical areas and help redress the aggregation of economic activity in the main urban centres (Callanan, 1999). In addition, the spread of SW can assist in improving the economic and employment opportunities of underdeveloped areas (Forgács, 2010).

4.3. Method

Since only limited empirical research on how organisations deal with the adoption of SW has been found an explorative approach has been chosen. Particularly, the research being reported in this chapter involved the case study of TIM Group (a telecommunication company) in the adoption of SW since 2015. Other scholars used the case study approach to examine SW [Gastaldi et al., 2014].

In this study, a single case is used, which is an appropriate way of establishing the field at the early stages of an emerging topic (Eisenhardt, 1989). Moreover, the single case study approach is normally preferred when an inductive approach can be adopted, using theory to explain empirical observations and also to inform refinements and extension of the theory (Berry et al., 1991; Otley & Berry, 1994; Yin, 1994).

The case study presented in this chapter aims to explore and to understand the configuration of SW and its outcomes at the individual, organisational and societal level.

According to our exploratory approach, we selected TIM Group as an exemplar case study (Yin, 1994), with unique circumstances. In particular, in TIM Group, the project on SW begun prior to the regulatory intervention by Italian legislation. Only in 2017 the Law n. 81/2017 clearly defined agile work and the purposes of its adoption within organisations. In this setting, we analyzed five different building blocks in order to understand both *why* and *how* SW has been adopted and what the outcomes obtained by a SW organisational model: a) context; b) ICT element; c) layout element; d) HR element; e) SW outcomes.

The information gathered during this research relates to the results of both the *trial* phase, which began in 2015 and was completed in 2016, and the *pilot* phase, which began in 2016 and it is still ongoing. From a methodological point of view, data and information collection period is particularly significant for our analysis, since it allows us to better define the nature and the relevance of the collected information. The longitudinal approach used in the observation of the project development led to the analysis of context, groups, and individuals dynamics, concerning the adoption of SW. To improve validity and reliability (Yin, 1994), of our finding and conclusions, we collected data from different sources. In relation to the four conceptual dimensions of analysis (ICT element, layout element, HR element and outcomes), a triangulation was carried out between documental information and interviews. The documents helped understanding the relevance given to the different phases and practices, the modes of interaction between actors and the technologies adopted for SW. Data have been collected by the "organisation co-author" also through interviews and continuous information flows. All information gathered provided also evidence on both the process of internal communication and the role of people involved in trialing and adopting SW. The interviews were conducted with some of the key organisational actors involved in the SW adoption process. The interviews were conducted to ensure that the case study is "bounded" (Yin, 1994) and to guarantee that the conclusions of this study are based upon specific observations (Maxwell, 1996). Thanks to a collaborative writing and analysis process between academics and organisation coauthor, the case study description has improved and the construct validity has increased (Yin, 1994).

4.4. The case study of the TIM Group: findings and discussion

TIM Group is one of the most important telecommunication company in Italy. In particular TIM is the leading telecommunications and ICT group and Italy's digital partner. Abroad it is one of the most important players on the Brazilian market. The Group is also active in Europe, Americas, Africa and Asia. Today, in Italy TIM Group manage 29.7 million mobile lines (12.5 million of which are BB users) and 11.2 million fixed connections (7.4 million of which are retail BB accesses, i.e. consumer & business). Moreover, in 2016 the Group generated 9.8 billion euros of social value. Through TIM Foundation the Group also promoted a vision of innovation and technology as social enablers. As a result of the social and environmental commitment TIM Group has, over the last 14 years, been included amongst the most important and selective stock market sustainability indexes worldwide.

In this setting, in 2015 Tim Group launched a trial to prepare the context for the development of a new way of working. Only in 2016 the pilot started and the SW model became a reality in the group. All the five subsidiaries (TIM, Sparkle, HR Services, Inwit) belonging to the Group are involved in the SW project.

The context for the adoption of SW in TIM Group

As stated before the context within the SW is adopted is one of the preliminary conditions to guarantee the effectiveness of the new working model. Looking at the internal context and – specifically – to the management philosophy – in 2015 (from october to december) TIM launched a *trial phase* in order to define a roadmap and to create the "right internal context" for the adoption of SW itself. Specifically, the trial was realized following the "manifesto of smart working" developed by Clapperton and Vanhoutte (2014). The authors proposed three relevant dimensions to adopt SW: 1) *Bricks*, the physical dimension, addresses all aspects of the physical work environment, 2) *Bytes*, the technological dimension, addresses all aspects concerning the use and application of ICT, and 3) *Behaviour*, the personal dimension, which addresses all aspects concerning the manager-employee relationship and the way the employee works and experiences his work. These dimensions define a new way of working: besides the freedom to work in any place and at any time, there is the need to the redesign of offices to accommodate taskbased workplaces, with concentration places and meeting places, and a result oriented way of working in which freedom and trust play an important role. Though the three dimensions can be applied in 'production and location based' work environments, they can best applied in the work environment of the 'knowledge worker' (Greene &

Myerson, 2011). However, in order to ensure the consistency of the new way of working with the business stratey, TIM Group decided to add another dimension that is called *"Business & Social"*: the "business" is referred to the need to combine a new way of working with the services supplied by the Group, the "social" dimension instead underlines the relevance of stakeholders involement in the SW project in order to promote commitment and collaboration, especially among smart workers.

The cities involved in this first experimentation are Roma, Milano, Torino, Bologna and Palermo, with a potential number of over 18,000 workers who have the opportunity to test SW as a new way of working. At the national level, the experimentation conducted in 2015 by TIM Group is one of the largest for its social and statistical dimensions. TIM workers involved in this experiment can choose to work from home or from various satellite locations. Data collection in this preliminary stage provided also a picture of the different working habits for smart workers.

Figure 2 summarizes all the elements defining the context in which SW is adopted.

Figure 2. The contextual elements.

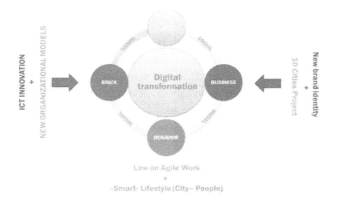

Source: TIM Group

The Smart Working Elements *in TIM Group.* From January 2016 the first pilot phase of SW started. Figure 3 shows the number of workers who decided to take part to the SW project along the time in wich the experimentation phase is conducted. As showed the number of smartworkers increased during the central phase (august 2016 and september 2016) and again in the last part of the experimentation (december 2016). However, the general trend remains constant starting to march 2016 until the end of the pilot phase. It's interesting to note the growing number of stakeholders from february 2016 to March 2016 (30%).

Figure 3. Smartworkers involved in the project.

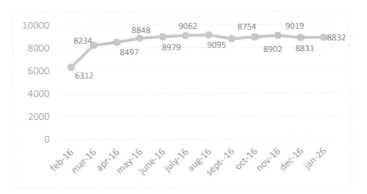

Source: our elaboration from data provided by TIM Group.

In order to complete the analysis related to the the extent to which employees adopt SW a focus can been made on the management level. Similarly, figure 4 shows the number of managers who decided to take part to the SW project along the experimentation period. The adoption trend of SW by managers in TIM seems to be very low; in addition the collected data show a costant decrease in the last three months of the experimentation period.

Figure 4. Managers involved in the SW project.

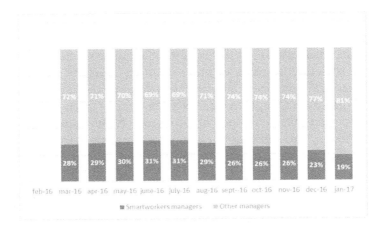

Source: our elaboration from data provided by TIM Group

Despite the presence of a supportive and mature digital infrastructure, TIM Group invested in the *ICT element* develpoing a "new" digital environment able to complete the HR strategy of letting people work whenever and wherever they wanted. Thus, in addition to some investments in unified communication and collaboration tools, a mobile workspace (constituted by a laptop, a smartphone and an internet connection) has been made available to all employees. Moreover, a set of cloudbased solutions has been developed to improve the performance, the reliability and the scalability of the applications used in day-by-day tasks. In this way the working place is highly simplified, and human resource can focus on one task at a time and boost both their efficiency and effectiveness. Moreover, the company is identinfying 31 new service solutions including the development of a set of apps allowing to book a meeting room on the run, release it, etc, the improvement of both the individual workstation and the internet connection.

Workers in TIM – using the corporate intranet – may book online the days in which they wish to work outside the office, indicating if he/she intend to use a personal workstation or one of the satellite locations (other than the home office) created by the company. In addition, using the smartphone workers are able to tethering and using the apn intelecomitalia.tim.it, to connect to the corporate intranet and to use the corporate mail as well as if in the office. Finally smart workers can use the microsoft lync social collaboration tool to collaborate with colleagues; the same tool is also used to attest the status of presence. In this way the company maintain some degree of control over employees.

The analysis of the *HR element* revealed that some new features have been introduced. Before to start with the pilot phase, in fact, a survey was conducted aiming to identify the most recurrent job profile identified according to the Activity Based Working (ABW). Presented as "the reorganisation of the work place to enable staff to be more productive and collaborate using shared workspaces or other locations" (Telsyte, 2015), it is remarked that ABW wishes to empower people to cultivate cross-functional skills and that it gives employees a choice about how, when and where they work (inside and outside the office). Moreover, ABW assumes all employees work flexibly and will seek out a range of different spaces to undertake different tasks. As such, these workspaces provide a range of work settings for different types of activities such as meetings, collaboration, private work, creativity and concentration. In TIM the management started from the idea that all tasks require a typical attention from workers, that is not uniform. For some tasks workers need to think creatively, for some activities will need to collaborate, and for others they simply need to do a couple of mundane chores. According to the four dimensions underpping this model (concentration, collaboration, communication and creativity) TIM identified four *job profile* in order: i) to assess the use of workspaces; ii) to understand for which profiles SW can be adopted; iii) to associate to each profile a working environment and a set of tools. The profiles identified are the following:

- *profile 1*: the most important dimension for performing tasks is reprensented by the concentration, consequently the worker may perform activties without collaboration using his work station (the 34,4% of workers in TIM belong to this profile);
- *profile 2*: the activities are characterized by all four dimensions (27,8%);
- *profile 3*: the activties required a lot of communication with other colleagueas, functional areas and customers, for these communications workers may use smartphone, e-mail, videos and conference call (18,2%);
- *profile 4*: the activities are mainly based on collaboration (7,1%).

In addition, on HR element TIM realized several training initiatives for supporting the change management process started trough the adoption of a SW model. The aim was to develop new competencies and capabilities necessary to efficiently and effectively accomplishing the new tasks and activities connected to new working model.

Finally, significant interventions are started on *layout element.* Following the management philosophy, work environments have to represent the company identity, meanwhile they are also conceptualized as "enablers" of a SW model. There was the necessity of changing the offices in order to fully benefit from SW models: a new design, in fact, may improve the creativity, the interactions, the exchange of ideas and the communication among people. TIM Group invested in layout and offices' design to reinforce its image as a dynamic, open and changing organisation able to ensure to its workers time and space to develop their ideas. Office layouts and design will be inspired by the organisational values and by the brand proposition. In this frame, TIM made a relevant investment in order to redesign the layout with the aims of rationalising the cost of facilities, improving the quality of the internal decision-making processes and stimulate creativity in individuals. The project on layout – called "10 Cities Project" since it firstly started in the 10 most important Italian cities – aims: a) to redesign the working environments identifying different spaces according to both the different purposes' activities and to the different moments of the working day; b) to favour the transition from separate offices (personal, closed, isolated and hard offices) to smart offices (common, open, aggregated and flexible); c) to divide working spaces in categories: single workstation, services to people on the floor (i.e. break area, etc.) and services to people at the workplace (i.e. meeting room, etc.).

Table 2. 10 Cities Project.

The numbers
10 cities
51 renovated buildings
400,000 renovated square metres
700,000 square metres in release
30,000 workers involved

Source: TIM Group

Individual, Organisational and Societal Outcomes within & outside TIM Group

The analysis of TIM Group case study confirms that SW is related to positive outcomes from personal, business and society perspectives.

At the *individual level*, perceived job flexibility, given a reasonable workweek, enables more employees to have work-family balance (personal and family benefit) and also enables employees to work longer hours before impacting work-family balance. Also in TIM perceived job flexibility is significantly and positively related to work-family balance. Given a workweek of reasonable length, employees who perceive flexibility in the timing and location of work have less difficulty with work-family balance. In addition, employees with perceived flexibility in the timing and location of work can work longer hours before work-family balance becomes difficult. In particular, one possible benefit of SW has to do with a reduction in the stress associated with the daily commute. Flexplace also provides more options for where an employee might choose to live. Smartworkers in TIM, in fact, may choose to work from home or from various satellite locations. In addition, many jobs include periods of peak work demands. In a rigid work environment, these times make it extremely difficult simultaneously to meet the demands of work and family life because the work has to be done physically from the work location. By contrast, in a flexible work environment, an employee can work the same long number of hours, but intersperse several hours of quality family time each day. For this last reasons remains unclear the choice to use SW by TIM Group managers. Finally, our analysis reveals that SW has a positive impact on individual productivity. The 99% of the smartworkers in TIM perceived an improvement of their productivity when they work at home. This perception is confirmed also by smartworkers which used a satellite location: in this case the 96% of the workers declared to be more productive recurring to SW.

The positive relationship between SW adoption and productivity remains valid also at the *organisational level*. On the one hand, in the case of remote SW, the 85% of the managers perceived an improvement of the team productivity; on the other hand, when smartworkers recurred to a satellite location, the perceived increase of team productivity is perceived by the 84% of the managers. Another issue at this level, may be the technology and, more in general, the role of the SW as one of the element support the digital transformation in TIM. Since TIM Group can be classified as a large company, it may have greater resources to support the technology required for flexplace. Moreover, with the SW adoption people in TIM are more aware of the use of digital technologies and the SW itself has became an opportunity in terms of organisational learning. Furthermore, in TIM the SW adoption required a different stratification processes and procedures in order to maintain the alignment among objectives, behaviours and tools. Another implication is related to the culture and the philosophy in TIM Group. The company that adopts SW also should move away from a "face-time" business culture to a "results-oriented" business culture, and performance evaluation systems must adapt to include more specifically measured objectives. The last, but not least, important aspect at the organisational level refers to the management of individual differences within the TIM Group, especially the gender differences. As suggested from some scholars, the analysis of the case study revealed (Figure 5) that gender differences associated with adoption of SW is insignificant, indicating a slightly lower proportion of men adopting SW.

Figure 5. SW and gender differences.

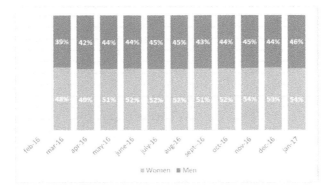

Source: our elaboration from data provided by TIM Group

The analysis of the case study shows significant evidences and outcomes also at the *societal level*. Looking at the environmental consequences and sustainability of SW, the experience conducted in TIM Group shows – first of all – that the new way of working has moderated private car use reducing environmental and socio-economical impacts of mobility on society. Congestion, air pollution, noise, the increase in time loss due to traffic and externalities linked to up-and downstream processes are the most well known transport related externalities. The data collected in TIM (Figure 6) show different level of SW adoption in the Italian cities and probably we can assume that these differences are due to the amount of externalities in the several cities: Roma results, in fact, the city where the number of smart-workers is higher than in other cities. More in general, trough the adoption of SW, the TIM Group could provide a significant externalities saving. The first estimates – made on 2016 – of the improvements realized by the TIM Group through the SW adoption reveal the savings of 1000 tons of Co_2 and a reduction of 248,000 hours of commuting time. Moreover, are created in urban relations since SW creates the conditions for a new and different "use" of neighborhoods, abandoning the concept of dormitory quarters.

Figure 6. SW and Italian cities.

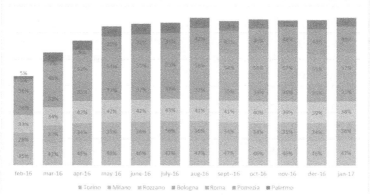

Source: our elaboration from data provided by TIM Group

4.5. Conclusions and limitations

SW represents a journey at both organisational and national level and this journey has only just begun. Starting from the assumption that there is not a unique path for developing a SW, but a set of potential paths that have to be designed taking into account the characteristics of the organisation investing in SW, this study highlights some considerations regarding the context, the elements and the outcomes characterising a SW model.

In particular, the analyzed case study help to understand that there are a number of pre-requisites for SW adoption and implementation in an organisation. The main reasons for which an organisation invests in SW tend to shape and being shaped by the investments accomplished in SW elements (Gastaldi et al. 2014). However, SW is not only a way to reduce costs: there is the need to go beyond the SW elements (ICT, layout and HR) analyzed in this chapter and to focus on the core beliefs and culture of the organisation as the underpinning factor that makes an organisation 'smart'.

Moreover, TIM Group case study suggests it is better to proceed through a gradual developmental process in order to identify the most effective solutions for creating value both for people and the organisation. The adoption of SW can be seen as a change management process. For this reason the design and the implementation of a SW model should be followed by the monitoring activities.

In conclusion, despite SW was studied in literature from using different perspectives, this chapter provides an important approach to how conceptualize and operationalize SW concept. The application of this conceptual framework, in fact, is important from a practical viewpoint when introducing SW in organisation as planners and implementers will consider the readiness to adopt, the SW options available and how their impact will be assessed before the implementation occurs.

Future research could better determine the nature of strategy, organisational structure and culture patterns during the adoption of a SW model. This case study showed that TIM Group begin implementing SW with a small group of smartworkers and anticipate scaling their efforts; future research could identify core factors that need to be considered during institutional scaling. Examples of such issues could include physical and technical infrastructure needs and the continued use of incentives to facilitate workers adoption.

Finally, as with many exploratory studies, several limitations should be taken into account. First, the results are derived from a single organisation operating in the telecommunication sector. It is thus not possible to predict the extent to which the results can be found in other telecommunication companies adopting a SW model in Italy. No attempt are be made, in this research phase, to generalize the obtained results to the wider Italian telecommunication sector. On this point, a next step of the research is to increase the number of case in order to compare different approaches for adopting SW.

References

Ahuja, M.K., Chudoba, K.M., Kacmar, C.J., McKnight, D.H., George, J.F. (2007). IT Road Warriors: Balancing Work-family Conflict, Job Autonomy, and Work Overload to Mitigate Turnover Intentions, *MIS Quarterly*, 31(1): 1-17.

Aycan, Z., Kanungo, R., Mendonca, M., Yu, K., Deller, J., Stahl, G., Kurshid, A. (2000). Impact of culture on human resource management practices: A 10-country comparison, *Applied Psychology*, 49(1): 192-221.

Baruch, Y. (2000). Teleworking: Benefits and Pitfalls as Perceived by Professionals and Managers, *New Technology, Work and Employment*, 15(1): 34-49.

Berry, A., Loughton, E., Otley, D. (1991). Control in a financial services company (RIF): A case study. *Management Accounting Research*, 2(2): 109–139.

Birkinshaw, J., Hamel, G., Mol, M. (2008). Management Innovation, *Academy of Management Review*, 33(4): 25-845.

Bondarouk, T., Brewster, C. (2016). Conceptualising the future of HRM and technology research, *The International Journal of Human Resource Management*, 27(21): 2652-2671.

Bondarouk, T. (2014). Orchestrating electronic HRM. Enschede: Twente University Press.

Brewster, C., Mayrhofer, W. (2012). Handbook of research on comparative HRM. Cheltenham: Edward Elgar.

Callanan, T.A. (1999). New Ways of Living and Working: Teleworking in Ireland. *Department of Enterprise Trade and Employment, Report of the National Advisory Council on Teleworking.*

Cameron, E., Green, M. (2012). Making Sense of Change Management: A Complete Guide to the Models Tools and Techniques of Organisational Change. London: Kogan Page Publishers.

Capobianco, M. (2017). Il lavoro agile tra proposte di legge e accordi di fatto. Lo stato di attuazione dello smart working in Italia e nell'U.E (forthcoming).

Chiaro, G., Prati, G., Zocca, M. (2015). Smart working: dal lavoro flessibile al lavoro agile, *Sociologia del Lavoro*, 138: 69-87.

Chudoba, K.M., Wynn, E., Lu, M., Watson-Manheim, M.B. (2005). How Virtual Are We? Measuring Virtuality and Understanding Its Impact on a Global Organisation, *Information Systems Journal*, 15(4): 279-306.

Clapperton, G., Vanhoutte, P. (2014). The Smarter Working Manifesto. Oxford: Sunmakers Eldamar.

Coenen, M., Kok, R.A.W. (2014). Workplace Flexibility and New Product Development Performance, *European Management Journal*, 32(4): 564-576.

Cooke, W.N. (2003). Multinational companies and global human resource management strategies. Westport: Quorum Books.

Costa, G., Åkerstedt, T., Nachreiner, F., Baltieri, F., Carvalhais, J., Folkard, S. (2004). Flexible Working Hours, Health, and Well-Being in Europe: Some Considerations from a SALTSA Project, *Chronobiology international*, 21(6): 831-844.

Duxbury, L. E., Higgins, C.A. (2002a). Telework: A Primer for the Millennium Introduction. In Cooper, C.L., R. Burke J. (Eds.) The New World of Work: Challenges and Opportunities (157-200). London: Sage Publications.

Duxbury, L.E., Higgins, C.A. (2002b). Work-Life Balance in the New Millennium: Where are We?: Where Do We Need to Go? *Canadian Policy Research Networks.*

Ehnert, I., Harry, W. (2011). Recent developments and future prospects on sustainable human resource management: Introduction to the special issue, *Management Revue*, 23(3): 221-238.

Eisenhardt, K. M. (1989). Building theories from case study research. *Academy of Management Review*, 14(4): 532-550.

Elsbach, K.D., Pratt, M.G. (2007). The Physical Environment in Organizations, *Academy of Management Annals*, 1(1): 181-224.

Flynn, G. (1995). Warning: Your Best Ideas May Work Against You, *Personnel Journal*, 74(10): 76-99.

Forgács, T. (2010). Empirical Research Findings on Telework: Management Experiences and Attitudes, *Business and Economic Horizons*, 1(1): 6-13.

Gastaldi, L., Corso, M., Raguseo, E., Neirottic, P., Paolucci, E., Martini, E. (2014). Smart Working: rethinking work practices to leverage employees' innovation potential. 15th International CINet Conference, Operating Innovation - Innovating Operations, Budapest, 7-9 September.

Glaister, S. (2008). Alternative View: Homeworking Won't Stem Rising Car Use. In Dwelly, T. Lake, A. (Eds.) Can Homeworking Save the Planet? How Homes can become Workspaces in a Low Carbon Economy (80-85). London: The Smith Institute.

Gooderham, P. N., Nordhaug, O. (2011). One European model of HRM? Cranet empirical contributions, *Human Resource Management Review*, 21(1): 27-36.

Greene, C., Myerson, J. (2011). Space for thought: designing for knowledge workers, *Facilities*, 29(1): 19-30.

Haines III, V.Y., Stoge, S. (2012). Performance management effectiveness: practices or context? The International Journal of Human Resource Management, 2(6): 1158-1175.

Hamel, G. (2012). What Matters Now: How to Win in a World of Relentless Change, Ferocious Competition, and Unstoppable Innovation. San Francisco: Jossey-Bass.

Hartog, K.L., Solimene, A., Tufani, G. (2015). The smart working book. Rome: Seedble.

Harvey, D. (2010). The enigma and capital: And the crises of capitalism. London: Profile Books.

Hill, E.J., Hawkins, A.J., Ferris, M., Weitzman, M. (2001). Finding an Extra Day a Week: The Positive Influence of Perceived Job Flexibility on Work and Family Life Balance, *Family Relations*, 50 (1): 49-58.

Himmelsbach, V. (1998). Working at Home Given Top Marks by Employees, *Computing Canada*, 24(47): 29.

Holland, P., Bardoel, A. (2016). The impact of technology on work in the twenty-first century: exploring the smart and dark side, *The International Journal of Human Resource Management*, 27(21): 2579-2581.

Howcroft, D., Taylor, P. (2014). Plus ca change, plus la meme chose? – Researching and theorising 'new' new technologies, *New Technology, Work and Employment*, 29(1): 1-8.

Huws, U., Robinson, W.B., Robinson, S. (1990). Telework Towards the Elusive Office. New York, NY: John Wiley & Sons.

Iacono, G. (2013). Smart Knowledge Working. Milan: Digitpub.

Jackson, S.E., Schuler, R.S., Jiang, K. (2014). An aspirational framework for strategic human resource management, *The Academy of Management Annals*, 8(1): 1-56.

James, P. (2004). Is Teleworking Sustainable? - An Analysis of Its Economic, Environmental and Social Impacts, *SUSTEL, Sustainable Telework*.

Kiesler, S., Siegel, J., McGuire, T.W. (1984). Social psychological aspects of computer mediated communication, *American Psychologist,* 39(10): 1123-1134.

Lindgreen, A., Swaen, V. (2010). Corporate social responsibility, *International Journal of Management Reviews*, 12(1): 1–7.

Mann, J. (2012), Transform the workplace with focus on bricks, behaviors and bits, *Gartner Report No. G0021229*.

Martin, G., Cerdin, J.-L. (2014). Employer branding and career theory: New directions for research. In Sparrow, P.R., Scullion, H., Tarique, I. (Eds.), Strategic Talent Management: Contemporary Issues in International Context (151-176). Cambridge: Cambridge University Press.

Martínez-Sánchez, A., Pérez-Pérez, M., De Luis, Carnicer, P., Vela, Jiménez, M.J. (2007). Telework, Human Resource Flexibility and Firm Performance, *New Technology, Work and Employment*, 22(3): 208-223.

Maxwell, J.A. (1996). Qualitative research design: An interactive approach. Thousand Oaks, CA: Sage.

Michelson, W. (2000). Home-Based Employment and Quality of Life: A Time-Use Analysis. In Diener, E., Rahtz, D.R. (Eds.), Advances in Quality of Life Theory and Research (183-203). London: Kluwer.

Morgan, J. (2014). The future of work: Attract new talent, build better leaders, and create a competitive organization. Hoboken, NJ: Wiley.

Nidumolu, R., Prahalad, C.K., Rangaswami, M.R. (2009). Why Sustainability is now the Key Driver of Innovation, *Harvard Business Review,* 87(9): 56-64.

Olsen, K.M., Dahl, S.Å. (2010). Working Time: Implications for Sickness Absence and the Work-Family Balance, *International Journal of Social Welfare*, 19 (1): 45-53.

Otley, D.T., Berry, A.J. (1994). Case study research in management accounting and control, *Management Accounting Research*, 5(1): 45-65.

Peters, P., Wetzels, C., Tijdens, K. (2008). Telework: Timesaving or Time-Consuming? An Investigation into Actual Working Hours, *The Journal of Interdisciplinary Economics*, 20: 421-422.

Rodriguez, J.K., Johnstone, S. (2015). Regulation of work and employment: Advancing theory and research, *The International Journal of Human Resource Management*, 26(13): 1782–1784.

Ruth, S., Chaudhry, I. (2008). Telework: A productivity paradox? *Internet Computing, IEEE*, 12 (6): 87-90.

Spillman, R.D., Markham, F.B. (1997). Telecommuting: Acceptance, Adoption and Application, *Journal of Computer Information Systems*, 37(4): 8-12.

Stone, D.L., Deadrick, D.L., Lukaszewski, K.M., Johnson, R. (2015). The influence of technology on the future of human resource management, *Human Resource Management Review*, 25(2): 216-231.

Taylor, S., Osland, J., Egri, C.P. (2012). Introduction to HRM's role in sustainability: Systems, strategies, and practices, *Human Resource Management*, 51(6): 789-798.

Telsyte, S., (2015). Activity based working is driving, *Sidney White paper*.

van Lier, T. De Witte, A., Macharis, C. (2012). The impact of telework on transport externalities: the case of Brussels Capital Region, *Procedia - Social and Behavioral Sciences*, 54: 240-250

Verbeke, A., Schulz, R., Greidanus, N., Hambley, L. (2008). Growing the Virtual Workplace: The Integrative Value Proposition for Telework. Cheltenham: Edward Elgar Publishing.

Von Bertalanffy, L. (1969). General systems theory. New York, NY: George Braziller.

White, P., Christodoulou, G., Mackett, R., Titheridge, H., Thoreau, R., Polak, J. (2010). The Impacts of Teleworking on Sustainability and Travel. In Manzi, T., Lucas, K., Jones, T.L., Allen, J. (Eds.), Social Sustainability in Urban Areas: Communities, Connectivity and the Urban Fabric (141-154). London: Earthscan Publications Ltd.

Wood, S., Van Veldhoven M., Croon, M., De Menezes, L.M. (2012). Enriched job design, high involvement management and organizational performance: The mediating roles of job satisfaction and well-being, *Human Relations*, 65(4), 419.

Yin, R.K. (1994). Case study research–design and methods. Thousand Oaks, CA: Sage Publications.

Yoo, Y., Henfridsson O., Lyytinen K. (2010). Research Commentary - The New Organizing Logic of Digital Innovation: An Agenda for Information Systems Research, *Information Systems Research*, 21(4): 724-735.

Chapter 5

WORK AUTONOMY, CONTROL AND DISCRETION IN INDUSTRY 4.0

Roberto Albano-Ylenia Curzi-Tommaso Fabbri

SUMMARY: 5.1. Introduction. – 5.2. Digital Taylorism and Electronic Panopticon. – 5.3. Digital Taylorism and Electronic Panopticon: empirical evidence. – 5.4. An alternative approach: "Living Labouring Capacity" and "Joint Regulation". – 5.5. Implications and future research directions. – References.

5.1. Introduction

The term Industry 4.0 was first mentioned in 2011 in Germany as a proposal for the development of an economic policy based on high-tech strategies to boost the competitiveness of the manufacturing sector. It refers to the industrial application of technologies such as cyber-physical systems, the Internet of Things and smart robots (e.g. embedded computers and networks, communication protocols and operating systems, learning machines, mobile phones, laptops, etc.), big data, and additive manufacturing. These technologies make it possible to use a virtual representation of physical processes for their control and surveillance. Moreover, they allow the real-time exchange of data between machines, humans, and humans and machines, and end-to-end ICT-based integration of the various activities of the value chain (inbound logistics, production, maintenance, outbound logistics, marketing, service, and transport) within and across organisational boundaries (Hermann *et al.*, 2015; Kagermann *et al.*, 2013; Pfeiffer, 2017; Roblek *et al.*, 2016; Valenduc and Vendramin, 2016).

Industry 4.0 appears to open up new opportunities for organisational change, at different levels. Some have argued that it would be associated with the fragmentation and integration of the value chain at the global level, the blurring of the boundaries between industry and service, the mass customisation of products and services, and the use of more streamlined, integrated and network-like organisational forms and structures.

The present chapter draws attention to the micro level of analysis, focusing on the potential implications of the increasing digitalization and automation of production systems for the regulation of the single work process or situation where the worker is involved. At this level of analysis, the technical change associated with Industry 4.0 appears to revitalize some classical questions in organisational theory: can human-based activities be completely formalised, codified and converted into algorithms? If this were the case, Industry 4.0 would inescapably reduce the opportunity for workers to exercise autonomy and discretion in the performance of their work, leading to the full automation of industrial operations and to the comprehensive standardisation and predetermination of work. Or, in contrast, shall we expect opposite trends, consistent with the predictions made by the socio-technical system scholars (Davis, 1971), back in the 1970s, when the introduction of electronics and information technology allowed companies to take the first steps toward the digitalisation of operations?

The empirical evidence necessary for a sound answer to these long-lasting questions is still lacking (Salento, 2016; 2017; Pfeiffer and Suphan, 2015; Pfeiffer, 2017) and therefore a lively debate is taking place leveraging some new exploratory studies on the impact of Industry 4.0 on work organization and job content.

Against this background, the present chapter focuses on the relation between Industry 4.0 and the regulation of work processes in terms of autonomy, discretion and control. Firstly (section 1.2), we discuss two theses that emerge from recent empirical research, *Digital Taylorism* and *Electronic Panopticon*, with their alleged implications for the future organization of work.

Secondly (section 1.3), we present the findings from a longitudinal analysis we have performed, using selected data and variables from the 1991-2015 European Working Conditions surveys (European Foundation for the Improvement of Living and Working Conditions, 2017), to test a number of hypotheses drawn from both the aforementioned theses.

Thirdly, in line with other authors (Salento, 2016; 2017; Pfeiffer and Suphan, 2015), we argue that further claims on the relationship between Industry 4.0 and the regulation of work should be based on stronger empirical foundations, and we suggest that a promising approach to the study and understanding of that relationship should be capable of keeping workers' competences at the forefront in the regulation of highly digitalized and automated production systems.

In this perspective, in section 1.4, we turn our attention to the *living labour capacity* approach (Pfeiffer, 2014) and we try to strengthen its analytical potential with some conceptual elements drawn from the *théorie de la régulation sociale* of Jean-Daniel Reynaud (Reynaud, 1988) and its further developments (Terssac, 1992; 2003).

The last section discusses some implications for the management of human resources in the context of Industry 4.0 and outlines some directions for future research.

5.2. Digital Taylorism and Electronic Panopticon

In this section, we provide an overview of the studies aimed at making predictions about the likely future developments in the organisation of work associated with Industry 4.0.

Firstly, we consider the studies that have used the term *Digital Taylorism* to account for the expected impact of intelligent algorithms and big data technologies on the regulation of work (Head, 2014; Staab and Nachtwey, 2016). According to these studies, management would leverage the opportunities opened up by the new wave of technological innovation to increase the standardisation and routinisation of work. This would reduce the role of human experience in work to a residual aspect playing only a temporary function, since experts on automation and data scientists would eventually be able to completely extract expert knowledge from daily work practices, and codify workers' experience into machine learning algorithms. Thereafter, machines would completely substitute human work, and production systems would function in a self-regulating way through simulation models and intelligent algorithms that capture products, industrial environments and operations conditions, examine the causes of production disruptions, predict impeding events, and identify the measures to improve outcomes and correct problems. The tendency towards an increasing standardisation and routinisation would affect all classes of work, from the shop floor to managerial, professional and technical jobs. In other words, Industry 4.0 would promise to realise the Taylorian utopia, namely the complete elimination of any opportunity for workers at all hierarchical levels to exercise autonomy, and the increasing reduction of their margin of manoeuvre.

Some theoretical studies (cf. Gorecky *et al.*, 2014), which describe the solutions for the technological assistance of workers in the Smart Factory, give some insights into how the introduction of cyber-physical systems and other digital applications may provide the technical support for the Taylorisation of industrial work. There is also some evidence to support the arguments outlined above, mostly from case studies, the most popular of which refers to the digitalisation of Amazon's "fulfilment centres" or factories around the world. Staab and Nachtwey (2016) and other scholars (Cattero and D'Onofrio, 2018; Spencer, 2017) report that operators in Amazon's warehouses perform small, simple and repetitive tasks which require little or no training and experience. Each picker (whose job is to collect the goods from various shelves) has a hand barcode scanner equipped with a microphone and camera that determines the route the worker has to take through the warehouse and serves as a kind of time card for clocking the time spent performing the task. Similarly, each packing station (where the job consists in preparing and labelling packages for shipping) is equipped with a monitor showing what order has to be handled and how. Employees' activities are constantly monitored by their supervisors and through the digital system used for managing all stages of the production process (from storing, to picking and packing operations). In fact, the company's digital system serves not only to register incoming goods, track the exact position of all goods stored, and collect data on current production processes, but also to comprehensively control where employees are, how many articles they handle in a given period of time, and how their performance compares to that of their colleagues. No autonomous or discretionary action is required of pickers and packers in the work process.

A similar logic appears to underlie the digitalisation of intralogistics operations within the Wittenstein Bastian's production facility in Fellbach, Germany. Some have argued that the production plant, which is organised according to the principles of lean production, is an example of the Smart Factory (Hermann *et al.*, 2015). Here, production planning and enterprise control systems, barcodes and scanners are used to record data on the real world (e.g. order documents, pallets, delivery, and pick-up spaces) in a digital form and to generate a virtual map of all materials in the production shop and of the necessary material flow. This map is then converted into a transport route, complete with departure times and stops, and displayed on the tablet of logistics operators who deliver parts to machines on the factory floor. This way, the digital system automatically guides the operator through the physical transport of goods between the various delivery and pick-up spaces in order to deliver parts for production just in time.

The advocates of *Digital Taylorism* argue that the tendency towards a comprehensive regulation of human work by digital technologies would concern not only the workers formally employed by the organisation. It would also apply to (formally) independent contractors and self-employed workers (Staab and Nachtwey, 2016) who are temporarily integrated into the company's production system through online platforms, which allow the company to outsource tasks and activities to a global base of third parties, while increasing the standardisation and fragmentation of activities and tasks. Some case studies have reported the increasing tendency among operating companies (e.g., Amazon and Uber) to use online platforms to establish a Tayloristic production logic. According to some scholars, this would represent a common trend across a wide range of industries, work processes (both abstract and physical such as transport) and jobs (both those involving tiny, simple, low-skilled, repetitive tasks and creative, qualified, highly skilled occupations traditionally involving complex tasks) (Bergvall-Kåreborn and Howcroft, 2014; Rosenblat and Stark; 2016; Schörpf *et al.*, 2017).

To sum up. The literature on *Digital Taylorism* predicts that Industry 4.0 would pave the way for the full routinisation of human work in production processes, with progressively narrower space for human experience in the work. Evidence for this thesis is mostly drawn from case studies based on qualitative interviews and observations, which do not primarily focus on the automation and digitalisation of industrial production. However, some scholars in this line of research have argued that these findings can be generalised to other cases and sectors (Staab and Nachtwey, 2016; Rosenblat and Stark, 2016) as they concern the practices of some key players in the digital economy (e.g., Amazon, Uber, etc.) that set the pace for the rest of the economy. Thus, other organisations in different sectors would be likely to converge on the same practices, via institutional isomorphic processes. *Digital Taylorism* would thus be likely to become the dominant approach to the digital transformation of work in all branches of the economy, irrespective of the sector, the content and nature of jobs, the level of skills required and the form of labour relations.

We now turn to a more heterogeneous body of literature that, like the one on *Digital Taylorism*, postulates a univocal impact of Industry 4.0 on work and organisation. It mainly consists of exploratory studies, mostly focused on the German industry (Bonekamp and Sure, 2015; Edwards and Ramirez, 2016, Hirsch-Kreinsen, 2014; 2016; Spath *et al.*, 2013). They provide a picture slightly different from the one emerging from the literature on *Digital Taylorism*, and unlike the latter, they are more cautious about the possibility of reaching definitive conclusions regarding the expected impact of Industry 4.0 on the world of work based on the current state of research on this topic.

These studies identify the possibility of the greater importance of teamwork and cooperation between different company's units in consequence of the full processes and system architectures integration determined by the Internet of Things and cyber-physical systems. They also draw attention to the greater decentralisation in decision-making at the executive and operative levels of the work organisation, and the greater demand for adaptability, flexibility, capacities in troubleshooting and improvisation to cope with unanticipated events and situations. For example, the tendency of intelligent algorithms-based production systems to change state "spontaneously" with non-transparent and unpredictable effects, and non-modelled aspects in sensors, control and actuation systems and software architecture that threaten the dependability of the technological system in normal operation.

However, the same studies also emphasise that Industry 4.0 might reduce workers' ability to shape the wider contours of the work system. More precisely, they point out that cyber-physical applications seem to lead to a fully configured system with linkages between the parts being defined by the technology, thereby giving workers the opportunity to make decisions only at the level of the specific task. Moreover, the aforementioned studies also identify the possibility that new technologies will make work processes, activities, and individual performance completely transparent and visible for management, thereby automating control and making it no longer necessary to have the traditional form of personal supervision by lower and middle-level managers. In addition, control and evaluation would be more concerned with quantitative and qualitative work outcomes (e.g. the achievement of predetermined performance targets) than with compliance to prescribed rules and procedures.

To sum up. Reviewing a number of heterogeneous studies, mostly focused on the German industry, the contours of a second thesis emerge. Using an *ante litteram* term, it can be called the *Electronic Panopticon*. The arguments outlined above resonate, in fact, with those of former studies in the literature on organisational surveillance (Sewell and Wilkinson, 1992; Wilson, 1999) which have echoed Foucault's (1977) use of the concept of the *panopticon* to explain how management can retain strategic control over decision-making processes while delegating responsibility to individual workers and teams, by using new technologies to erect an electronic surveillance system providing constantly and immediately updated information about individual and collective action on the shop floor to a central point controlled by an elite group (Sewell and Wilkinson, 1992). New technologies would make the overarching visibility of work possible, as well as potentially omnipresent surveillance leading to a less obtrusive mode of control based on the *possibility* of constant surveillance and making power relationships invisible. This would enable management to minimise the opportunities for workers to make negative divergences, while harnessing positive divergences. In this sense, the tendency towards decentralisation would go along with enhanced centralised control, and rather than being synonymous with the autonomy of individuals, it would reflect *"earlier industrial reforms which were identified by Braverman (...) as 'representing a style of management rather than a genuine change in the position of the worker. They are characterised by a studied pretence of worker 'participation', a gracious liberality in allowing the worker to adjust a machine, to replace a light bulb, and to have the illusion of making decisions by choosing among fixed and limited alternatives designed by a management which deliberately leaves insignificant matters open to choice"* (Wilson, 1999).

Like the empirical evidence for the *Digital Taylorism*, the one for the *Electronic Panopticon* mostly comes from exploratory, qualitative research (e.g. the study by Bonekamp and Sure (2015) is exclusively based on qualitative interviews to experts).

Therefore, assessing the validity of both the above theses would also require testing them against data from quantitative studies, which at present are still lacking. However, there are some large-scale datasets which, though not primarily focused on Industry 4.0, can nonetheless be used to take a preliminary step in this direction. The next section thus presents the findings from some empirical tests of a number of hypotheses drawn from both the above theses that we have performed using selected data from a major repeated cross-sectional survey conducted among European workers from 1991 onwards, namely the European Working Conditions Survey (European Foundation for the Improvement of Living and Working Conditions, 2017).

5.3. Digital Taylorism and Electronic Panopticon: empirical evidence

The theses discussed in the previous section are enunciative: they make very precise statements about trends that would characterize work (in general) in the current transformation phase. Therefore, they can be translated into hypotheses to be tested empirically. Let's start from the hypotheses.

The literature on *Digital Taylorism* that we have reviewed leads us to formulate the following general hypothesis:

Hyp1: *in work with intensive use of digital technologies there is an increase in direct hierarchical control and a progressive reduction in the margin of manoeuvre allowed to workers; increasing fragmentation and simplification of tasks derived from a greater dependence of human performers on formalised and automated rules makes the role of individual experience more and more irrelevant.*

In another type of literature, more heterogeneous and overall less inclined to set forth a clear thesis such as that of *Digital Taylorism*, we have acquired elements that can be collapsed in a second general hypothesis:

Hyp2: *in work with intensive use of digital technologies one can observe over time an increase in the indirect monitoring of workers and their performance as compared to general standards; alongside an increase in the demand for flexibility in execution, there is a simultaneous reduction of workers' chances to influence the organisation of production processes; the rhetoric of empowerment tends to conceal that a true autonomy is by now possible only over negligible aspects of work.*

Hypothesis 1 (*Digital Taylorism*) and 2 (*Electronic Panopticon*) are less abstract than the theses from which they are derived, but they still need further operational translation in order to be empirically tested. Here are the sub-hypotheses we have elaborated on the two general ones[1]: *in work with intensive use of digital technologies,*

Hyp1.1: *the complexity of tasks tends to decrease.*

Hyp1.2: *the possibilities for the worker to choose his/her own work methods tend to diminish.*

Hyp1.3: *job execution is depending more and more on the speed of a machine.*

Hyp1.4: *the autonomous search for solutions to unexpected problems by the operator tends to shrink.*

Hyp1.5: *the pace of work is increasingly dependent on direct hierarchical control.*

Hyp 2.1: *the pace of work is increasingly dependent on production and performance obligations.*

Hyp 2.2: *the discretion of the worker in taking a break tends to shrink.*

Hyp 2.3: the *worker's involvement in setting working goals tends to shrink.*

Hyp 2.4: *the involvement of the operator in improving the processes of his/her department or organisation tends to disappear.*

Hyp 2.5: *the possibilities for the employee to influence important decisions for his/her work are reducing.*

As for the empirical testing, we have identified the European Working Conditions Survey (EWCS, Integrated Data File 1991-2015) (European Foundation for the Improvement of Living and Working Conditions, 2017) – a periodic research carried out in European countries where the units of observation are workers – as an adequate database because it contains numerous variables that can be considered either operative translations or proxies of the concepts contained in our hypotheses. We selected data from four countries: first of all Italy, then France and Germany as two major industrial powers that have launched important government programs to support Industry 4.0, and Great Britain, due to the distinctiveness of its labour market system as compared to continental European countries. Then we further selected data, picking up only those industrial and logistic sectors, as more relevant for our purposes[2]. Here's (Table 1 and 2) what we found.

---

[1] Our operationalization takes into consideration the available variables that we have found in an adequate dataset for a secondary trend analysis. Obviously, several other sub-hypotheses could be derived and tested, in principle, using other available and adequate data on the aforementioned topics.

[2] After ascertaining that SMEs and large enterprises (in the selected sectors) do not differ substantially in the intensity of ICTs use, we have abandoned this distinction to avoid having overly small numbers and therefore overly uncertain estimates. In 2015, the percentage of workers using ICTs for at least ¾ of their working time was about 37% in SMEs and 44.5% in large companies.

Table 1. Test of the hypotheses derived from the *Digital Taylorism*.

% of "yes" Hps1/Item	1995 - 2nd EWCS	2000 - 3rd EWCS	2005 - 4th EWCS	2010 - 5th EWCS	2015 - 6th EWCS
H1.1 Your job involves complex tasks (Reverse)	62.50% 75.30%	55.80% 71.40%	58.20% 75.90%	56.40% 75.20%	60.00% 81.30%
H1.2 You are able to choose/change your methods of work (Rev.)	63.50% 81.40%	59.60% 79.40%	57.20% 76.20%	55.50% 76.10%	60.00% 80.70%
H1.3 Your pace of work depends on automatic speed of a machine	29,60% 24.60%	35.90% 26.70%	38.40% 17.90%	36.50% 21.10%	35.80% 20.20%
H1.4 Your job involves solving unforeseen problems on your own (Rev.)	78.70% 94.60%	78.90% 92.50%	73.30% 89.10%	77.20% 90.20%	76.00% 91.30%
H1.5 Your pace of work depends on the direct control of your boss	41.90% 38.90%	41.70% 37.30%	42.20% 43.50%	44.50% 42.00%	36.00% 38.10%

Value at the bottom of each cell: % of workers using ICTs for at least ¾ of the time; value at the top of each cell: other workers.
Reverse = the content of the statement contradicts the general hypothesis.
Source: Authors' own elaboration based on EWCS data.

According to interviewed workers, there is no important reduction in the complexity of the assigned tasks and in their leeway in executing tasks and handling unanticipated criticalities. Moreover, no increased dependence of the worker on automated rules emerges from the interviews, nor increased direct hierarchical control.

Therefore, at present, given the limitations of the available self-reported data and within the selected sectors, there seems to be no empirical evidence for the *Digital Taylorism* hypothesis. No doubt such situations are documented by several case studies. What does not emerge from the "stylized facts" of our analysis is a clear general trend, a convergence towards a model of digital neo-Taylorism[3].

Going on to examine the second general hypothesis, we notice different, even conflicting tendencies (Tab. 2).

---

[3] Comparing the percentage of ICT-intensive workers in the last wave reporting that their job involves solving unforeseen problems on their own with the one in the 2nd wave (91.3 and 94.6% respectively), it can be said that hypothesis 1.4 is actually confirmed. However, the fact that more than ninety percent of workers in both waves declare that they handle unforeseen criticalities, makes the difference unimportant for the theoretical framework.

Table 2. Test of the hypotheses derived from the *Electronic Panopticon.*

Hps2/Item	1995 - 2nd EWCS	2000 - 3rd EWCS	2005 - 4th EWCS	2010 - 5th EWCS	2015 - 6th EWCS
H2.1 Your pace of work depends on numerical production targets or performance targets (% of 'yes')	51.60% 41.10%	47.50% 48.60%	60.10% 61.60%	58.90% 55.60%	55.10% 52.20%
H2.2 You can take a break when you wish (% of 'always' + 'most of the time') (Rev.)	n.d. n.d.	40.80% 55.40%	39.20% 59.70%	41.60% 64.30%	40.30% 60.40%
H2.3 You are consulted before objectives are set for your work (% of 'always' + 'most of the time') (Rev.)	n.d. n.d.	n.d. n.d.	n.d. n.d.	36.60% 49.00%	34.70% 49.60%
H2.4 You are involved in improving the work organisation or work processes of your department or organisation (% of 'always' + 'most of the time') (Rev.)	n.d. n.d.	n.d. n.d.	n.d. n.d.	33.90% 53.00%	36.90% 54.00%
H2.5 You can influence decisions that are important for your work (% of 'always' + 'most of the time') (Rev.)	n.d. n.d.	n.d. n.d.	n.d. n.d.	29.40% 39.40%	37.70% 48.70%

Value at the bottom of each cell: % of workers using ICTs for at least ¾ of the time; value at the top of each cell: other workers.
Reverse = the content of the statement contradicts the general hypothesis.
Source: Authors' own elaboration based on EWCS data.

At a first glance, hypothesis 2.1 seems to be confirmed: work pace appears to be increasingly subject to indirect control, even by means of implicit obligations. However, it should also be pointed out that:

- an increase in indirect control is no more marked in ICT-intensive work; on the contrary, on average, it seems to happen most in non-ICT-intensive work.
- from 1995 to 2005, this kind of control has grown a lot, especially in ICT-intensive work, then it has significantly shrunk in the next two waves.

The other variables selected to test this second hypothesis do not reveal a growing perception of working in a kind of *panopticon* among workers whose job involves intensive use of digital technologies. Nor do they appear to exercise autonomy only over negligible aspects of work. On the contrary (always with the caution imposed by the available data limitations), it seems that workers' involvement in decision-making on general and important aspects of organisational processes is increasing.

Here, more than in the previous case, it could be argued that these responses are the result of a widespread ideology, or false consciousness. The forms of indirect control are, in fact, less visible than the control exercised directly, and those who are subject to such control may have little awareness of it. This consideration leads us to examine a further variable, which is an indicator of compulsive behaviour in the fulfilment of labour obligations.

Interviewees were asked, unfortunately only in 2015, "How often have you kept worrying about work when you were not working"; the percentage of those who answered "always" or "most of the time" is 10.5% for those who work with ICTs for less than ¾ of the time and 13.3% for ICT-intensive users. These findings, certainly alarming, are a sign of *workaholism* and over-commitment to work, negative phenomena well-known to work and organisational psychology, but at present they still seem to concern a minority, and in any case not specifically those who intensively use ICTs at work.

5.4. An alternative approach: "Living Labouring Capacity" and "Joint Regulation"

The findings presented in the previous section not only fail to corroborate a number of hypotheses drawn from the theses in the current debate postulating a univocal impact of Industry 4.0 on work and organisation. They also appear to suggest that the intensive use of digital technologies may open opportunities for workers to use their competences to influence decisions concerning important and general aspects of work organisation. Managers may or may not decide to take such an opportunity. In any case, the central question that emerges is what approaches and conceptual elements can be draw from the literature to bring into focus the role of human action in the regulation of highly digitalised and automated work.

What is referred to as the *living labouring capacity* approach (Pfeiffer, 2014; Pfeiffer and Suphan, 2015) appears to be promising. It does not aim at developing general and univocal prognoses of the expected impact of

Industry 4.0 on work content and work organisation[4]. Rather, it aims at improving the way we study and evaluate the relationship between Industry 4.0, work and organisation. In this regard, this approach has two main merits.

At the methodological level, it starts from the assumption that neither qualitative nor quantitative methods alone can generate insights into the changes taking place inside firms, triggered by Industry 4.0, in the organization of work and in the content of job, if they work in isolation. The *living labouring capacity* approach thus represents a first, careful attempt to combine information from qualitative studies at the micro-level of analysis with large-scale data from quantitative research at the macro-level.

On the theoretical level, it draws attention to the key role that experience-based knowledge and judgement of competent workers play in routine work. The multiple case-study research carried out by Pfeiffer (2016) highlights that experience plays a crucial role in highly standardised and formalised work processes to cope with unexpected disruptions in apparently robust procedures (including those embedded in advanced manufacturing technologies) and to pro-actively prevent them through anticipatory interventions. Experience finds expression in the workers' ability to make decisions alone or in cooperation with others, to ensure quality control of their own activities, upstream processes, materials, process steps, and to contribute to the continuous reconfiguration of the whole production process. Experience is considered as a dynamic resource that is continuously renewed and developed through the performance of apparently routinised work, which thus cannot be conceived as static and unchanging[5]. Pfeiffer (2014) has developed the concept of *living labouring capacity* as a category for qualitative and quantitative research aimed at analysing the relationship between knowledge, work and experience, the role of workers' experience even in highly routinised and standardised work, and the qualitative changes in work and work organisation associated with Industry 4.0.

Living labouring capacity indicates "*all the capabilities that are needed for the confrontation with the world – i.e. for appropriation processes in the*

---

[4] Pfeiffer and Suphan (2015) have explicitly stated that they "... do not believe that such prognoses can be made with any accuracy". In a later work, Pfeiffer (2017) has clarified the point, pointing out that the ways new technologies will affect work ultimately depend on the specific settings as defined by factors such as the characteristics of national economies and institutional settings, product complexity, value chains, the prevailing criteria of economic rationality in different companies. Otherwise formulated, changes in work and work organisation associated with Industry 4.0 are conditioned by additional factors, the number and peculiar nature of which rule out any possibility of making robust predictions.

[5] In organisational theory, Zamarian (2010) has proposed a similar concept of routine.

broadest sense". It encompasses *"the comprehensive forming and application of the senses, living working knowledge with its objectifiable (but not yet objectified) and non-objectifiable shares of experiential knowledge and, finally, capabilities of the situational concretising application of theoretically-grounded knowledge or of theoretically-grounded procedures and methods"*. (Pfeiffer, 2014). Pfeiffer has emphasised that this concept is related to that of *subjectifying work action*, set forth by Böhle (2013). The latter refers to informal, tacit, experiential skills, knowledge and capabilities, and includes four dimensions of human action: physical and sensorial perception, associative and intuitive thought, intuitive and dialogical action, and an empathetic relationship towards one's environment (persons, tools, objects, and technical systems). *"Subjectifying work action is of great significance as an autonomous form of action and knowledge both for planning and practical action as well as for creative, innovative processes that form the basis for coping with unforeseen circumstances"* (Pfeiffer, 1999; 2014).

Both concepts refer to the qualities of human work in action, which always elude complete formalisation, standardisation, abstraction, and objectification. Any management attempt to transform them into objectified labour produces a requirement for appropriation by the working subjects, and eventually renews the need for a new formation of *living labouring capacity* and *subjectifying work action*. In this sense, *living labouring capacity* is dialectically connected with *labour power* (part of the knowledge, experience and work that is objectified and formalised in consequence of successful transformation, proving to be amenable to management control) and both are in motion. Even in the digital era, the recursive, albeit endless and never fully accomplished transformation of *living labouring capacity* into *labour power* is the key inherent characteristic of capitalism.

The *living labouring capacity* approach makes an important contribution to the development of a method for grounding the study of the changes in the organisation of work associated with Industry 4.0 on strong empirical foundations. However, its conceptual categories do not help clearly distinguish between the assertion of autonomy by individual workers or work groups and the prescription of discretion imposed on them by management. The lack of this conceptual distinction hampers a correct understanding of the conditions under which workers can develop new knowledge and competences in the performance of work and play a key role in the regulation of highly digitalised and automated work. In this regard, we thus suggest taking into consideration the *théorie de la régulation sociale* of Jean-Daniel Reynaud (Reynaud, 1988), and its further developments (Terssac, 1992; 2003).

Like the *living labouring capacity* approach, this conceptual framework emphasises that work individuals actually perform does not completely coincide with their prescribed tasks, and that the competences ensuring the effectiveness of work processes develop, at least in part, in and through the performance of work. In addition, it considers the actual regulation of work processes as a *régulation conjointe* (joint regulation) reflecting a permanent dialectic between control and autonomy. The former finds expression in the rules set up by the organisation's top management team to prestructure significant aspects or parts of the organisational process as a whole. Autonomy finds expression in rules different from those defined by management, reflecting work groups' agency. Work groups may assert their autonomy, by elaborating innovative solutions to cope reactively with unforeseen specific production problems that could adversely affect the work process effectiveness. But work groups may also assert their autonomy, by carrying out exploration activities aiming at expanding the future range of potential solutions through the proactive search for new practices alternative to those already available. While individual workers and work groups produce autonomous rules, they simultaneously assert their professional identities and develop new competences, which are source of professional development. Autonomous rules may either oppose or supplement control rules.

In any case, work groups demand management to recognise that their rules are valid and effective as much as control rules. Such a recognition may find expression in two forms. On the one hand, management may acknowledge the need for the continuous development of autonomous rules and new competences to ensure long-term organisational process effectiveness, and thus may refrain from hampering work groups and individual workers from exercising their autonomy. On the other hand, management recognition may consist in the codification of part of the tacit knowledge underlying the autonomous rules that have proven effective into procedures embedded in expert systems, thus in the transformation of autonomous rules into control rules. However, the empirical studies carried out by de Terssac (1992) have highlighted that it is more than likely that, even in this case, workers and groups do not stop elaborating and asserting new autonomous rules.

What we have just outlined above should make it clear that the permanent dialectic between control and autonomous rules revolves around experience and competences and that, at any given time, the actual regulation of work is the result of a local, temporary compromise between control and autonomy based on the development of new competences.

In addition, the aforementioned studies have also paved the way for the elaboration of the key analytical distinction between autonomy and discretion (Maggi, 2003/2016). The former refers to the capability of an individual or collective subject to produce his own rules and manage his own organisational processes. On the other hand, discretion indicates room for action in a regulated process where the subject is obliged to decide and choose from a set of alternatives already predetermined by heteronomous rules. Unlike autonomy, discretion involves no possibility for the subject to regulate work. Unlike discretion, autonomy refers to situations where workers make decisions about the regulation of work mostly in cooperation with others, and decision-making opens the opportunity for them to develop new knowledge and experience, and not only to apply those they have already accumulated. New knowledge and experience may concern the object, the means of work, and the modes of coordinating actions and people that perform them. Thus, unlike discretion, autonomy is a source of organisational learning, technical and organisational innovation, and makes the performance of work a real occasion for workers' training and professional development.

The distinction between autonomy and discretion can prove useful to strengthen the analytical potential of the *living labouring capacity* approach. In particular, we believe that such analytical categories can help understand whether the performance of highly digitalised and automated work provides real opportunities for the workers involved to play a key role in the regulation of work, and thus whether it makes room for them and the organisational process as a whole to develop new competences.

5.5. Implications and future research directions

We have started this chapter by drawing attention to some key questions in the current debate about the likely future changes in the regulation of work processes associated with Industry 4.0, and namely in the relationship between autonomous and control rules. Throughout the chapter, we have provided arguments to call into question the possibility of making solid predictions in this regard. The new digital technologies are just one of the elements that create the conditions in which changes take place. Technology is an opportunity for change 6. In any new wave of technological innovation (thus in the coming stage of industrial revolution called Industry 5.0 as well), technology is an element that creates a space of organisational possibilities for change. However, the actual changes will be the result of how new technological opportunities will interact with other conditioning factors. Namely, the dynamics of the economy and the social relationships between productive forces as shaped by the choices made at different levels by many different actors (workers and their representative bodies, policy makers, and other

---

[6] This concept of technology as an opportunity for change has been put forward by Masino (1997, 1999, 2000).

institutional actors). This means that there is no single Industry 4.0. In this regard, the longitudinal analysis, that we performed using selected data from the 1995-2015 European Working Conditions surveys (European Foundation for the Improvement of Living and Working Conditions, 2017), shows no evidence for the hypotheses in the current debate postulating a univocal impact of new digital technologies on work and organisation. Our findings do not indicate that in the industrial sectors and logistics of some potential leading European countries in Industry 4.0, the intensive use of digital technologies is associated with a clear general trend towards the Taylorisation of work or a regulation of work where control rules allow workers to exercise autonomy exclusively over negligible aspects of work.

In line with other scholars (Pfeiffer and Suphan, 2015; Salento 2016; 2017), we thus believe that an alternative approach is needed if our understanding of the relationship between Industry 4.0 and the regulation of work has to be advanced. Namely, an approach that helps us understand how and why, even in highly digitalized and automated work settings, workers may participate in the regulation of work and develop new experience and competences on the job. An approach that considers routine work as ever-changing work, that continuously calls for new competences and forges new experience (Pfeiffer, 2014; 2016; Pfeiffer and Suphan, 2015), and in which autonomy and discretion in the regulation of work are clearly distinguished.

Such a distinction can also be the cornerstone of a conceptual framework for human resource management updated to Industry 4.0, in which "organization personalities" (Barnard, 1938), that describe the individual contribution to the organization, are identified according to the peculiar combination of enacted autonomy and expected discretion, and the new temporal and spatial modes of work, allowed for by last-generation ubiquitous ICTs, are accordingly clarified and associated with a legal type. From such a conceptual framework, implications might be drawn for selection, training, and development of workers in the context of Industry 4.0.

While further research is needed, the analysis conducted so far provides some tentative policy clues with respect to education and training for Industry 4.0. If digital technologies, as an ingredient of the ongoing industrial revolution, enact organizational change opportunities, and if work is an ever-changing process that requires the continuous development of new competences part of which in the actual practice of work, then education policies, aimed at addressing the demand for new Industry 4.0 skills, should focus on computational skills as well as on practical abilities. This calls for dual training pathways jointly designed and implemented by a network of different actors (not only education institutions, but also companies, workers and their representative bodies). It also calls for methods for certifying the skills learned on the job. And finally, but no less important, it calls for participatory approaches allowing workers to autonomously assess, individually and in groups, the competences they have developed in specific work settings, and their own specific training needs.

This chapter is the result of the joint work of the authors. However, sections were authored as follows: 5.1. Introduction by Roberto Albano and Tommaso Fabbri; 5.2. Digital Taylorism and Electronic Panopticon by Ylenia Curzi; 5.3. Digital Taylorism and Electronic Panopticon: empirical evidence by Roberto Albano; 5.4. An alternative approach: "Living Labouring Capacity" and "Joint Regulation" by Ylenia Curzi; 5.5. Implications and future research directions by Tommaso Fabbri.

References

Barnard, C.J. (1938). *The Functions of the Executive*, Harvard University Press, Cambridge, MA.

Bergvall-Kåreborn, B., Howcroft, D. (2014). Amazon Mechanical Turk and the commodification of labour, *New Technology, Work and Employment*, 29(3): 213-223.

Böhle, F. (2013). *'Subjectifying Action' as a Specific Mode of Working with Customers*, in Dunkel, W., Kleemann, F. (eds.), *Customers at Work*, Palgrave Macmillan, London, 149-174.

Bonekamp, L., Sure, M. (2015). Consequences of Industry 4.0 on Human Labour and Work Organisation, *Journal of Business and Media Psychology*, 6 (1): 33-40.

Cattero, B., D'Onofrio, M. (2018), *Organizing and Collective Bargaining in the Digitized "Tertiary Factories" of Amazon: A Comparison Between Germany and Italy*, in Ales, E., Curzi, Y., Fabbri, T., Rymkevich, O., Senatori, I., Solinas, G. (eds.), *Working in Digital and Smart Organizations. Legal, Economic and Organizational Perspectives on the Digitalization of Labour Relations*, Palgrave Macmillan.

Davis, L.E. (1971). The coming crisis for production management: technology and organization, *International Journal of Production Research*, 9 (1): 65-82.

Edwards, P., Ramirez, P. (2016). When should workers embrace or resist new technology?, *New Technology, Work and Employment*, 31 (2): 99-113.

European Foundation for the Improvement of Living and Working Conditions (2017). *European Working Conditions Survey Integrated Data File, 1991-2015*, [data collection], 4th Edition, UK Data Service, SN: 7363.

Foucault, M. (1977). *Discipline and punish: The birth of the prison*, Penguin Books, London.

Gorecky, D., Schmitt, M., Loskyll, M., Zühlke, D. (2014). Human-Machine-Interaction in the Industry 4.0 Era, 12th IEEE International Conference on Industrial Informatics (INDIN), 289-294.

Head, S. (2014), *Mindless: Why Smarter Machines Are Making Dumber Humans*, Basic Books, New York.

Hermann, M., Pentek, T., Otto, B. (2015). Design Principles for Industrie 4.0 Scenarios: A Literature Review, Working Paper No. 01, Technische Universität Dortmund, Fakultät Maschinenbau and Audi Stiftungslehrstuhl Supply Net Order Management.

Hirsch-Kreinsen, H. (2016). Digitization of industrial work: development paths and prospects, *Journal of Labour Market Research*, 49 (1):1-14.

Hirsch-Kreinsen, H. (2014). Welche Auswirkungen hat "Industrie 4.0" auf die Arbeitswelt?, *WISO direct*, December: 1-4.

Kagermann, H., Wahlster, W., Helbig, J. (2013). *Recommendations for implementing the strategic initiative INDUSTRIE 4.0*. Final report of the Industrie 4.0 working group.

Maggi, B. (2003). *De l'agir organisationnel. Un point de vue sur le travail, le bien-être, l'apprentissage*, Octarès, Toulouse (TAO Digital Library, Bologna, 2016, 2nd ed.).

Masino, G. (2000). *Nuove tecnologie e azione organizzativa. Riflessioni teoriche e casi aziendali*, Isedi, Torino.

Masino, G. (1999). Information technology and dilemmas in organizational learning, *Journal of Organizational Change Management*, 12 (5): 360-376.

Masino, G. (1997). *Nuove regole di progettazione. Opportunità tecnologiche e scelte organizzative*, Nuova Italia Scientifica, Roma.

Pfeiffer, S. (2017). The Vision of "Industrie 4.0" in the Making – a Case of Future Told, Tamed, and Traded, *Nanoethics*, 11: 107–121.

Pfeiffer, S. (2016). Robots, Industry 4.0 and Humans, or Why Assembly Work Is More than Routine Work, *Societies*, 6 (16): 1-26.

Pfeiffer, S. (2014). Digital labour and the use-value of human work. On the importance of labouring capacity for understanding digital capitalism, *TripleC-Journal for a Global Sustainable Information Society*, 12 (2): 599-619.

Pfeiffer, S. (1999). Ignored and Neglected – Work in Cybersociety, in Armitage, J., Roberts, J. (eds.), *Exploring Cybersociety. Social, Political, Economic and Cultural Issues*, Vol. 2, University of Northumbrian, Newcastle.

Pfeiffer, S., Suphan, A. (2015). *The Labouring Capacity Index: Living Labouring Capacity and Experience as Resources on the Road to Industry 4.0*, Working Paper 2015 No. 2, University of Hohenheim, Chair for Sociology, Stuttgart.

Reynaud, J.D. (1988). Les régulations dans les organisations: régulation de contrôle et régulation autonome, *Revue française de sociologie*, XXIX, 1, 5-18.

Roblek, V., Meško, M., Krapež, A. (2016). A Complex View of Industry 4.0, *Sage Open*, April-June: 1-11.

Rosenblat, A., Stark, L. (2016). Algorithmic Labor and Information Asymmetries: A Case Study of Uber's Drivers, *International Journal of Communication*, 10: 3758-3784.

Salento, A. (2017). Industria 4.0, imprese, lavoro. Problemi interpretativi e prospettive, *Rivista Giuridica del Lavoro e della Previdenza Sociale*, anno LXVIII, No. 2: 175-194.

Salento, A. (2016). Note sui problemi di ricerca su Industria 4.0 e sulle conseguenze per i lavoratori e le lavoratrici, *Inchiesta*, 191 (gennaio-marzo): 44-49.

Schörpf, P., Flecker, J., Schönauer, A., Eichmann, H. (2017). Triangular love–hate: management and control in creative crowdworking, *New Technology, Work and Employment*, 32(1): 43-58.

Sewell, G., Wilkinson, B. (1992). 'Someone to watch over me': surveillance, discipline and the just-in-time labour process, *Sociology*, 26(2): 271-289.

Spath, D., Ganschar, O., Gerlach, S., Hämmerle, M., Krause, T., Schlund, S. (2013). Produktionsarbeit der Zukunft-Industrie 4.0, Fraunhofer Verlag, Stuttgart.

Spencer, D. (2017). Work in and beyond the Second Machine Age: the politics of production and digital technologies, *Work, Employment and Society*, 31 (1): 142-152.

Staab, P., Nachtwey, O (2016). Market and Labour Control in Digital Capitalism, *TripleC*, 14(2): 457-474.

Terssac, G. de (1992). *Autonomie dans le travail*, Presses Universitaires de France, Paris.

Terssac, G. de (2003). *Travail d'organisation et travail de régulation*, in Id. (s/d), *La théorie de la régulation sociale de Jean-Daniel Reynaud. Débats et prolongements*, La Découverte, Paris, 121-34.

Valenduc, G., Vendramin, P. (2016), *Work in the Digital Economy: sorting the Old from the New*, ETUI Working Paper, 2016.03.

Wilson, F. (1999). Cultural control within the virtual organization, *The Sociological Review*, 47 (4): 672-694.

Zamarian, M. (2010). Le routine organizzative tra dimensione operativa e dimensione generativa: modi di riproduzione dell'agire organizzativo, *Rassegna Italiana di Sociologia*, Anno LI, n. 2, aprile-giugno: 233-253.

Chapter 6

WORK CONTROL AND SURVEILLANCE IN THE AGE OF DIGITAL

Andrea Carugati-Aurélie Leclercq-Vandelannoitte-Joao Vieira da Cunha

SUMMARY: 6.1. Introduction. – 6.2. Foundations for a dramaturgical model of control. – 6.2.1. Personal control. – 6.2.2. Bureaucratic control. – 6.2.3. Social control. – 6.3. A dramaturgical model of control. – 6.4. Conclusion. – References.

6.1. Introduction

Is control something that people have or something that they do? In functional models of organizational control, it appears as control is something that managers have over employees (Das, 1993; Lange, 2008; Snell, 1992). In contrast, other models specify control as a joint accomplishment, such that managers assess compliance using representations of work that employees produce (e.g., Anteby, 2008; Burawoy, 1979; Kipnis, Schmidt, & Wilkinson, 1980; Orlikowski, 1996; Webb & Palmer, 1998). We propose a dramaturgical model of control that complements the functional model by exposing opportunities for employee participation in control processes, as it is evident in corporate ethnographies but not in literature on organizational control (e.g., Rosen, 1985; Roy, 1960; Sewell, 2008).

As a noun, control is defined as the power to influence or direct people's behavior or the course of events (all definitions in this article come from the New Oxford American Dictionary, unless otherwise noted). As a verb, it means to determine the behavior or supervise the running of somebody or something. Thus defined, control differs from other attempts to shape the behavior of others, because it focuses on monitoring the very actions it seeks to affect. Most research on control indicates that managers enforce compliance by turning organizations into a stage, such that everything employees do is open to scrutiny (Allen, Hart, & Walker, 2007; Ezzamel & Willmott, 1998; Sewell, 1998). Such studies explain control as processes of compliance and resistance. Thus the effects on employees' compliance with prescribed procedures stem from the orders that managers issue (e.g., Anteby, 2008; Barker, 1993; Kohli & Kettinger, 2004). Such exposure also influences employees' resistance to company procedures or managers' orders (Ball & Wilson, 2000; Doolin, 2004; Ezzamel, Willmott, & Worthington, 2001). These studies adopt a functional model of control by establishing a link between the control that managers have and the work that employees do.

However, research on information technology (IT) and change (Orlikowski, 1996), street-level bureaucracy (Kipnis et al., 1980), and workplace deviance (Lawrence & Robinson, 2007; Mars, 1983) also reveals that control can affect how employees present their work, not just how they do their everyday work (Cunha and Carugati, 2017). These studies note that employees might present an image of compliance, even if they do not follow prescribed procedures or obey managers' orders. Thus a dramaturgical model might be appropriate, to emphasize that control is imposed on representations of work, not the work itself, and to underscore the role of employees in producing the representations that managers use to assess compliance.

Modern digital work tools like enterprise social media and social media in general afford multiple forms of collaboration but also allow for multiple forms of work expression and multiple forms of control (e.g. Fonstad and Mocker, 2016). Defining control as an activity that managers perform on the representations of the work produced by employees, offers various opportunities for employees using modern digital tools, to participate in their own control, beyond compliance or resistance. We explore these opportunities in relation to personal, bureaucratic, and social forms of control, and in so doing, we develop a dramaturgical model of control that accounts for the gap between work and representations of work. Failing to account for this gap leads to underestimations of the power that employees have to improve and embellish representations of their work, which are what managers use to monitor and enforce compliance. That is, employees offer evidence of their compliance with procedures that they actually refuse to follow, because they produce representations of their work that are loosely coupled with their actions. Our dramaturgical model is based on Goffman's (1959) dramaturgical theory of interaction.

6.2. Foundations for a dramaturgical model of control

The functional model of control contrasts the wide range of strategies that managers use to exert control over employees with the narrow range of tactics that employees use to react to managers' control attempts (Ball & Wilson, 2000; Ezzamel & Willmott, 1998; Lange, 2008). The etymological origin of "control" provides a starting point for restoring a balance between the agency of managers and employees over the control of work (cf. Oxford English Dictionary):

Control, noun: From the French contrôle, earlier contrerolle 'the copie of a roll (of account, etc.), a paralell of the same qualitie and content with th' originall; also, a controlling or ouerseeing' (Cotgr.), corresp. to med.L. contrrotulus, f. contr against, counter (cf CONTRA) + rotulus ROLL.

Control, verb: From the French contrôler (16th c. in Littré), earlier contreroller (c 1300 in Anglo-Fr.) 'to take and keepe a copie of a roll of accounts, to controll, observe, oversee, spie faults in.'

These etymological roots offer a compelling argument for research to recognize the gap between work and its representation in explanations of organizational control. That is, both definitions suggest that control is not exercised directly but rather is mediated by a "counter-roll," which is the representation of work. When employees participate in the production of representations of work, which managers then use to establish control, they are no longer simply objects of control but also become agents with as much power as managers over the dynamics of control.

To specify control as something that employees do together with managers, we need a model that defines how people produce the representations that others will use to monitor and assess their performance. Goffman's (1982) dramaturgical model of interaction provides a good foundation for building such a model.

Goffman's dramaturgical model of action. According to Goffman, interaction is a process in which people achieve expression through what they say and what they do, and then others use those expressions to form impressions. He thus emphasizes the power that people have to shape others' impressions:

> [D]uring the period in which the individual is in the immediate presence of others, few events may occur which directly provide others with ... conclusive information they will need if they are to direct wisely their own activity.... They will be forced to accept some events as conventional or natural signs of something not directly available to the senses.... . The security that they justifiably feel in making inferences about the individual will vary, of course, depending on such factors as the amount of information that they already possess about him, but no amount of such past evidence can entirely obviate the necessity of acting on the basis of inferences (Goffman, 1959: 2-3).

That is, others form impressions on the basis of the expressions that people give (i.e., sayings and doings) and the expressions that they give off (i.e., appearance and demeanor) to an audience.

Audiences add independent information to the expressions actors give and give off, including "the past life and current round of activity of a given performer [which] typically contain at least a few facts which, if introduced during the performance, would discredit or at least weaken the claims about self that the performer was attempting to project as part of the definition of the situation" (Goffman, 1959: 209). However, audiences routinely refrain from tapping into this information, to preserve the definition of the situation that guides their own behavior in an interaction (Goffman, 1959).

Control of work as an instance of Goffman's dramaturgical model of interaction. In specifying the control of work as an instance of Goffman's dramaturgical model, the managers become the audience, and employees are the actors. It is a demanding instance; Goffman (1959) emphasizes that audiences are more likely to reify, rather than scrutinize, people's expressions. Control research cites various motivations—such as interests (Zweig & Webster, 2002), identity (Covaleski, Dirsmith, Heian, & Samuel, 1998), and domination (Barker & Cheney, 1994)—for managers to police employees' work to find evidence of deviance instead of accepting superficial evidence of their compliance.

By developing a dramaturgical model of control, we hope to move beyond the dichotomy of compliance versus resistance and specify difficulties created by a stricter specification of Goffman's model, while also emphasizing the opportunities that employees have for expressing compliance with procedures that they refuse to follow and goals that they are not committed to achieving. These opportunities depend on the type of control that managers use to monitor and enforce compliance. Perrow (1972) and Child (1973) define three types of control that appear in several taxonomies (e.g. Das, 1993; Orlikowski, 1991; Ouchi, 1979; Pennings & Woiceshyn, 1987). Specifically, managers enforce prescribed procedures and orders through three forms of control: personal control, bureaucratic control, or social control.

6.2.1. Personal control

Personal control consists of "a dyadic relationship between supervisors and subordinates, having its usual expression in direct supervision where one individual assumes authority over the actions of others and closely monitors that action to ensure compliance with orders" (Orlikowski, 1991: 10). It is prominent in both the everyday, face-to-face supervision of work and the punctuated, face-to-face evaluation of performance (e.g., Akerlof & Kranton, 2008; Mayer & Davis, 1999).

First, supervision consists of monitoring and enforcing compliance by taking advantage of the material properties of the workplace, typically including digital tools, to scrutinize employees' work. Andrzejewski (2008: 86) describes factories in Victorian America in which "supervision from an elevated platform served as the primary means of work discipline." Ethnographies of factory work also emphasize that employees must escape to regions that their supervisor's gaze cannot reach to deviate from prescribed procedures (Anteby, 2008; Beynon, 1973). Today work is no longer supervised from elevated platforms. Digital tools, electronic reporting, contactless badges are the modern encarnation of the elevated factory platform.

Second, through performance evaluations, managers monitor and enforce compliance by taking advantage of employees' disclosure of their achievements, failures, strengths, and weaknesses, then encouraging them to establish a plan to achieve normative levels of performance (Townley, 1993a). As Rose (1990: 240) describes, "in compelling, persuading, and inciting subjects to disclose themselves, finer and more intimate regions of personal and interpersonal life come under surveillance and are opened up for expert judgment, normative evaluation, classification and correction." Like digital tools allow for continuous control, performance evaluations are also nowadays computer madiated. Performance is only achieved if the "computer says so".

The two types of personal control thus constitute modern instances of Goffman's dramaturgical model of interaction. In digitally mediated face-to-face interactions, managers form impressions of employees' compliance that are based on the expressions that employees give and give off while performing their everyday work, as well as the accounts that employees give about their accomplishments during performance evaluations. A dramaturgical specification of personal control therefore must emphasize that the dynamics of control in these interactions are joint accomplishments by supervisors and employees. It also should reveal the opportunities available to represent obedience with orders and compliance with procedures, without actually doing either.

Dramaturgical opportunities in the practice of personal control. Goffman's dramaturgical model of interaction suggests that people can cloak deviance with an image of compliance, because others are lenient when they form impressions of people's actions. Goffman (1959) suggests that others take claims about behaviors and motivations at face value, rarely seeking independent information to disconfirm the image that people try to present. They also dismiss small transgressions that could jeopardize that image. Personal control, as an instance of this model, suggests that when managers assess employees' compliance, they compromise on their commitment to enforcing rules and procedures, for the sake of lenience.

The notion of such an obliging audience contrasts with research on control that portrays supervisors as exercising personal control over employees (cf. Jermier, 1998). In these studies, supervisors have a stake in employees' compliance with their orders, which prompts them to scrutinize employees' work for any evidence of deviance. A comparison of Goffman's audiences with supervisors in theories of control suggests that the reactions of supervisors to infringements might occur along a continuum of increasing lenience. Theories of control place managers at the stricter end; some empirical studies of factory work and research on how leaders supervise managers instead place them at its most tolerant end.

In addition, early ethnographic research on supervision in factories (e.g., Gouldner, 1954), sales departments (e.g., Benson, 1986), and government bureaucracies (Crozier, 1964) emphasizes that supervisors know enough about the situated conditions of employees' everyday work to forgive transgressions that employees must commit to comply with the spirit, if not the letter, of their company's goals. According to these early studies, supervisors are close enough to employees' work to understand the recurrent contingencies, unspecified by prescribed procedures, that employees need to address. For example, Lipsky's (1980) research on street-level bureaucracy and Blau's (1955) investigations of social workers reveal that supervisors in government agencies allow employees to deviate from prescribed procedures that fail to match local contingencies. Such evidence supports Goffman's (1959) finding that the audience may exclude what it interprets as legitimate transgressions from impressions formed on the basis of people's actions.

Finally, performance appraisal research shows that supervisors exclude deviations from their impressions of employee compliance (Giangreco, Carugati, Sebastiano, & Al Tamimi, 2012). Fealty relationships, as documented by Jackall (1989), Kanter (1993), and Watson (2001), pervade power dynamics in organizations, such that organizational cliques can develop their own norms of behavior, with varying tolerance for deviations from the procedures they impose on junior members. This research in turn evokes Goffman's (1959) findings that some audiences are more flexible than others in their formed impressions, because they adopt positive images using expressions that other audiences would employ to form negative images.

Dramaturgical opportunities in the reactions to personal control. Goffman (1959) argues that the expressions that people give and give off can be contrived, to present an image that differs from their actual accomplishments and interpretations but is close to the achievements and beliefs that their audience prefers. Specifying personal control as an instance of Goffman's model thus suggests that employees present an image of compliance while deviating from procedures and disobeying orders, even from a strict supervisor.

Prior research on control instead suggests a much tighter link between employees' actions and the expressions that they give and give off to managers (e.g., Sewell & Wilkinson, 1992). These studies afford employees little opportunity to contrive the behaviors that their supervisors observe. They argue instead that the materials and procedures that constrain people's everyday work, as well as avowal procedures in performance appraisals, hinder attempts to represent compliance while disobeying orders or deviating from prescribed procedures (Barker & Cheney, 1994; Townley, 1993a). In contrast, research on employee deviance (e.g., Mars, 1983), IT implementation (e.g., Gwillim, Dovey, & Wieder, 2005), and corporate politics (e.g., Buchanan, 1999) shows that employees can widen the gap between their everyday work practices and the expressions that they give and give off to managers. Employees' appropriation of the spatial arrangements that support direct supervision and the process of avowal that supports performance appraisal thus offer a continuum of increasing opportunities for concealed deviance.

Moreover, employees might use performance appraisals as opportunities to present an image of compliance that does not reflect their everyday practices. Such evaluations often rely on questionnaires that encourage employees to provide evidence of their own compliance with the projects that their managers enforce (Townley, 1993b). As Kanter (1993) notes, people also might adjust their appearances and demeanor when interacting with managers to improve their façade of compliance and thus present themselves in ways that appear to comply – when instead they are distancing themselves from the identification processes that their companies use to control them. People can also use these interactions to voice allegiance to and present an image consistent with managers' expectations, even while they reject the behaviors that upholding such images would demand (Jackall, 1978; Weeks, 2004).

The opportunities that employees have to produce self-serving expressions of obedience in interactions and managers' lenience toward these employee efforts thus highlight the limitations of a functional approach to control through supervision and performance reviews. The dynamics of personal control outlined in the functional model represent a specification of the dramaturgical model of control in which managers show no lenience to employees and employees make no attempt to create a gap between their work practices and the image that they give and give off to their supervisors. A dramaturgical model of control instead suggests that managers' appropriations of interactions with employees constitute an instance of Goffman's dramaturgical model of interaction. This model includes a specification in which employees can contrive the expressions that they give and give off, which supervisors use to form generous impressions of their actions and accomplishments.

6.2.2. Bureaucratic control

Bureaucratic control refers to "indirect control through rules, regulations and reports" (Perrow, 2005: 163), such that "performance is evaluated according to specified and measurable criteria, hence managers' judgments of work achieve 'objective' status and serve to reinforce the apparent neutrality of the policies, procedures, and rules" (Orlikowski, 1991: 12). Managers can enforce bureaucratic control by using reports to assess compliance (Ball & Wilson, 2000) or adopting information technologies that encode prescribed procedures (DeSanctis & Poole, 1994; Orlikowski, 1991).

With reports of employees' work, managers can detect and punish deviations from procedures, because the information systems record and broadcast the details of employees' practices. Zuboff's (1988: 345) research on the effects of surveillance shows that when employees are thus exposed, "the behavioral expectations of [managers] can be so keenly anticipated by [employees] that the foreknowledge of visibility is enough to induce conformity". Research on IT implementation also attributes employees' resistance to new technologies to the increased visibility that managers have over their work, which hinders their everyday improvisations with prescribed procedures (Ball & Wilson, 2000; Doolin, 2004).

Reports of employees' use of digital tools also help managers monitor and enforce compliance with information systems that impose procedures embedded in technologies. When reporting systems expose people's use of technology, they enable "a disciplinary matrix of knowledge and power", in which people "lose the ability to reflect on the assumptions, rules, and concepts that facilitate and constrain their work", because they already are incorporated in the tools that they use in their everyday practice (Orlikowski, 1991: 35). The enforcement of prescribed technologies in a consulting company, for example, meant that:

> The autonomy and self-regulation of individual practitioners is undermined by the focus on leverage, substitutability of individuals, and enforcement of disciplined work practices. While methodologies and tools may afford consultants some technical autonomy vis-a-vis their clients, those same methodologies and tools limit their professional autonomy not only to better serve client needs, but also to serve the public good. (Orlikowski, 1991: 37).

The two types of bureaucratic control, reports and compliance, represent instances of Goffman's dramaturgical model of interaction in which managers form impressions of employees from independent information, such as that found in performance reports, instead of relying on the expressions that employees give and give off in interactions. A dramaturgical specification of bureaucratic control also specifies performance reports as a medium employees can use to impress their managers with an image of compliance. It explores any gaps between work and its representation, to find opportunities for presenting an image of compliance without following procedures or using prescribed technologies.

Dramaturgical opportunities in the practice of bureaucratic control. Goffman (1959) underestimates the role of independent information – that is, information about people that does not come from their expressions – in determining the impressions that others form of behavior. He instead emphasizes the reluctance of audiences to access and assess such information during interactions, because of the difficulty and effort of doing so. He argues that people take advantage of the limited information that others have about their accomplishments and intentions to present an image that is inconsistent with what they actually have done and intend to do but consistent with others' expectations. However, by specifying bureaucratic control as an instance of Goffman's model, we might suggest that managers use a fraction of the performance information available about what employees have done.

This willingly ignorant audience contrasts with the appetite for detailed and exhaustive data about employees' work that research on control in organizations attributes to managers (Coombs, Knights, & Willmott, 1992; Dandeker, 1990). Such studies posit that managers implement information systems to improve their ability and reduce their effort to monitor and enforce compliance, beyond the level of surveillance offered by personal control. Comparing the picture of relative audience ignorance in Goffman's dramaturgical model of interaction with the omniscience granted by digital tools (Orlikowski, 1996) in models of bureaucratic control, we find a continuum of increasing visibility. Research on control locates managers at the most knowledgeable end (Elmes, Strong, & Volkoff, 2005; Gomez & Jones, 2000), while research on implementation and adoption of technologies that produce records of employees work suggest managers sit at the most ignorant end (Cunha and Carugati, 2017).

In studies that focus specifically on IT implementation, managers often specify a process for producing reports that limits their ability of scrutiny. The data provided in reports depends on more than managers' need for information; it also reflects the struggles for power in organizations (Hart & Sunders, 1997), pet solutions to organizational problems (Thomas, 1994), and managers' own attempts to impress their superiors (Jackall, 1989). Zuboff's (1988) surveillance research shows that managers can sabotage information systems to present only limited data, which protects them from their leaders' surveillance. Research on post-implementation reviews (Gwillim et al., 2005) also shows that managers can choose uses of information systems that hide employees' resistance and misuse, to present their role in the implementation of the IT in a positive light. These studies echo Goffman's (1959) findings that audiences accept access to a limited set of information to verify the image that people present. However, in IT research, the limitation stems not from managers' lenience but rather from their attempts to protect their own image and interests (Cunha, 2013).

Furthermore, research on how managers use and implement information systems indicates that managers use IT to weaken the link between work and its electronic representation. Mintzberg (1975) notes that managers prefer information that they obtain in interactions with others over that which they obtain from reports produced by information systems (see also Stubbart, 1989). Ackoff's (1967) research on executive information systems confirms that managers use a handful of the many measurements available in information systems (see also McBride, 1997). The evidence in these studies supports Goffman's claim that others use a limited amount of information to form impressions, even if more data about people's accomplishments and intentions are available. However, the reason is not to reproduce the conditions for interactions with employees. Rather, their limited data use enables these managers to enact their own preferences for making sense of their company's performance.

Dramaturgical opportunities in the reactions to bureaucratic control. In IT adoption research, records and reports can be promoted from a potential, still underused source of independent information to a medium for giving expressions that substitutes for face-to-face interactions (Orlikowski, 1996). In this case, Goffman's dramaturgical model of interaction is a specification of a broader model that includes a specification in which the stage on which actors perform consists of electronic representations of their behavior.

Research on control also portrays reports as stages for impression management, though according to these studies, employees have very little power to change information about their work recorded in IT (Ball & Wilson, 2000). To improve the image that reports give of them, employees thus must comply with prescribed procedures (cf. Stanton & Barnes-Farrell, 1996). However, other evidence indicates that employees take advantage of report production to represent their compliance with prescribed procedures, without actually doing so (e.g., Marakas & Hornik, 1996; Webb & Palmer, 1998). The same processes that allow digital tools to make some employee actions visible to managers also makes the rest of their everyday practices invisible (a managers may use enterprise social media to have an idea of the work done by employees but it will never be a complete picture of a work day ... on the other side what is reported in enterprise social media may be the result of an attempt to project a better image og oneself). On this electronic back stage, employees deviate from and improvise around prescribed procedures, without being detected.

These contrasts suggest a continuum in the representations of work, with decreasing exposure and increasing potential for impression management. For example, employees might reduce exposure by resisting information systems and hindering managers' surveillance attempts (Doolin, 2004). When employees do so, they prevent managers from monitoring their work but also provide evidence of their lack of compliance with prescribed information systems that produce reports about their work. Employees also might sabotage rather than openly resist information systems, to hide evidence of their attempts to reduce their exposure and avoid sanctions for deviating (Zuboff, 1988). Research on resistance and sabotage suggests broadly that when expressions are given and impressions are formed through reports, employees expand the back stage where they act without risking their presentations of images of commitment and compliance to managers.

Moreover, research on people's appropriation of reporting procedures is rife with evidence that people take advantage of reports to improve the image of their compliance. In Orlikowski's (1996) study, customer service representatives used digital tools to present an image of expediency and effectiveness to their managers. This empirical support confirms that performance reports can be used to give off expressions of compliance that are as malleable and powerful in shaping others' impressions as are expressions in face-to-face interactions.

The dramaturgical opportunities for the practice and reaction to bureaucratic control thus underscore the limitations of a functional approach. Employees can produce self-serving representations of their work, bolstered by the restricted selection of performance data that managers use to monitor their work. The functional model is a specification of the dramaturgical model of bureaucratic control, in which managers exhaust the possibilities of surveillance and employees reproduce the potential of exposure through technologies that report on their work. A dramaturgical model of control instead suggests that managers' appropriation of reports and employees' attempts to shape the information therein are best specified as an extension of Goffman's dramaturgical model of action. Then, bureaucratic control allows employees to give expressions of compliance by improving the representation of their work in performance reports and give off expressions of compliance by taking advantage of the procedures that managers enact to produce and incorporate those reports into their own practices.

6.2.3. Social control

Social control consists of a "shared ideology [that] obviates the need for extensive and explicit procedures and rules, providing a philosophy of interests and norms from which members can deduce an almost limitless number of specific rules to suit varying conditions" (Orlikowski, 1991: 21). It has two manifestations: managers' punctuated efforts to socialize employees collectively into the company's values and beliefs (Hatch & Schultz, 1997; Schein, 1983; Trice & Beyer, 1984) and continuous efforts by employees to enforce these values and beliefs on one another (O'Reilly & Chatman, 1996; Wenger, 2000).

Rituals enforce compliance with corporate culture by compelling employees to affirm and confirm their identities using the set of values and beliefs prescribed by the organization. Rohlen's (1974) ethnography of socialization in a Japanese company shows how such processes prompt newcomers to examine and disclose their selves, using language and categories provided by the company culture (Rose, 1988). Rites and rituals transform individual disclosure into a shared process of self-classification that makes individuals more amenable to normalization.

The continuous visibility that employees have with one another – augmented by digital tools like social media – enables them to monitor and enforce shared values and beliefs (Barker, 1993). Sewell (1998: 421) explains that employees can "creat[e] a climate in which a horizontal disciplinary force, based on peer scrutiny, operated throughout the team, as members sought to identify and prevail upon those who were jeopardizing its overall performance." Ethnographies of peer control emphasize how difficult it is to escape peer scrutiny and endure peer pressure that employees impose among themselves (Berk, 1966; Birnberg & Snodgrass, 1988).

These two types of social control then extend Goffman's dramaturgical model to a setting in which interactions are not one-to-one but one-to-many. In a flow of face-to-face encounters, employees join in forming impressions of others' allegiance to corporate values and beliefs, based on the expressions that each gives and give off as they carry out their everyday work. Therefore, the dramaturgical perspective on social control emphasizes that the expressions that employees give and give off in the course of their everyday work are not unintended outcomes of action but rather deliberate attempts to present a consistent and positive image of themselves. It also highlights how employees give and give off expressions of compliance with values and beliefs, even when they reject those values or procedures.

Dramaturgical opportunities in the practice of social control. Solidarity arises among people who see themselves as members of the same group (Goffman, 1963). When a group, such as employees of the same firm or in the same department, give collective expressions to another group, such as their managers, they stop enforcing shared values and beliefs on one another so that they can present a positive image to their audience. This solidarity contrasts with the policing that research on social control expects employees to perform on one another (cf. Kunda, 1992). In these studies, each employee is an agent of the practices, values, and beliefs that managers prescribe, such that they have a stake in one another's compliance with prescribed values and beliefs and monitor others' commitment to the company's culture (Barker, 1999).

Comparing the lenience that Goffman suggests in groups of peers with the strictness that research on social control attributes to employees, we find a continuum of increasing employee collusion. Research on social control places employees at the end with little collusion, because employees enforce compliance on peers who deviate. In contrast, several studies of employees' appropriation of corporate culture and production of subcultures suggest that employees also occupy the other end of the continuum, by joining together to resist managers' attempts to delegate the surveillance of compliance to them (e.g., Jermier, Slocum, Fry, & Gaines, 1991; Orr, 1990; Smith & Simmons, 1983). Still other studies show that companies host a multiplicity of subcultures and countercultures (e.g., Gagliardi, 1986; Jermier et al., 1991). Each fragmented subculture imposes its own values and beliefs on its members, which weakens the effect of the corporate culture. These studies extend Goffman's (1959) model of interaction by suggesting that teams may refuse to present an image of compliance to their audience and thereby avoid imposing audiences' expectations on their members.

Finally, studies of corporate culture (e.g., Benson, 1986) and broader theories of cultural adoption (e.g., Certeau, 1988) suggest that even members of integrated cultures dismiss and conspire to weaken the values and beliefs imposed by managers, to substitute for personal and bureaucratic control. Thus, employees might not adopt but rather adapt the culture to match their identity, interests, and interpretations (cf. Gagliardi, 1986). This process of appropriation can lead employees to dismiss the messages and metaphors that managers use to convey values and beliefs, by ignoring or mocking them. Smith and Simmons (1983) show how a group of employees resisted change by taking advantage of the metaphor that their leader used to implement it; in Cunha and Orlikowski's (2008) study, employees used an online forum to mock managers' attempts to introduce a new organizational culture after a merger and instead framed it as a threat to their identity. These extensions of Goffman's (1959) findings reveal that teams can not only refuse to impose audiences' expectations on members but also flaunt their resistance to those norms and interpretations.

Dramaturgical opportunities in the reactions to social control. Impressing a group of peers with expressions of compliance, without practicing such compliance, may be more difficult than impressing managers with expressions of compliance or through information systems. As Goffman (1959) argues, groups of peers have substantial visibility and thus cannot be deceived easily by misrepresentation. Research on culture in organizations supports this specification of team performance by highlighting the difficulties that employees face when attempting to feign compliance with values and beliefs to their peers (Louis, 1983; Posner, Kouzes, & Schmidt, 1985; Smircich, 1983).

However, research on resistance in everyday life suggests that impression management is possible even under continued observation. Certeau (1988: xiii) describes how native South American Indians appropriated the culture that Spanish colonizers attempted to impose on them:

The ambiguity that subverted from within the Spanish colonizers' "success" in imposing their own culture on the indigenous Indians is well known. Submissive, and even consenting to their subjection, the Indians nevertheless often made of the rituals, representations, and laws imposed on them something quite different from what their conquerors had in mind; they subverted them not by rejecting or altering them, but by using them with respect to ends and references foreign to the system they had no choice but to accept. They were other within the very colonization that outwardly assimilated them; their use of the dominant social order deflected its power, which they lacked the means to challenge; they escaped it without leaving it.

Scattered evidence in organizational research suggests people's ability to enact similar practices to impress their peers with regard to their compliance with a culture to which they do not subscribe (e.g., Barker, 1993; Ezzamel & Willmott, 1998; Mortensen & Hinds, 2001). Thus, employees' participation in interactions in which peers assess their acceptance of values and beliefs can be placed along a continuum of increasing opportunities to pretend compliance.

In the regionalization of workplaces, employees may find or create spaces and times at work in which their actions and their utterances do not get incorporated into their images of one another. Such times and places allow people to prepare a façade of compliance and release the tension associated with presenting themselves as members of a culture that they reject. Fayard and Weeks's (2007) research on interactions around water coolers and photocopiers in an office setting shows that employees use these places to prepare performances of prevalent norms and values or to release the tension from faking compliance with corporate culture in interactions with others. According to Van Maanen (1992) and Rosen (1988), corporate parties and informal meetings in which employees interact while intoxicated allow them to act outside their roles as compliant members of their organization but then deny that they have done so afterward.

Furthermore, research on the role of appearance and demeanor in interactions at work reveals that employees can create façades of compliance that obfuscate others' scrutiny of their obedience. A wide range of tactics enable people to take advantage of the gap between their intentions and others' interpretations of them; they appear not only plausible but also necessary in organizations as means to cope with the dynamics of power and politics. Jackall (1989) and Kanter (1993) document how managers must act, and even require family members to act, to express compliance with prescribed of values and norms and thereby avoid scrutiny of their everyday practices, if they want to establish a career for themselves in the organization.

The dramaturgical dynamics for social control thus highlight additional limitations to the functional approach. A façade of compliance can discourage scrutiny, especially when supported by opportunities to prepare presentations of compliance at times and places in which others suspend their assessments. This façade can be attacked, but it also can be protected by the reluctance of employees to impose prescribed values and beliefs on one another. The functional model of social control offers a specification of dramaturgical model, in which employees do not attempt to improve the image that others have of them beyond their actual accomplishments. Instead, employees expose all of their actions and genuine motivations to peers, who scrutinize them to ensure compliance with corporate values and beliefs. The dramaturgical dynamics in social control instead suggest that employees' appropriation of their company's culture and ability to hide any deviance behind a façade of compliance constitute an extension of Goffman's dramaturgical model of interaction that includes tactics people use to impress their peers and escape the pressure to comply with their company's or occupation's norms.

Table 1 outlines the outcomes of the practices of managers and employees, contrasting personal, bureaucratic, and social control scenarios.

Table 1. Dramaturgical opportunities in personal, bureaucratic, and social control.

	Practice of control	Reactions to control
Personal control	1. Supervisors exclude some deviations from procedure from their impressions of employees' compliance, because they interpret these deviations as necessary to deal with specific conditions for action. 2. The norms and dispositions that supervisors draw on when forming impressions of their employees cause them to be lenient to deviance, even when they do not interpret it as a necessary response to situated conditions for action.	1. Employees can take advantage of spatial arrangements of work and the temporal structure of supervision to escape the scrutiny of their managers. 2. Employees can take advantage of the reliance of appraisal interviews on self-reports to present an improved image of their accomplishment and themselves.
Bureaucratic control	1. Managers can limit their visibility of employees' work to reduce the visibility that their own leaders have over their work. 2. Managers can limit their visibility of employees' work with practices of using reports to monitor market dynamics and company performance.	1. Employees resist or sabotage information systems that produce reports to reduce managers' visibility over their work. 2. Employees manipulate information systems that produce reports to improve the image that they give of their work and accomplishments.
Social control	1. Peer employees can impose subcultures that dilute the power of the corporate culture. 2. Peer employees can join together in dismissing the events and messages that managers use to communicate corporate values and beliefs.	1. Employees can find spaces where they are safe from scrutiny of their compliance with values and beliefs. 2. Employees can present a façade of compliance with values and beliefs that discourages scrutiny.

6.3. A dramaturgical model of control

Dramaturgical opportunities afforded by digital tools across personal, bureaucratic, and social forms of control suggest an overall dramaturgical model of control that contrasts with but also complements functional models of control. In this dramaturgical model, control is something that supervisors (managers in personal and bureaucratic control, other employees in social control) and employees perform together, instead of something that supervisors exert over employees. The dramaturgical model also highlights how control is mediated by digital tools, the modern *counter-roll* that may be linked only loosely with everyday work, and which employees may produce solely for the benefit of supervisors.

Extending Goffman's model of interactions to a digitally mediated dramaturgical model of control. The dramaturgical model of control represents a specification of Goffman's model of interaction according to the relationship between supervisors and employees. It defines supervisors as agents of control who form impressions of employees to assess their compliance with company procedures or direct orders, according to the expressions that employees give and the reports that employees produce. Employees as agents of control produce expressions and reports of their compliance.

A dramaturgical model of control also entails a three-pronged extension of Goffman's model of interaction. The dramaturgical dynamics in personal control suggest extending Goffman's model to include interactions in which others scrutinize the expressions that people give for evidence of inconsistency. Research on personal control further highlights that managers use spatial arrangements and employees' disclosure of their work and achievements to monitor compliance. Managers may be lenient toward, and even expect, deviations from procedure because of the situated challenges that employees face in their everyday work. However, research on personal control also emphasizes that the identity and career prospects of managers relate to their ability to enforce procedures, or at least present an image of being able to do so. A dramaturgical model of control therefore must account not only for lenience but also monitoring that is far stricter than expected by Goffman.

The dramaturgical dynamics in bureaucratic control also extend Goffman's model to include interactions mediated by material artifacts. In this sense, the model exposes the dramaturgical opportunities and dramaturgical challenges associated with the decreasing role of face-to-face supervision in managers' control over employees' work, due to the increasing use of reports. A dramaturgical model of control therefore must include the role of reports and the information systems that produce them as the chief inputs into managers' impressions of their employees and the primary medium by which employees express their compliance with procedures and their obedience to orders.

Finally, the dramaturgical dynamics in social control suggest that employees can join supervisors in exerting surveillance on one another. Thus, the dramaturgical model of control extends Goffman's model of interaction by integrating competitive and cooperative dynamics in team performance. Companies become social contexts in which employees struggle and are capable of deviating from the norms that they enact collectively with peers. The dramaturgical approach to social control highlights that even when employees refuse their company's norms, they may replace them with norms of their own, which they enforce on one another. The collusion that Goffman expects from team members who present a collective image to an audience is one possible specification of team performance, which is easiest to conduct when the collective performances are limited in duration. If teams of employees must maintain collective performance for extended periods, such as when members present a collective image of compliance in IT to their managers, team members will be less forgiving of inconsistencies in others' enactment of their parts.

The role of supervisors in the dramaturgical model of control. This dramaturgical model of control specifies the role of supervisors (i.e., audiences): They form impressions from a counter-roll of expressions or reports produced by employees using digital tools. The dramaturgical dynamics in personal, bureaucratic, and social forms of control suggest in combination that supervisors exert three structuring effects on control.

First, supervisors define the image that employees need to present. The dramaturgical dynamics in personal control suggest that managers may demand compliance with prescribed procedures, but they also may enforce a set of behaviors and goals that differ from or even are at odds with those specified by the organizations. Dramaturgical dynamics in bureaucratic control and social control are similar. That is, managers may monitor much less information about employees in reports than is necessary to assess their compliance with prescribed procedure, and employees also might enforce a subculture on one another that conflicts with or even resists their company's culture.

Second, supervisors define the level of exposure of employees' work. The dramaturgical dynamics in personal and bureaucratic control show that the exposure employees endure depends on the practices that their supervisors enact to assess compliance with procedures and orders. Managers may not use all of the potential visibility afforded by information systems or spatial arrangements in their organization, in which case they waste the surveillance potential of panoptical technologies and workspaces. The dramaturgical dynamics in social control also show that employees can reproduce some times and places as liminal occasions for suspending assessments of one another's compliance with shared norms.

Third, supervisors define the level of lenience granted to employees by specifying how much of their exposed work practices influence the supervisors' impressions of employees' compliance. The dramaturgical dynamics in personal, bureaucratic, and social control all suggest that supervisors use only some of the practices and achievements of employees to assess their compliance. Supervisors exclude deviance that supports their own interests or in circumstances in which supervisors regard deviance as acceptable or necessary. The dramaturgical dynamics in the three forms of control also emphasize that control is not a process of observation in which supervisors assess deviations but rather is a process of interpretation so that managers can form impressions. The behaviors and goals that determine compliance are not fixed work procedures or targets but changing actions and accomplishments, interpreted in context.

The role of employees in the dramaturgical model of control. Employees produce a counter-roll of expressions of compliance, both given and given off. When control is specified this way, the dramaturgical dynamics in personal, bureaucratic, and social control define two structuring effects of employees on control.

First, employees join supervisors in stipulating the exposure of their everyday work. According to the dramaturgical dynamics in personal, bureaucratic, and social control, employees find and create back stages for themselves where their actions are more difficult to scrutinize. In these places, employees establish their own space and become exempt from the gaze of managers or peers who supervise them. Employees also might sabotage information systems that supervisors use to monitor their work, or at least keep some of their actions and achievements out of these information systems to hinder supervisors' attempts to expose all the work they want to monitor. By enacting some spaces and representations of work as front stages and keeping others as back stages, employees reduce the overall exposure of their everyday practices. Thus exposure is a joint, competitive accomplishment between supervisors and employees, achieved in everyday interactions in which one group forms impressions from the expressions of compliance that others give by displaying some actions and hiding others.

Second, employees define the level of exposure by regionalizing experience. The dramaturgical dynamics in social control show that employees hide their own interpretations and intentions by framing their actions and achievements specifically for supervisors. Certau's (1988) example of native Indians' image of compliance with Christian rituals, even as they continued to worship their own gods, effectively illustrates how the supervised carve out back stages for themselves, in plain sight of those who exert surveillance. Exposure in a dramaturgical model of control thus is an interpretive process by which employees provide expressions of compliance and attempt to shape how supervisors make sense of those expressions.

6.4. Conclusion

In this chapter we show that the functional model of control represents only an instance of a broader dramaturgical model of control. In this specification, supervisors expose as much of employees' work as the available information systems and spatial arrangements allow, then use all of that information to assess employees' compliance with every prescribed procedure. Thus, supervisors expose their successes, as well as their failures, in enforcing the company's procedures and goals. Furthermore, employees do everything on well-exposed digitally created stages, they do not hide from or deceive their supervisors, and do not to deviate from prescribed procedures. This functional model therefore is one instance of the dramaturgical model of control, in which supervisors and employees choose to, happen to, or must act against their own interests for the sake of the company's goals.

Such a specification of the functional model as an instance of the dramaturgical model of control reveals that research on control in organizations could be improved with some alternative specifications of the dramaturgical model in which managers and employees put their own interests ahead of the interests of their organization. These specifications can help researchers explore and explain how employees take advantage of opportunities to present a façade of compliance when their managers enact personal, bureaucratic, or social controls. Such research also might improve the relevant insights by exploring conditions that produce different functional specifications of this model. When employees and managers enact a certain specification, they may be acting against their own interests (Jackall, 1989; Sewell & Wilkinson, 1992). If managers hinder the improvisations that employees use to adapt prescribed procedures to their situated challenges, they reduce employees' ability to comply with prescribed procedures and goals. Employees who expose all the evidence of their inability or unwillingness to comply with managers' expectations and orders invite sanctions that punish them for noncompliance. Yet it remains difficult to find a model of behavior that justifies the extent to which managers and employees jeopardize their own interests when they enact this variation of control, whereas many studies provide evidence of managers and employees enacting functional variations of the dramaturgical model of control (e.g., Dandeker, 1990).

Future research on control in organizations also should explore how managers co-participate through digital tools in personal, bureaucratic, and social forms of control to impress their leaders with their ability to enforce compliance. A functional model of control looks at managers as a community of practice who blame deviations from prescribed procedures on employees (Ball & Wilson, 2000; Barker & Cheney, 1994; Bloomfield & Coomes, 1992). But ethnographic studies suggest an alternative specification, in which managers' careers feature a permanent state of probation, and any evidence of their inability to enforce prescribed procedure jeopardizes their ambitions to access informal networks of influence or climb formal structures of power (Kanter, 1993). Therefore, managers' attempts to impress their leaders likely define how they exercise control over employees. Exploring the choices that managers make, the constraints they face, and the tactics they improvise can advance research on control by explicating the double bind supervisors face.

Finally, another extension of research on control in organizations could explore how managers use representations of their employees' work strategically. For example, when using digital tools, the data and observations that managers use to monitor employees' compliance with procedures and orders also can reveal organizational strengths and weaknesses and competitive threats and opportunities in their markets (Rosen & Baroudi, 1992; Yates, 1989). However, the dramaturgical model of control suggests that this information may be little more than a façade of compliance, designed to impress managers. Supervisors can be not only accessories but also instigators of the enactment of control processes. When they thus participate in organizational control, they hinder the production of accurate data about their company and its competitive context, which often is used to determine a strategy for their unit or the organization as a whole. Exploring how supervisors might improve on or replace these performance data to determine an appropriate strategy would expand research on organizational control by specifying how managers produce and reproduce the link between representations of their employees' work that they use for control and the information they use to guide their strategy process.

References

Ackoff, R. (1967). Management misinformation systems. Management Science: 147-156.

Akerlof, G.A., & Kranton, R.E. (2008). Identity, supervision, and work groups. The American Economic Review, 98(2): 212-217

Allen, M.W., Hart, J.L., & Walker, K.L. (2007). Workplace surveillance and managing privacy boundaries. *Management Communication Quarterly*, 21(2): 172-200.

Andrzejewski, A.V. (2008). Building power: Architecture and surveillance in Victorian America. Knoxville, TN: University of Tennessee Press.

Anteby, M. 2008. Identity incentives as an engaging form of control: Revisiting leniencies in an aeronautic plant. *Organization Science*, 19(2): 202-220.

Ball, K., & Wilson, D.C. (2000). Power, control and computer-based performance monitoring: Repertoires, resistance and subjectivities. *Organization Studies*, 21(3): 539–565.

Barker, J.R. (1999). The discipline of teamwork: Participation and concertive control. Thousand Oaks, CA: Sage Publications.

Barker, J.R. (1993). Tightening the iron cage: Concertive control in self managing teams. *Administrative Science Quarterly*, 38: 408-437.

Barker, J.R., & Cheney, G. (1994). The concept and the practices of discipline in contemporary organizational life. Communication Monographs, 60: in press.

Benson, S.P. (1986). Counter cultures. Urbana, IL: University of Illinois Press.

Berk, B.B. (1966). Organizational goals and inmate organization. *American Journal of Sociology*, 71(5): 522-534.

Beynon, H. (1973). Working for Ford. London: Allen Lane.

Birnberg, J.G., & Snodgrass, C. (1988). Culture and control: A field study. Accounting, Organizations and Society, 13(5): 447-464.

Blau, P.M. (1955). The dynamics of bureaucracy: A study of interpersonal relations in two government agencies. Chicago: University of Chicago Press.

Bloomfield, B.P., & Coomes, R. (1992). Information Technology, control and power: the centralization and decentralization debate. Journal of Management Studies, 29(4).

Buchanan, D. (1999). Politics and organizational change: The lived experience. Human Relations, 52(5): 609-629.

Burawoy, M. (1979). Manufacturing consent: Changes in the labor process under monopoly capitalism. Chicago: University of Chicago Press.

Certeau, M. (1988). The practice of everyday life. Berkeley, CA: University of California Press.

Child, J. (1973). Predicting and understanding organizational structure. Administrative Science Quarterly, 18: 168-185.

Coombs, R., Knights, D., & Willmott, H. (1992). Culture, control and competition: Towards a conceptual framework for the study of information technology in organizations. Organization Studies, 13: 51-72.

Covaleski, M.A., Dirsmith, M.W., Heian, J. B., & Samuel, S. (1998). The calculated and the avowed: Techniques of discipline and struggles over identity in Big Six public accounting firms. *Administrative Science Quarterly*, 43: 293-327.

Crozier, M. (1964). The bureaucratic phenomenon. Chicago: University of Chicago Press.

Cunha, J. (2013). A Dramaturgical Model of the Production of Performance Data. *Mis Quarterly*, 37(3).

Cunha, J., & Carugati, A. (2013). Systems of transfiguration and the adoption of IT under surveillance. In International Conference on Information Systems.

Cunha, J., & Orlikowski, W.J. (2008). Performing catharsis: The use of online discussion forums in organizational change. Information and Organization, 18: 132-156.

Dandeker, C. (1990). Surveillance, power, and modernity: Bureaucracy and discipline from 1700 to the present day. Cambridge, UK: Polity.

Das, T.K. (1993). A multiple paradigm approach to organizational control. International Journal of Organizational Analysis, 1(4): 385-403.

DeSanctis, G., & Poole, M.S. (1994). Capturing the complexity in advanced technology use: Adaptive structuration theory. Organization Science, 5(2): 121-147.

Doolin, B. (2004). Power and resistance in the implementation of a medical management information system. Information Systems Journal, 14(4): 343-362.

Elmes, M.B., Strong, D.M., & Volkoff, O. (2005). Panoptic empowerment and reflective conformity in enterprise systems-enabled organizations. Information & Organization, 15(1): 1-37.

Ezzamel, M., Willmott, H. (1998). Accounting for teamwork: A critical study of group-based systems of organizational control. *Administrative Science Quarterly*, 43: 358-396.

Ezzamel, M., Willmott, H., & Worthington, F. (2001). Power, control and resistance in 'the factory that time forgot'. *Journal of Management Studies*, 38(8): 1053-1079.

Fayard, A.-L., & Weeks, J. (2007). Photocopiers and water-coolers: The affordances of informal interaction. *Organization Studies*, 28(5): 605-634.

Foucault, M. (1980). Power/knowledge: Selected interviews and other writings. New York: Pantheon Books.

Foucault, M. (1977). Discipline and punish: The birth of the prison. London: Allen & Lane.

Friedman, W.A. (2004). Birth of a salesman: The transformation of selling in America. Cambridge, MA: Harvard University Press.

Gagliardi, P. (1986). The creation and change of organizational cultures: A conceptual framework. *Organization Studies*, 7(2): 117-134.

Giangreco A., Carugati A., Sebastiano A., & Al Tamimi H. (2012). War outside, ceasefire inside: An analysis of the performance appraisal system of a public hospital in a zone of conflict, Evaluation and Program Planning, 35: 161-170.

Giddens, A. (1986). The constitution of society: An outline of the theory of structuration. Berkeley, CA: University of California Press.

Goffman, E. (1982). The interaction order: American Sociological Association, 1982 presidential address. *American Sociological Review*, 48: 1-17.

Goffman, E. (1963). Behavior in public places: Notes on the social organization of gatherings. New York: Free Press.

Goffman, E. (1959). The presentation of self in everyday life. Garden City, NJ: Doubleday.

Gomez, P.-Y., & Jones, B.C. (2000). Conventions: An interpretation of deep structure in organizations. Organization Science, 11(6): 696-708.

Gouldner, A.W. (1954). Patterns of industrial bureaucracy. New York: Free Press.

Gwillim, D., Dovey, K., & Wieder, B. (2005). The politics of post-implementation reviews. *Information Systems Journal*, 15: 307-319.

Hart, P., & Sunders, C. (1997). Power and trust: Critical factors in the adoption and use of electronic data interchange. *Organizational Science*, 8(1): 23-42.

Hatch, M.J., & Schultz, M. (1997). Relations between organizational culture, identity and image. *European Journal of Marketing*, 31(5): 356-365.

Hollinger, R.C., & Clark, J.P. 1982. Formal and informal social controls of employee deviance. *The Sociological Quarterly*, 23(3): 333-343.

Jackall, R. (1989). Moral mazes: The world of corporate managers. New York: Oxford University Press.

Jackall, R. (1978). Workers in a labyrinth. Montclair, NJ: Allanheld, Osmun & Co.

Jermier, J.M. (1998). Introduction: Critical perspective on organizational control. *Administrative Science Quarterly*, 43(2): 235-256.

Jermier, J.M., Slocum, J.W., Jr., Fry, L.M., & Gaines, J. (1991). Organizational subcultures in a soft bureaucracy: Resistance behind the myth and facade of an official culture. *Organization Science*, 2(2): 170-194.

Kanter, R.M. (1993). Men and women of the corporation, 2nd ed. New York: Basic Books.

Kipnis, D., Schmidt, S.M., & Wilkinson, I. (1980). Intraorganizational influence tactics: Explorations in getting one's way. *Journal of Applied Psychology*, 65(4): 440-452.

Kohli, R., & Kettinger, W. (2004). Informating the clan: Controlling physicians' costs and outcomes. *Management Information Systems Quarterly*, 28(3): 363-394.

Kunda, G. (1992). Engineering culture: Control and commitment in a high-tech corporation. Philadelphia, PA: Temple University Press.

Lange, D. (2008). A multidimensional conceptualization of organizational corruption control. *Academy of Management Review*, 33(3): 710-729.

Lawrence, T.B., & Robinson, S.L. (2007). Ain't misbehavin: Workplace deviance as organizational resistance. *Journal of Management*, 33(3): 378-394.

Lipsky, M. (1980). Street-level bureaucracy: Dilemmas of the individual in public services. New York: Russell Sage Foundation.

Louis, M.R. (1983). Organizations as culture-bearing milieux. In L.R. Pondy, P.J. Frost, G. Morgan, & T.C. Dandridge (Eds.), Organizational symbolism (pp. 39-54). Greenwich, CT: JAI Press.

Marakas, G.M., & Hornik, S. (1996). Passive resistance misuse: Overt support and covert recalcitrance in IS implementation. *European Journal of Information Systems*, 5: 208-219.

Mars, G. (1983). Cheats at work: An anthropology of workplace crime. London: Unwin Paperbacks.

Mayer, R.C., & Davis, J.H. (1999). The effect of the performance appraisal system on trust for management: A field quasi-experiment. *Journal of Applied Psychology*, 84(1): 123-136.

McBride, N. (1997). The rise and fall of an executive information system: A case study. *Information Systems Journal*, 7: 277-287.

Mintzberg, H. (1975). The manager's job: Folklore and fact. Harvard Business Review, 53(4): 49-61.

Mortensen, M., & Hinds, P. (2001). Conflict and shared identity in geographically distributed teams. *International Journal of Conflict Management*, 12(3): 212–238.

O'Reilly, C.A., & Chatman, J. (1996). Culture as social control: Corporations, cults, and commitment. In B.M. Staw, & L.L. Cummings (Eds.), Research in organizational behavior, Vol. 18 (pp. 157-200). Greenwich, CT: JAI Press.

Orlikowski, W.J. (1996). Improvising organizational transformation over time: A situated change perspective. Information Systems Research, 7(1): 63-92.

Orlikowski, W.J. (1991). Integrated information environment or matrix of control? The contradictory implications of information technology. Management and Information Technology, 1(1): 9-42.

Orr, J. (1990). Sharing knowledge, celebrating identity: War stories and community memory in a service culture. In D.S. Middleton, & D. Edwards (Eds.), Collective remembering: Memory in society (pp. 35-47). Beverly Hills, CA: Sage.

Ouchi, W.G. (1979). A conceptual framework for the design of organizational control mechanisms. Management Science, 25(9): 833-848.

Pennings, J.M., & Woiceshyn, J. (1987). A typology of organizational control and its metaphors. Research in the Sociology of Organizations, 5: 73-104.

Perrow, C. (2005). Organizing America: Wealth, power, and the origins of corporate capitalism. Princeton, NJ: Princeton University Press.

Perrow, C. (1972). Complex organizations. Glenview, IL: Scott Foresman.

Posner, B.Z., Kouzes, J.M., & Schmidt, W.H. (1985). Shared values make a difference: An empirical test of corporate culture. Human Resource Management, 24(3): 293-309.

Riley, P. (1983). A structurationist account of political-culture. *Administrative Science Quarterly*, 28(3): 414-437.

Rohlen, T.P. (1974). For harmony and strength: Japanese white-collar organization in anthropological perspective. Berkeley: University of California Press.

Rose, N. (1988). Calculable minds and manageable individuals. History of the Human Sciences, 1(2): 179-200.

Rose, N.S. (1990). Governing the soul: The shaping of the private self. London: Routledge.

Rosen, M. (1985). Breakfast at Spiros: Dramaturgy and dominance. *Journal of Management*, 11(2): 31-48.

Rosen, M. (1988). You asked for it: Christmas at the bosses' expense. *Journal of Management Studies*, 25(5): 463-480.

Rosen, M., & Baroudi, J.J. (1992). Computer-based technology and the emergence of new forms of managerial control. In A. Sturdy, D. Knights, & H. Willmott (Eds.), Skill and consent: Contemporary studies in the labor process (pp. 213-234). London: Routledge.

Roy, D.F. (1960). Banana time: Job satisfaction and informal interaction. Human Organization, 18: 156-168.

Schein, E.H. (1983). The role of the founder in creating organizational culture. Organizational Dynamics, 12(1): 13-28.

Sewell, G. (2008). The fox and the hedgehog go to work: A natural history of workplace collusion. *Management Communication Quarterly*, 21(3): 344-363.

Sewell, G. (1998). The discipline of teams: The control of team-based industrial work through electronic and peer surveillance. *Administrative Science Quarterly*, 43(2): 397-428.

Sewell, G., & Wilkinson, B. (1992). "Someone to watch over me": Surveillance, discipline and the just-in-time labour process. Sociology, 26: 271-289.

Smircich, L. (1983). Studying organizations as cultures. In G. Morgan (Ed.), Beyond method: Strategies for social research (pp. 160-172). Beverly Hill, CA: Sage.

Smith, K.K., & Simmons, V.M. (1983). A Rumpelstilskin organization: Metaphors on metaphors in field research. *Administrative Science Quarterly*, 28: 377-392.

Snell, S.A. (1992). Control theory in strategic human resource management: The mediating effect of administrative information. *Academy of Management Journal*, 35(2): 292-327

Stanton, J.M., & Barnes-Farrell, J.L. (1996). Effects of electronic performance monitoring on personal control, task satisfaction, and task performance. *Journal of Applied Psychology*, 81(6): 738-745.

Stubbart, C.I. (1989). Managerial cognition: A missing link in strategic management research. *Journal of Management Studies*, 24(4): 325-347.

Thomas, R.J. (1994). What machines can't do: Politics and technology in the industrial enterprise. Berkeley: University of California Press.

Townley, B. (1993a.) Foucault, power/knowledge and its relevance for human resource management. *Academy of Management Review*, 18: 518-545.

Townley, B. (1993b.) Performance appraisal and the emergence of management. *Journal of Management Studies*, 30(2): 221-238.

Trice, H.M., & Beyer, J.M. (1984). Studying organizational culture through rites and ceremonies. *Academy of Management Review*, 9(4): 653-669.

Van Maanen, J.E. (1992). Drinking our troubles away: Managing conflict in a British police agency. In D.M. Kolb, & J.M. Bartunek (Eds.), Hidden conflict in organizations: Uncovering behind-the-scenes disputes (pp. 32-62). Newbury Park, CA: Sage.

Watson, T.J. (2001). In search of management: Culture, chaos and control in managerial work (Rev. ed.). London: Thomson Learning.

Webb, M., & Palmer, G. (1998). Evading surveillance and making time: An ethnographic view of the Japanese factory floor in Britain. *British Journal of Industrial Relations*, 36(4): 611-627.

Weeks, J. (2004). Unpopular culture: The ritual of complaint in a British bank. Chicago, IL: University of Chicago Press.

Wenger, E. (2000). Communities of practice and social learning systems. *Organization*, 7(2): 225-246.

Yates, J. (1989). Control through communication. Baltimore, MD: John Hopkins University Press.

Zuboff, S. (1988). In the age of the smart machine. New York: Basic Books.

Zurcher, L.A.J. (1965). The sailor aboard ship: A study of role behavior in a total institution. Social Forces, 43(3): 389-400.

Zweig, D., & Webster, J. (2002). Where is the line between benign and invasive? An examination of psychological barriers to the acceptance of awareness monitoring systems. *Journal of Organizational Behavior*, 23(5): 605-633.

Chapter 7

THE FUTURE ROLE OF MACHINE LEARNING IN HR DEVELOPMENT

Roberto Bernazzani-Franca Cantoni-Mariacristina Piva

SUMMARY: 7.1. Introduction. – 7.2. Managerial decision making applied to performance measurement and potential evaluation. – 7.3. About machine learning. – 7.3.1. How machine learning works. – 7.3.2. Machine learning tools. – 7.4. Possible scenarios and critical considerations. – 7.5. Conclusions. – Acknowledgements. – References.

7.1. Introduction

Using a Gaussian process classifier, Frey and Osborne (2017) examine how jobs are susceptible to computerisation in the US labour market by estimating the probability of technological replacement for 702 detailed occupations. The non-neutrality of technology and computerisation in labour markets, in general, is acknowledged in the literature (for a survey, see Piva & Vivarelli, 2017). Indeed, an increasing number of empirical studies (Marcolin et al., 2016) documents the decline of employment in routine intensive jobs, i.e., jobs mainly consisting of tasks following well-defined procedures that can be easily performed by sophisticated algorithms. Our research focuses on a specific occupation, the human resources (HR) manager, which is positioned at the 28th place out of the 702 occupations in the Frey and Osborne study. This evidence suggests that this occupation is hardly replaceable by technology (Chui et al., 2015). However, by disentangling the different tasks included in this occupation, we mainly focus on a complex and non-routine lever in human resource management (HRM) that requires intuition and discretionality, i.e. potential evaluation. By using a precautionary approach, this work tries to understand if machine learning (ML) can be effectively used in executing potential evaluation and consequently whether it might assist or even replace HR managers.

7.2. Managerial decision making applied to performance measurement and potential evaluation

HRM is all about making decisions that directly influence organizations' competitiveness (Walger et al., 2016; Lacombe & Tonelli, 2001). Indeed, the functions of the HR department have direct relevance to both the definition and implementation of organizational strategies. Its strategic role is evident in the necessary alignment between HR and organizational strategy, as well as in the fact that HR strategies, policies, and practices are always required (Wright & Snell, 1998; Lacombe & Tonelli, 2001; Bosquetti & Albuquerque, 2005). Management decisions made in the HR department affect the organization's entire value-creation process. HRM line managers play a central role because they are asked to face situations where taking complex (Fish & Hardy, 2015) and non-routine[1] decisions is the norm. In many organisations, a myriad of HR-related tasks, such as filling out performance forms, interviewing candidates for employment, making salary increase recommendations, and breaking employment-related news to employees require HR managers to have the ability to act in a situation of opalescence (incomplete and asymmetric information) and with the employment of discretion (ability to choose between different options) (López-Cotarelo, 2011). Human resource development, the framework for helping employees to develop their personal and organizational skills, knowledge, and abilities (Hassan, 2007; Swanson, 2001; Koike, 1997), is one of these activities, because the pieces of information available to managers are always fragmentary and incomplete, and decisions require them to choose among different options.

Human resource development leverages on two processes (Lebas, 1995; Micheli & Mari, 2005): performance measurement (PM) and potential evaluation (PE). While PM is connected to the formal determination of an individual's job-related actions and outcomes within a particular position or setting, PE is a future-oriented appraisal whose main objective is to identify and evaluate the potential of employees to assume higher positions and responsibilities in the organizational hierarchy (Brown & Benson, 2010). Differences between the two processes are clear:

- "performance" refers to output results and their outcomes obtained from processes, products, and services that permit measurement on the basis of numerical information (outcomes);
- "potential" is typically used to suggest that an individual has the qualities (e.g., characteristics, motivation, skills, abilities, experiences, etc.) to effectively perform and contribute in broader or different roles in the organisation at some point in the future. Potential is associated with possibilities for the future rather than with problems in the current performance.

---

[1] "Non-routine" refers to unique and non-repetead situations, such as creative problem solving and decision making (Marcolin et al., 2016).

In contrast to performance, PE requires specific forward-looking measurement tools and measures. While backward-looking measures (tool: performance matrix) and measures of the present (tools: behaviour ratings, simulations, competency-based interviews, 360° assessments) can be used for performance measurement, forward-looking measures are needed for potential evaluation (tool: potential appraisal, self-appraisals, peer appraisals, superior appraisals, Management By Objectives, psychological and psychometric tests, management games like role playing, leadership exercises, etc.) (Micheli & Mari, 2005).

This illustrates quite clearly that PE, unlike PM, requires the use of discretion in areas characterized by information scarcity and subjectivity, such as motives, values, personality and cognitive abilities.

Our contribution stems from an attempt to identify a scientific response to a shared doubt about the use of technology in the execution of those activities that are characterized by a high degree of discretion and non-routine work (Holland & Bardoel, 2016).

Given the fact that computerisation is no longer confined to routine tasks that can be written as rule-based queries but will soon spread to non-routine tasks as large databases become available (Brynjolfsson & McAfee, 2011; Frey & Osborne, 2017), we are interested in understanding if machine learning (ML) – here intended as the ability of a machine to learn and therefore to improve its performance from the experience – can be effectively used in executing PE.

7.3. About machine learning

There is an increasing trend in automating jobs currently done by highly trained and experienced white-collar workers, thanks to the advance of ML and various forms of artificial intelligence. The broad idea that manual work can be carried out by machines is already familiar; as early as the 19th-century industrial revolution, the fear of "technological unemployment" induced English textile workers to destroy machines under the charismatic lead of Ned Ludd (Hobsbawm, 1968). Today, smarter machines can perform even more sophisticated tasks (McAfee & Brynjolfsson, 2014). Generally speaking, what makes workers vulnerable to automation is less whether their work is manual than whether it is repetitive and routinized. Machines that can already do many forms of routine manual labour are improving their performances in some routine cognitive tasks, too.

It is important, first of all, to formally define ML. One widely accepted definition is offered by Tom Mitchell: "*A computer program is said to learn from experience E with respect to some class of tasks T and performance measure P, if its performance at tasks in T, as measured by P, improves with experience E"* (Mitchell, 1997).

In the academic world, the topic has been investigated since the 1950s (e.g., Samuel, 1959); however, ML has received more and more attention in the last few years mainly because of two factors. The first one is the availability of data. As we will see, ML algorithms are trained using data and, usually, the more data they receive as input, the better their output in terms of accuracy. The huge increase in the volume of data produced (including data from social networking sites, smartphones, and devices belonging to the "Internet of things"), which has characterized the last few years, has therefore positively affected the adoption of ML techniques. The second factor is the availability of computational power. Although ML algorithms often require vastly expanded computational resources, during the last years the availability of such resources has increased both in volume and flexibility (e.g., Amazon Elastic Compute Cloud, https://aws.amazon.com/ec2), and such improvements have positively affected the trend toward ML adoption.

7.3.1. How machine learning works

We can explain how ML works with the help of some examples. A typical ML problem, for example, is spam filtering. It is a classification problem in which a ML algorithm can be trained with a set of email messages, pointing out which of them are spam messages and which are not; at the end of the training, the algorithm should be able to correctly classify new messages, having learned from experience.

We can see an important difference with respect to classic computer programming. In the above example, there is no sequence of instructions (algorithm) that explicitly tells the machine how to detect spam (for example, by providing a data set of specific text patterns); the machine, instead, uses a set of examples to "learn" the rules autonomously.

One of the most challenging parts in this process is defining how to represent the objects (observations) belonging to the training set. For document classification tasks, for example, a bag-of-words model can be adopted: each document can be represented as a vector of words, together with the frequency with which they appear.

Another example of ML application is sentiment analysis. A company, for example, might be interested in measuring the "sentiment" (positive or negative) toward a brand or a product by using, as a data source, public Twitter posts related to a brand or product. Even in this case, the sentiment is not computed according to predefined rules; after the system has been trained by the introduction of a manually classified set of tweets (training set), it should be able to automatically classify the new tweets according to the actual text. The same approach can be applied to any kind of content: reviews, comments, posts.

The examples of spam filtering and sentiment analysis are binary classification problems solved using a supervised ML algorithm. More complex classification tasks can involve more than two classes. A well-known multinomial classification problem, for example, is handwriting recognition, where the number of classes is equal to the number of letters in the alphabet.

Besides classification, another typical class of problems that can be solved using ML is regression analysis, where the output is not a class belonging to a finite set of values (e.g., spam vs. not spam – binary classification) but a value belonging to a continuous range. Typically, regression analysis is used to statistically predict the (unknown) value of a variable, according to (known) values of other variables. Applications of regression analysis in business are very common. Predictions of how sales change according to advertising, for example, can help with investment planning; and insurance companies can use regression analysis to predict future medical expenses of their customers based on several variables, including past medical expenses and demographic data.

All of these examples are supervised ML problems; a training set, containing both the input values and the desired output (that's the reason for the term "supervised"), is provided to the algorithm to "train" it. After the training phase, the algorithm can predict the output from input values not available in the training set.

With unsupervised ML problems, instead, no training set is provided. The ML algorithm analyses the input data and finds results without any additional training or help.

A typical unsupervised problem is clustering. A machine is provided with a set of objects (observations) having some characteristics (features), and the algorithm tries to group or cluster objects in order to maximize the similarity among them. A real-world problem that can be solved using unsupervised clustering techniques is customer segmentation. Each customer is described according to some characteristics, and the algorithm tries to group similar customers into segments. Segments can then be analysed in order to define different marketing strategies.

As we have seen in our examples, a ML problem normally involves a number of observations and features. If we think about spam filtering, the messages are observations and the words used to represent these messages (each word having a specific frequency) are the features. When working with high-dimensionality data, i.e., data having a large number of features and in particular a number of features higher than the number of observations, we face at least two problems. First, data noise, i.e. having some data that cannot be correctly interpreted by machines, can affect the accuracy of ML algorithms; second, the amount of storage space and computational power could become excessive. In these cases, an additional subfield of ML, dimensionality reduction, can alleviate those problems. Dimensionality reduction is an unsupervised ML technique that is often applied to a data set before applying classification or regression methods; its goal is to reduce the number of features while retaining most of the relevant information, thus limiting the amount of storage space and computational power needed and removing the data noise. Furthermore, representing data through a few features can also facilitate data visualization (Raschka, 2015).

Finally, the last ML method we would like to mention is reinforcement learning. In reinforcement learning, a software agent interacts with the environment and receives rewards signals, which are evaluations of its performances. Based on such reward signals, the agent can modify its action to improve the performances. For example, after having learnt from negative feedback that a classification is wrong, the agent can adjust its classification strategy (Raschka, 2015).

7.3.2. Machine learning tools

An additional reason for the spread of ML techniques has probably been the availability of libraries that allow practitioners to take advantage of the most common algorithms without re-implementing them. Two well-known examples are the scikit-learn library for the Python programming language (http://scikit-learn.org) and the Statistic and Machine Learning toolbox for Matlab (https://www.mathworks.com/products/statistics.html). Other examples are Caffe (http://caffe.berkeleyvision.org) and TensorFlow (https://www.tensorflow.org). Caffe is a deep-learning framework mainly developed by the Berkeley Vision and Learning Center, and TensorFlow is a library developed by Google for its commercial products and then released to the public under an open-source license.

Furthermore, because coding can be intimidating for people without technical skills, there are now some utilities that provide MLaaS (Machine Learning as a Service), allowing noncoders to solve some ML problems easily, through a user-friendly graphical interface and without the necessity of writing code. Two examples are Rapidminder (https://rapidminer.com) and BigML (https://bigml.com).

After having described the scope and operating principles behind ML, in the next section possible scenarios driven by the following question "besides the conventional tools and techniques used for PE in HRM, could ML play a key role?" will be depicted.

7.4. Possible scenarios and critical considerations

We can imagine two possible scenarios for this question: ML fully replacing managers in HRM decisions, and a milder scenario in which ML only supports managers while they retain the final decision-making authority. Of these scenarios, which is more likely to bring about?

As highlighted above, we face a new wave of automation whose main effect is machines replacing humans in routinized tasks. Until a few years ago, it was commonly understood that only manual labour could be affected by machine replacement. Nowadays, it is quite obvious that the discrimination between replaceable and non-replaceable jobs is not linked with the classical organizational hierarchy; as Jerry Kaplan from Stanford University says, "*automation is now blind to the colour of your collar*" (in "Rise of The Robots"[2], Martin Ford 2015). Vulnerability to automation is now determined less by a role's manual or mechanical functionality than by its repetitiveness or routinization.

For jobs to survive in this new wave of machine replacement, they must require creativity, empathy, or social interaction, where (at least right now) humans are still better than machines. Thus, the next step is to investigate whether managerial decision making in HRM retains at least one of these characteristics. As highlighted in Section 2, we cannot deal with HRM as a whole but must distinguish between at least two main areas: PM and PE.

PM is mainly related to analysing numerical data with retrospective origins. Thanks to recent technological advancements, it is quite easy to collect data about workers' performance and outcomes. These collection tools produce a large amount of data that can be analysed by an algorithm in a shorter time and with much more accuracy than by humans. Therefore, PM tasks have all the characteristics of a routine job, with a high risk of being replaced by computers. This process, however, does not strictly require automation through ML.

By contrast, PE is strictly related to forward measures (such as motives, values, personality measures, and cognitive abilities), requiring the use of discretion in areas characterized by information scarcity and subjectivity. Looking at the most commonly used techniques in potential evaluation (potential

---

[2] Ford, M., 2015. (2015). The Rise of the Robots. *Marginal Revolution (blog)*. Retrieved June 22, 2015.

appraisal, self-appraisals and appraisals by peers and superiors, MBO, psychological and psychometric tests, management games like role playing, leadership exercises, etc.), it is clear that they require managers to trigger soft skills like sensitivity, psychological awareness, empathy, and creativity.

However, to some extent PE could take advantage of ML. It is probably difficult to build a precise formula that computes an individual's potential according to characteristics and personality. If we had such a formula, we could simply apply it and compute the potential for every individual. However, a ML algorithm could learn how to evaluate potential using some examples as input.

Let's try to imagine how it could work. The algorithm would produce as output the potential of an individual, represented as a value between 0 and 1 (where 1 is the maximum potential). Each individual is described using characteristics (descriptors) like age, school transcripts, artistic skills, mathematical skills, and others. The system needs a training set to work, i.e., a set of individuals whose potential has been evaluated by a human expert. The ML algorithm, finally, will use the examples to guess the potential of individuals not evaluated by humans. This process is based on the assumption that individuals having similar scores for the same descriptors will probably have the same potential (if the descriptors are well chosen).

It should now be clear that an unsupervised technique is not applicable in this context; (human) managers would still have a dual role: finding the best descriptors and training the machine (i.e., creating the training set by evaluating some individuals). The first task is very important; a ML algorithm can work only if the input items are described using characteristics that are relevant to the final goal. Although it is tricky to find a precise formula that computes an individual's potential, there is probably a hidden rule that links the descriptors to the output, and it can be discovered (although it might remain opaque) during the ML process itself.

7.5. Conclusions

We started this chapter with the following research question: "Could machine learning overtake managerial decisions in HRM, specifically in PE?". We then discussed how the field of HRM is too complex to give a single yes/no answer. In fact, HRM needs to be distinguished by the different leverages involved, mainly PM and PE tasks. While PM could be effectively performed by computers (even without the adoption of ML techniques), potential appraisal tools could take advantage of ML but will probably require a partnership between humans and machines.

Artificial intelligence can play a crucial role in supporting the decisions of HR managers, but at the same time managers are critical for training machines and correcting their mistakes. Therefore, we argue that managers will probably need to acquire more and more data science skills in order to be competitive in the future.

It is likely that the same conclusion can be extended to most of the managerial roles in companies. In a 2016 report, "Automation and Independent Work in a Digital Economy", the Organisation for Economic Co-operation and Development concluded that

> No matter how advanced artificial intelligence becomes, some jobs are always likely to be better done by humans, notably those involving empathy or social interaction. In many cases, there are legal as well as ethical obstacles that may prevent such a substitution or at least substantially slow down its pace (OECD, 2016).

This is particularly true in the HR field, where a wrong decision could lead to an employee's salary reduction, or, even worse, to dismiss him. Individual and social implications of these mistakes are clear. Therefore, before giving this power to an algorithm, we should be 100% sure it can play the role better than humans.

Acknowledgements

The Authors would like to thank Eugenio Tacchini for the precious comments and insights received.

References

Bosquetti, M.A., Albuquerque, L.G. (2005). Gestão estratégica de pessoas: visão do RH x visão dos clientes. ENANPAD, XXIX, 2005, Brasília. *Anais Eletrônicos,* GPR-A951. Rio de Janeiro: ANPAD, 2005.

Brown, M., Hyatt, D., Benson, J. (2010). Consequences of the performance appraisal experience, *Personnel Review,* 39(3): 375-396.

Brynjolfsson, E., McAfee, A. (2011). *Race against the machine: how the digital revolution is accelerating innovation, driving productivity, and irreversibly transforming employment and the economy.* Lexington, MA: Digital Frontier Press.

Chui, M., Manyika, M., Miremadi, M. (2015). *Four fundamentals of workplace automation.* McKinsey Quarterly.

Fish, S., Hardy, M. (2015). Complex issues, complex solutions: applying complexity theory in social work practice, *Nordic Social Work Research,* 5(1): 98-114. http://dx.doi.org/10.1080/2156857X.2015.1065902

Frey, C.B., Osborne, M. (2017). The future of employment: how susceptible are jobs to computerisation?, *Technological Forecasting & Social Change,* 114: 254-280.

Hassan, A. (2007). Human resource development and organizational values, *Journal of European Industrial Training*, 31(6): 435-448.

Hobsbawm, E.J. (1968). *Industry and empire: An economic history of Britain since 1750*. Harmondsworth Middlesex: Penguin Books.

Holland, P., Bardoel, A. (2016). The impact of technology on work in the twenty-first century: exploring the smart and dark side, *The International Journal of Human Resource Management*, 27(21): 2579-2581.

Koike, K. (1997). Human resource development. *Japanese Economy & Labour Series 2*. Tokyo: Japan Institute of Labour.

Lacombe, B.M.B., Tonelli, M.J. (2001). O Discurso e a prática: o que nos dizem os especialistas e o que nos mostram as práticas das empresas sobre os modelos de gestão de recursos humanos, *RCA*, 5(2): 157-174.

Lebas, M.J. (1995). Performance measurement and performance management, *International Journal of Production Economics*, 41(1–3): 23-35.

López-Cotarelo, J. (2011). HR discretion: understanding line managers' role in human resource management. Academy of Management annual meeting, 12th-16th August 2011, San Antonio, Texas.

Marcolin, L., Miroudot, S., Squicciarini, M. (2016). Routine jobs, employment and technological innovation in global value chains, *OECD Science, Technology and Industry Working Papers*, No. 2016/01. Paris: OECD Publishing.

McAfee, D., Brynjolfsson, E. (2014). *The second machine age: work, progress and prosperity in a time of brilliant technologies*. New York: W.W. Norton & Co.

Micheli, P., Mari, M. (2005). The theory and practice of performance measurement, *Management Accounting Research*, 25(2):147-156.

Mitchell, T. (1997). *Machine learning*. New York: McGraw Hill.

OECD (2016). *Automation and independent work in a digital economy: Policy brief on the future of work*. Paris: OECD Publishing.

Piva, M., Vivarelli, M. (2017). *Technological change and employment: Were Ricardo and Marx right?*, IZA Discussion Paper 10471.

Raschka, S. (2015). *Python machine learning*. Birmingham: Packt Publishing Ltd.

Samuel, A.L. (1959). Some studies in machine learning using the game of checkers, *IBM Journal of Research and Development*, 3(3): 210-229.

Swanson, R.A. (2001). Human resource development and its underlying theory, *Human Resource Development International*, 4(3): 293-312.

Walger, C., De Dea Roglio, K., Abib, G. (2016). HR managers' decision-making processes: a "reflective practice" analysis, *Management Research Review*, 39(6): 655-671.

Wright, P.M., Snell, S.A. (1998). Toward a unifying framework for exploring fit and flexibility in strategic human resource, *Academy of Management Review*, 23(4): 756-772.

Part III
LEVERAGES

Chapter 8

INDIVIDUAL VERSUS ORGANIZATIONAL LEARNING FOR KNOWLEDGE IN INNOVATION 4.0 ERA

Paolino Fierro-Paola Briganti-Luisa Varriale

SUMMARY: 8.1. Introduction. – 8.2. Individual learning versus organizational learning in the traditional era. – 8.3. Organizational learning in the digital era. – 8.3.1. Organizational learning for innovation: applications and techniques. – 8.4. Organization learning for innovation: managerial implications and final remarks. – References.

8.1. Introduction

Industry 4.0, also called the 'digital revolution', focuses on all digital technologies which are able to increase interconnection and cooperation between resources (people or IT systems) without limiting itself to one sector rather than another.

Over the years, and even more so in the near future, organizations face many challenges mostly due to the technological changes from the unpredictable effects that will trigger the introduction of new organizational models, requiring a serious reflection on different professional roles, management, necessary skills, and leadership. The success of digital transformation within companies will depend first and foremost on the parallel enhancement of human resources.

The Cloud, the Internet of Things (IoT), the Big Data, the digitization of companies and the world of work have set itself as both a destructive and regenerating acceleration. They are changing processes, learning models and organizations themselves.

In such an outline, it is necessary, adopting an organizational perspective, to rethink the relationship between individuals, knowledge and learning.

The main purpose of this chapter is to investigate the relationship between individual learning and organizational learning with respect to the creation of new knowledge, intangible assets of organizations, in a highly dynamic and uncertain environment, such as Industry 4.0.

The first part of the chapter will examine the main paradigms usually developed and used in the literature to explain the complex inter- organizational relationship between individual and organizational learning.

The second part of the chapter will analyze organizational variables that affect the innovative learning level of organizations (human resources, integration, coordination) and techniques or tools that can be an enabling factor. This analysis will be the starting point for identifying the main ways in which organizations learn to reconfigure, replace old standards, improve their information flows, and revitalize their creative skills (managerial implications).

8.2. Individual learning versus organizational learning in the traditional era

The issue of knowledge as fundamental organizational resource to the process of organizational action, especially in reference to complex and uncertain concepts, has characterized the first half of the Nineties resource (Grant, 1996; Kogut and Zander, 1996; Spender and Grant, 1996; Nahapiet and Ghoshal, 1998).

In the prevalent literature knowledge has been recognized as the key factor for the competitive advantage, long-term sustainability and success of firms (Prahalad and Hamel, 1990; Nonaka and Takeuchi, 1995; Grant, 1996; Stewart, 1997; von Krogh, 1998; Hackbarth, 1998; Alavi and Leidner, 1999, 2001). The capacity to create and maintain knowledge has been considered as the most important ability of firms (Smith, Collins & Clark, 2005).

"Knowledge is a multifaceted concept with multilayered meanings" (Nonaka, 1994: p. 15). Knowledge represents a complex topic, because of being abstract, difficult to define and quantify. In any organizational settings knowledge tends to be fuzzy in nature and it is usually deeply and closely attached to the individuals who hold it (Davenport et al., 1998), thus this issue is challenging to define, measure and manage (Ipe, 2003).

Scholars usually tend to focus on some components of knowledge more measurable, such as the attributes and variables of any knowledge development activity through which the same knowledge manifests itself. Consequently, researchers try to define and measure knowledge taxonomy such as meta, milieu, tacit, contingent, informal, formal and instrumentality, and so on (Ramachandran, 2003).

Overcoming the debates related to the Greek philosophy, in the different research fields the attention has been paid to the several and most significant definitions provided by the scholars, mainly viewing knowledge as "a dynamic human process of justifying personal beliefs as part of an aspiration for the truth" (Nonaka, 1994: 15). Specifically, according to Nonaka (1994) and Huber (1991), knowledge has been conceived as the specific and justified belief of an individual that is able to increase his/her capacity to take effective action.

In the numoreous and variegated studies on knowledge topic, two main knowledge dimensions have been identified (Polanyi, 1966; Nonaka and Takeuchi, 1995): explicit and tacit, and the main characteristics of such variable have been specified, with reference to the importance of knowledge management in the processes of change.

In general, such a debate can be split into two tendencies. The first, regarding content models, highlights the set of schemes and definitions of knowledge. The study by Polanyi (1966) on tacit knowledge and other distinctions among other dimensions of knowledge, which have been already described, belongs to this tendency. The other orientation, which seems to be more significant and refers to process models, discusses the modalities of creation, spreading, and socialization of knowledge. The contributions by Nonaka (1991) and Weick (1979) follow this tendency.

In complex contexts, the critical problem of managing organizational change is codification of implicit knowledge, with reference to the scarce appropriability, to subjectivity (human resources) with very high correlated transaction costs. As a consequence, human resources represent the only real competitive barrier. They represent the main tool for planning and making organizational learning processes, which help to set and root the relevant implicit knowledge in the structure.

Indeed, this traditional contrast between objectified and reificated knowledge (which becomes property of the organization) and people knowledge (that traditional organizations have historically tried to reduce and codify), seems to tend towards a view stimulating the synergy and the convergence of any knowledge.

For the first time since Fordism, all the different dimensions of knowledge become, in the United States, Japan as well as in Europe, the single object of strategies, professional management and development of organizations, and in some cases, of the public administration and schools. When in one organization, the competitive context is highly uncertain, when goals are changeable and very difficult to achieve, when processes are uncertain and cross a network-shaped organization, when technology and re-engineering shake up the organization, when innovation derives mostly from people, when cooperation is required even among people in remote positions, when knowledge becomes strategic and it is necessary to make reificated and people knowledge converge, only then every "knot in the network", at any level of the "network", has to strengthen not only knowledge, but also its own co-operation and communication system and makes community and organization to converge (Butera, 1990). Knowledge management is going to be a subject of organizations' policies or public policies. Knowledge management means identifying, managing and exploiting what the organization knows and could know, that is people's skills and experience, files, documents and libraries, relationships with customers, suppliers and other people and information stored into electronic databases (Davenport et al., 1996). In this case it's necessary to promote and start integrated development programs of strategies for assessing and exploiting knowledge, ITC systems, competencies management modalities and ways of communication. Knowledge management means also planning of work organization and macro-organization models.

Because of the different forms and dimensions of knowledge, specifically, the strategic importance, the size and the variety of knowledge make most of the previously developed typologies of organizations inappropriate. A concept of shared knowledge arises, as pointed out by Butera (1990), who includes the shared and simultaneous use of:

- all the forms of knowledge: both those embedded and encoded (including in data, information of texts, databases, software, and so forth) and those embrained, embodied and encultured (knowledge based on experience, values, competencies and vision which are all in people's brain);
- all the kinds of people knowledge: both explicit and tacit knowledge (Nonaka and Takeuchi, 1995), and those deriving from specific context;
- all the processes of acquisition, distribution retrieval and sharing of knowledge ;
- all the processes of knowledge ("knowing").

Such knowledge represents an essential requirement to "ignite" the radical learning process, which fosters any changes. But, at the same time, knowledge acquisition is necessary but insufficient prerequisite for taking place of organizational learning (Aguilera, 2007; Argote & Ingram, 2000). Indeed, adopting an organizational learning perspective, firms need to possess a significant level of concrete absorptive capacity to capitalize on knowledge acquisition from external sources and for facilitating organizational learning (Argote, 1999). As we clarify later, realized absorptive capacity has been defined as a firm's ability to exploit externally generated knowledge, to transform and commercially apply knowledge that creates firm value, as source of compettive advantage (Zahra & George, 2002).

Focusing the attention on the main constructs of knowledge and clarifying its link to learning process, we evidence that Huber (1991) distinguished four different constructs: Knowledge acquisition, Information distribution, Information interpretation and Organizational memory. Instead, Nevis and colleagues (1995) have identified three-stage model: knowledge acquisition, knowledge sharing and knowledge utilization. Independently from the categorization, in the knowledge management process, the assimilation process or organizational memory have been considered as the most difficult parts (Nevis et al., 1995; Huber, 1991).

Then, this process arises through four steps, where the organization takes on a relevant role, as it is able to learn on its own. The first step consists of the acquisition of knowledge and its constitution, which can take place through different learning modalities; the second one consists of information spreading; the third step is the interpretation of the distributed information through the creation of cognitive maps, using the echo of the media for communicating and also by unlearning.

Huber (1990) focuses much attention on this latter process as he claims that the accumulation of new rules and procedures substantially depends on the degree of unlearning of the previous principles. He defines unlearning as "the effect of development of a common mind among the different units of an organization". A common trend derives from homogeneity of interpretation and of validity judgements assigned to the event; it determines therefore both a reduction and an extension of the possible behaviours; on the one hand, such decreased diversity makes a better internal cooperation possible, which enlarges the available repertoire (Butera, 1990).

Unlearning fosters the search of new scripts or beliefs which can replace the displaced one: When the need of change becomes relevant and widely perceived, and the pre-existing beliefs start to crumble, new learning is easier.

The fourth and last step is the constitution of the memory, through information retrieval and storage, and the constitution of a computerized organizational memory.

In terms of organizational action, instead, learning is a process identifying and correcting mistakes and it takes place through exploiting solutions given to the problem tackled in the time, and translates into the redefinition of the organization, of its behaviours, in response to the new action context and the changed values (Marziliano, 1995).

This theoretical approach has been proposed by Argyris and Schon (1978), who claim that knowledge derived from the action is codified in individual and organizational action theories, as they reckon that the grounds for any behaviour or action, either individual or organizational, is on a cognitive basis, included in an action theory.

An action theory has two basic elements: the declared theory and the use theory. The declared theory corresponds to the explicit statements or the values and the goals which drive the subject's behaviour and corresponds to officially and commonly shared values. The use theory includes implicit assumptions, images and representations which have an objective role in organizational behaviours.

It is a kind of program or scheme of the action by which the agent is prepared to achieve goals and affects context variables. The use theory in not always consistent with the declared one. In fact, the organizational learning happens when there is a continuous change in the use theories and in the behavioural models. It occurs when individuals "acting from their maps and images, discover matches and discrepancies between expectations and outcomes, which confirm or invalid the use theory of an organization" (Argyris e Schon, 1978). Also, organizational learning has been often linked to the capacity of firms to develop of knowledge or insights that are relevant in their behavioral change (Hurley & Hult, 1998). Thus, organizational learning generally includes specific aspects, that is the processes of creating, retaining, and transferring knowledge (Argote, 1999; Argote & Ingram, 2000). Furthermore, Meyers (1990) defined organizational learning as the ability of firms to observe, assess and act upon internal and external stimuli to the organization in cumulative, interactive and purposeful ways. With reference to the different and growing complexity and degree of innovation four types of organizational learning can be identified: maintenance learning, adaptive learning, transitional learning and creative learning.

Otherwise, most scholars focus on organizational learning trying to defining this concept identifying its dimensions and functions within any organizations (March, 1991; Cohen & Levinthal, 1990; Levitt & March, 1988), but also others tend to recognize a kind of link between exploitation and exploration in organizational learning, in terms of innovative activities (Kim, Son & Nerkar, 2012; Sorenson & Stuart, 2000).

The organizational learning represents a process or a set of organizational processes. "If we conceptualize each component of knowledge as a stock, then, the underlying learning processes that create them represent flows" (Garud, 1996). The different flows can be differentiated through their occurrence levels (McKee, 1992; Senge, 1990; Argyris & Schon, 1978), as single-loop (or corrective), double-loop (or generative) and meta - (or institutional) learning.

According to Argyris e Schon (1978), different learning models and cycles can be distinguished: Single-loop and double-loop learning models.

The single-loop consists of adding some modifications to the corporate behaviour as some difficulties occur. To solve them, the organization looks for alternative actions. These are conditioned by fundamental assumptions and values. In this case, learning tends to keep the existing cultural structures and to include the differences and the exceptions which take place when the event is being experienced.

The double-loop, implies a modification of the organizational laws and, then a deeper change which involves the fundamental values and the culture of the organization. This implies strategies and cognitive assumptions restructuring and organization reframing. In order to make an organizational, and not only individual, learning takes place, it is necessary that such changes are generalized and spread to the whole organization through their codification in maps and organizational memory.

According to this perspective (Argyris e Schon, 1978), organizational learning must necessarily happen through the individual learning. The above-mentioned approaches seem to be interactive and complementary, as they point out both the subjective nature of the knowledge creation processes and the objective one of the learning change processes which occur within organizations which live in very complex and uncertain contexts. Most researchers argue that knowledge is created by individuals (Spender, 1996) existing outside of the organization, but any organizations also learn through their individuals (Grant, 1996; Spender, 1996; Huber, 1991; Argyris & Schomn, 1976). On the other side, organizational learning has been conceived as more than the sum of learning by individual members of each organization (McKee, 1992).

One most relevant aspect in analysing the relationship between organizations and knowledge is the concept of cognitive dimension of the organization. On the one hand, if the historical analysis of the size of organizations and degree of bureaucratization, and on the other hand, the concepts of physical and real size of the organization are weakened in reference to a broader idea, which includes different factors: that is the virtual size, the enlargement of the borders, or better, of the possibilities to control complex systems of relationships, external to the organization. A lot of these factors allow the organization to be "big while remaining small", thanks to the ability to manage large information flows through new technologies. The fact, that the new notion of size is nowadays more faded than in the past, does not imply that the size variable has lost its importance from an economic point of view. But it is necessary to understand what kind of variable is and why it is relevant from the economic point of view, that is from the point of view of value generation and of competitive advantage. For economists, the link between size and organizations pivots around the idea that the big organization allows the achievement of scale economies, which are denied to small organizations. Economies of scale are one of the determinants to the growth of the organizations, with reference both to the broadening of its borders and to the growth of internal compactness.

Even though the market seems to reward small organizations, characterized by the continuous search for quality, by productive flexibility, by product innovation, in the industrial sector the competition is based on scale economies, which are considered with a more sophisticated significance, focusing on the idea that some cost advantages can be achieved from the same knowledge based on another area of activity (Di Bernardo, 1997). At planning level, the repetition economies depend directly on the division of labour, as a complex problem is divided into smaller parts, allowing the specialists to focus, at a cognitive and experimental level, on a limited part of the problem. Consequently, the costs and the learning time decrease and then, the larger such a "specialistic decomposition" is, the more the advantages deriving from repetition economies. Here that's why a strong link exists between size and organization division of labour. Apart from the size of the whole organization, what really counts is the size of the circuit of division of labour. Actually, this principle is valid for the Fordist enterprise too, as in this case, the size of circuit of division of labour matches with the one of the whole organization, as it is carried out inside the organization's borders.

A question may arise on the reason why some different size circuits of division of labour exist and the largest circuit does not prevail on the others. The answer is in the fact that the division of labour is not spontaneous, but it is imposed by the organization that, through long established values and the setting of standards, protects the circuit, so that it will be suitable to transfer knowledge, from a specialist to another and allows managing the interdependency among them (Rullani, 1994). From one specialist to another, it has a twofold task: on the one side, to plan communication media which permits to understand the codes that knowledge is expressed in and on the other side, to make the division of labour reliable, developing a network of institutional and non-institutional relationships, which guarantee the availability of knowledge at a certain time and through a certain modality. Thus, the organization looses its physical features, resulting in a cognitive and decisional process which constantly reviews and feeds the entrust and communication circuits to allow the internal actors to manage their interdependency (Di Bernardo, 1997).

At this point, the relationship between organization and size should be clear, as it is the cognitive and decisional process which is at the basis of the organization which guarantees the efficiency and the extension of the division of labour, and then, the importance of repetition economies within organizations becomes a centre of collective knowledge, which allows to overcome the limits linked to individual learning; such limits would hinder the efficient selection and review of information. In this context the size acquires features of virtuality, as it depends on the ability of the organization to create relationships with other cognitive systems which can produce and supply information at multiple levels. From the economic point of view, then, it is the virtual size that becomes relevant, rather than the real one, as the larger the circuit of the division of labour, the more consistent the repetition economies. The organizations, considered as cognitive systems, work embedded in complex relationship networks, which have a crucial role transferring knowledge through codification channels.

In such an outlined context, as above mentioned, learning becomes central, so the organization can be considered and analysed as a "learning organization". Having placed the organization in a dynamic context, under a continuous evolution process, where technology innovation brings nonstop uncertainty and change, has strongly affected the organizational action. The organization takes on an active role using its own resources to survive and/or to keep and consolidate its competitive advantage by modifying and updating knowledge, competencies and routines.

In this framework, dynamic abilities, meaning the ability to keep up performance in different contexts, should be learned and nourished.

The competency theory points out the multidimensional feature of learning; the organization learns according to several modalities: the production of knowledge goes through the innovation that the organization develops, through research, product development, market research; but learning can happen even without production, through external absorption of new forms of knowledge. It is not always free and automatic, but it is often costly and it is the result of organizational choices.

The vision of learning adopted in the competency theory highlights its local nature and its path dependence. The idea of path dependence recognizes that an organization's history is important to determine future development, decisions, and the direction of the learning process. An organization's past history shapes the conceptual network, which in turn, conditions future perception and elaboration of external information.

Path dependence, which characterizes the learning process, is linked to the organization's past history: the experience and knowledge stored inside a particular technology pattern and inside a particular core business, condition relevantly possibility and direction.

The local nature of the learning process implies the difficulty for the organization to modify and quickly adapt to business and technology change. Organizations tend to walk on the same path and meet relevant difficulties and rigidities as they decide to change it. Thus, the shift from a technology pattern to another or from a core business to another is costly and time expensive.

An important consequence of local nature and path dependence of the learning process consists of the trend within organizations to specialize in previously explored cognitive fields instead of others; it follows a limited capacity of diversification. The entrance in new markets and the introduction of radical innovation become difficult.

Competencies and knowledge of one organization are limited; each organization develops knowledge along certain paths and at the same time lacks in some competencies.

Inside the competency theory, the organization's cognitive basis may develop in a number of ways; sometimes the organization learns unconsciously and costlessly, sometimes it needs to activate resources and means.

It is possible to recognize two different categories of learning: internal learning and external learning (Campanini, 1998; Cohen & Levinthal, 1990; Lewitt & March, 1988).

Internal learning implies the production of knowledge inside the organization, and it is linked to a number of business functions. Internal learning develops through forms of: *learning by doing*, by using and by searching. *Learning by doing* is linked to the production process of the organization; it generates improvements, incremental modifications and innovations, both in processes and products. *Learning by using* is linked, instead, to the adaptation of the organization to new technologies, incorporated in new equipment, unfinished products or industrial goods. It implies a better and more efficient use of scarce resources, of materials and intermediate goods. *Learning by searching* is the most intentional process of learning, as it represents an activity institutionalized and targeted by the organization to this aim.

The second learning modality available to the organization depends on the possibility to acquire and absorb knowledge developed outside the organization. *Learning by interacting*, *learning by imitation* and *learning from advantages* in science and technology (Campanini, 1998) represent the three kinds of external learning. *Learning by interacting* develops through the interaction and the relationships among users and suppliers of the organization. *Learning by imitation* is generated by the reproduction of the innovation introduced by other organizations. Finally, *learning from advantages* in science and technology depends on the exploitation of knowledge developed outside the organization in the scientific community (Tab. 1).

Table 1. The three kinds of internal/external learning.

INTERNAL LEARNING	EXTERNAL LEARNING
Learning by doing,	learning by interacting
Learning by using	learning by imitation
Learning by searching	learning from advantage in science and technology

Source: Adapted by Campanini, 1998.

It is important to point out that there is a strong interaction between internal and external learning; a sound internal cognitive basis is a necessary condition to the acquisition of external knowledge, which, in turn, is fundamental to increase the capacity of internal learning.

The production of knowledge is closely linked to the activities connected to the solution of problems. As the organization realizes that its goals cannot be achieved, it must check its capacity to fill the gap between current performance and the optimal one. The trial and error process, which comes from this check, generates knowledge: in fact, once the problems are recognized, it is necessary to identify a number of possible solutions, testing them in order to find the best one. Through all these activities, called problem solving activities, knowledge is created and developed.

Problem solving activities are not the only way to develop and increase the cognitive basis in the organization. The capacity to absorb new external knowledge, and the capacity to include it in the organization take on a relevant role.

The competency to recognize relevant external knowledge, to incorporate it and to exploit it is called absorptive capacity.

The capacity of absorption determines the amount of external knowledge that can be stored and exploited in the organization. External knowledge must, in fact, be first of all identified and later absorbed and integrated in the cognitive basis, and finally exploited and turned into competitive advantage.

The absorptive capacity can be the result of the research and development activity or it can be developed intentionally through efforts directed to feed it.

The recourse to partnerships and other forms of external co-operation, which has grown recently, is due to the awareness that being self-sufficient may result in an unrealizable practice in competitive contexts which require flexibility, innovation and strategic focus. In rapidly developing technological regimes no single organization owns all the necessary competencies for sustainable success.

The search for the discriminants of competitive advantage has tried to clarify learning and knowledge generation mechanisms, which can be defined as "interaction kind". Different contributions have explored relational practices pointing out how extensive and anticipative networkization by third actors have allowed the organization to focus on its own distinctive competencies and to get to accelerate learning. At the basis of partnerships there is the awareness that co-operation improves the capacity of learning .

A further step in the analysis must be made with reference to the addressees of the process, that is individuals and organizations. The distinction between individual and organizational learning is crucial to organizations, where individual learning is not enough, as already outlined especially considering the continuous and very complex changes occurred because of technologies and innovations introduced within organizations; it is necessary on the one hand, that the whole organization must learn, and on the other hand, that the results of individual learning can be shared throughout the whole organization.

A definition of individual learning can be one which considers learning as acquisition of competencies and knowledge with reference to the ability to perform tasks or acquire new know-how, which implies the psychophysical ability to draw "conceptual understanding" from the experience .

The relationship between thought and action shows that learning takes place when new knowledge is transformed into different individuals' repeatable behaviours . For this reason, it is important to consider what individuals learn (know-how), and how they absorb and apply what they have learnt (know why). Individual learning can also be defined as the improvement of an individual's abilities to carry out effective actions.

It has been observed that a person acts on the basis of real experience, makes observations and considerations over such experience, forms abstract concepts and generalizations based upon considerations and experiments, these new ideas in new situations leading to new experience.

8.3. Organizational learning in the digital era

Scholars and practitioners, engaged in knowledge management and innovation processes, are already aware that implementing Knowledge Management Information Technology Systems (KMITS) doesn't significantly support the increase and development of organizational knowledge. Knowledge innovations are fundamentally created, shared and implemented thanks to social interactions (Rupčić, 2017). At the same time, within firms, organizational learning makes one important job, that is to address rapidly changing environments, interactions between systems of innovation inside and outside the same firms (Hu, Ma & Xu, 2009).

One of the most challenging aspects of implementing learning organizations is reaching the stage where organizational members implement learning networks, shared systems thinking fundamental to create and manage knowledge innovations (Rupčić, 2017).

Conceiving Human Resource Management (HRM) as a learning network means to focus on: Work-related learning (employees), organized Human Resource Development (HRD) processes (employee initiatives and managerial engagement), and career development (combination of individual and organizational needs and preferences). The ways to develop learning networks should be predominantly: thematizing (determining a work-related learning path, setting learning goals, problemsolving, experimentation); operating explicitly strategically (learning driven by individual values, norms, and insight; network of internal and external colleagues and experts); problematizing (emphasis placed on developing career prospects, and/or gaining other dimensions of knowledge and experience). The development of meaning and purposefulness should represent the underlying shared motivation in employee-colleague-expert-management interactions and negotiations (Rupčić, 2017).

According to this perspective, SECI model (Socialization Externalization Combination Internalization) (Nonaka & Takeuchi, 1995) conceptualizes specific phases such as socialization, externalization, combination and internalization of knowledge and innovation. To introduce systems thinking to the SECI model, Sasaki (2017) identified systems intelligence (SI) as a kind of human intelligence based on systems thinking in knowledge and innovation processes: individuals should be encouraged to act as intelligent agents and perceive themselves as a part of the whole, so it's necessary to study the influence of the whole upon themselves and to examine their possible influence on the system as a whole (Sasaki, 2017). Examples of intelligent human behavior, specifically individual system intelligence behavior, are represented by: Socialization Managers that walk around and observe, start conversations with employees to determine their opinion and feelings, share tacit knowledge with them; employees, who search for new opportunities to interact with customers and colleagues, look also for new ways to gain and share knowledge; Externalization Managers and employees: willingly externalize tacit knowledge with stakeholders, stimulate them to express their tacit knowledge, feelings, insight; Combination Managers and employees: use IT systems even when other shun them and motivate others to do the same; Internalization Managers and employees: nourish the belief that new individually gained tacit knowledge has potential in practical usage and further socialization.

In a learning network perspective Human Resource Management (HRM) activities paly a key role, and they need a broader approach to organizing employees systems thinking, that become the main stakeholders in designing strategically HRM activities. Many managers agree that HRM process is very difficult in practice, often yielding dubious results. In this regard, some authors (Poell and Van Der Krogt, 2017) present a conceptual framework in which they identify limited and one-sided conceptualization of organizing HRM as one of the main reasons why HRM still produces poor results. Employee training, education and development are often considered the most effective ways to stimulate and manage organizational learning and innovation, but managers should keep in mind that their role in all HRM and development activities is crucial: they are responsible for providing organizational infrastructure, but they mainly should help employees gain a better understanding on how those activities can contribute to their development, in a pivotal way.

In a more comprehensive way, to let organizational learning and innovation through employees individual and group development, HRM should not be limited to training, which is related to the direct work of employees: employees can and should surely learn from their primary work processes, both routine and project-based, which can help them gain a diversity of knowledge and experience, and employees should also take part in programs focusing on the development of their careers. Planning managerial career for individuals by developing their talents through challenging and interesting tasks, increases their motivation, and also it provides more favorable labor contracts and improves their employability. Besides taking courses and attending seminars and conferences, employees should be stimulated to interact with other individuals and groups (colleagues, experts, etc.) as well as engage in a self-study and reflect on their own performance.

The two forms of organizational learning, single and double-loop learning, as already outlined, represent two extremes of the organizational learning continuum, with a wide range of nuanced behavior between them. That is why it is beneficial that managers examine the propensity or likelihood of the described behavior in their organizations as well as in inter-organizational collaborations, as both have merits.

Both types of organizational learning, as well as possible collaborative forms (structural arrangements) and collaborative modes (functional arrangements), as described by Simonin (2017), should work at a macro, meso, and micro level of learning and innovation processes.

At a macro level, Simonin (2017) outlined in his research, using a large sample of technology firms, that double-loop learning significantly and positively affects the development of collaborative know-how.

Therefore, companies excelling in double-loop learning can tap into a greater variety of opportunities and implement different modes of collaboration, which can subsequently create new learning opportunities and stimulate collaborators to develop new organizational routines to better match environmental conditions. On the other hand, while excellence in single-loop learning can be beneficial in a certain period, it can cause companies to become stuck in the so-called "competency traps", when implemented routines become irrelevant or even counter-productive.

Simonin (2017) tested "N-loop learning" in international strategic alliances, Poell and Van Der Kroght (2017) focused on HRD, Hillon and Boje discussed dialectics in the context of higher education, Sasaki (2017) emphasized the importance of System Intelligence (SI) in knowledge management (KM), and Goktürk and colleagues (2017) investigated error management practices in two state university departments. Simonin (2017) proposed and tested a model capturing single- and double-loop learning and their influence on collaborative knowhow in international strategic alliances. Inter-organizational collaborations are established for numerous reasons, which can be summarized in three somewhat overlapping groups: minimization of production and transaction costs; profit maximization through joint strategic approach; and knowledge acquisition and transfer. As international enterprises operate in different and changing environments, capability to adapt quickly is key to their success and survival. However, the adaptability is highly learning dependent.

That is why it has become interesting to examine international enterprises as learning organizations and study their ability to engage in organizational learning and KM.

Practitioners in any organizations, as well as those engaged in various forms of inter-organizational collaborations, should put special emphasis on single- and double-loop organizational learning. When engaging in single-loop learning, organizations learn incrementally by detecting variations from established goals, norms and routines and introducing corrective measures. In inter-organizational collaborations, single-loop learning can refer to incremental adjustments in different collaborative activities, such as joint Research&Development (R&D). On the other hand, double-loop organizational learning results in major departures from existing routines as a response to challenging situations. New solutions, such as structural and functional changes, are often a product of experimentation and can result in new forms or modes of collaboration and a higher-order collaborative know-how.

8.3.1. Organizational learning for innovation: applications and techniques

Organizational learning concern presents very large area in terms of determinants, techniques and applications due to its high and direct involvement in the deep changes due to technologies and innovation which significantly introduced new ways for individuals and organizations to develop, enrich, improve and acquire new knowledge and competences. As already evidenced, organizational learning in the perspective of knowledge creation and transfer process in the digital area assumes different and more challenging dimensions, requiring an increasing attention to some specific features and tools.

Thus, we observe that scholars and practitioners in any organizational contexts, especially in higher education, search for new ways to conceive and develop "organizational learning" in the digital era also considering innovative and more interesting and specific tools and techniques. This growth focus on new visions of organizational learning better can respond to the needs of learning organizations, also because in this challenging and turbolent century all the organizations, for profit firms or not, institutions, and so forth, need to develop themselves as learning organizations in one continuous development process of knowledge and skills.

Hillon and Boje (2017) further elaborate modalities of practice by introducing dialectic reasoning and implementing it in the context of higher education. Thus, this study is especially interesting for practitioners in higher education, particularly deans and administrators facing various challenges. Introduction of dialectics is also very interesting for academics and practitioners developing learning organizations. Organizations develop and evolve through individual and group interactions characterized by debate and rhetoric.

While debate is aimed at persuading the other party of the validity of one's arguments and does not make way for compromising or adopting collaborative solutions, the intent behind using rhetoric is to inform and motivate the audience, which makes it a milder form of persuasion.

While techniques are useful and important in organizational life, dialectics is very effective to learn organizational philosophy. Dialectics is a process in which parties involved try to discover the truth about something: opposing arguments are not considered mutually exclusive, and their integration is welcome, according to perspective of reality that is ever evolving.

This view is consistent with modern organizational practice that is under the influence of a variety of internal and external factors, which are interrelated and interacted with one another through various mediators. Practitioners wishing to develop and sustain a learning organization should nourish dialectics as a learning process leading to change that could match environmental complexity. Storytelling is one of the tools to accomplish that goal.

Higher education organizations have the potential to cultivate learning organization ideas. However, higher education has become a highly competitive business facing many challenges, especially resource scarcity, which has led to the so-called "academic capitalism". Instead of inducing a collective dialogue and action among stakeholders based on the implementation of dialectics, many higher education institutions have decided to implement business process reengineering, despite evidence of its detrimental effects in business. The introduction of consultants and the top-down approach, while excluding engagement of other stakeholders, led to equally miserable outcomes in colleges. The main argument for such actions was the TINA ("There is No Alternative") narrative. Higher education practitioners are encouraged to review case studies presented by Hillon and Boje (2017) to avoid similar pitfalls in their institutions.

Training can be personalized using online resources to determine an individual's learning preferences and personality characteristics. This study provides an overview of learning style, personality types, and multiple intelligences theories; lists and describes selected testing instruments available on the Internet; and provides strategies for teaching and learning, considering different learning styles (Vincent and Ross, 2001).

In 4.0 companies, the transformation of firms from resource-based-view to knowledge-based-view is crucial to strategically extend the importance of organizational learning through transformational leadership with indirect effect of knowledge management process capability and interactive role of knowledge-intensive culture.

Imran and colleagues (2016) examine the importance of organizational learning in the context of innovative ability, competitive advantage, creativity and organizational performance. The results of Imran and colleagues research (Imran et al., 2016) are clearly depicting that transformational leadership has significant positive impact on organizational learning and knowledge management process capability, and partially mediates the relationship between transformational leadership and organizational learning. Additionally, knowledge-intensive culture has strengthened the relationship between transformational leadership and knowledge management process capability: management has to initiate steps to induct transformational leaders, develop knowledge-intensive culture and introduce knowledge management processes to boost learning environment in organizations.

According to this perspective, and forwarding the conceptual traditional framework of organisational learning, some scholars (Wang and Ahmed, 2003) identify five main features/topics of the concept and practices within the existing literature, namely, focus on collectivity of individual learning; process or system; culture or metaphor; knowledge management; and continuous improvement. In line with current 4.0 industrial contexts, they redefine the concept of organisational learning, incorporating the aspect of radical innovation and creativity.

Chang and Lee (2007) investigate the relationship among leadership, organizational culture, the operation of learning organization and employees' job satisfaction, following a quantitative methodology, and the research results show that the various operation extents of learning organization have significant difference under the dimensions of leadership, organizational culture and the operation of learning organization; both leadership and organizational culture can positively and significantly affect the operation of learning organization. In addition, the operation of learning organizations has a significantly positive effect on employees' job satisfaction. The study adopts the experimental methodology to observe the learning achievement within the business organizations in Taiwan. The study shows that, with the increasing number of knowledge workers in Taiwan, it is impossible for business administrators to satisfy employees' demands by means of conventional leadership. Instead, they are required to enhance their own skills in transformational leadership and, through setting a good example to employees, encouraging innovation and learning activities, developing employees' potentials, giving education and training activities, etc, more money incentives, this is necessary to keep people with excellent talents; an attempt is made by Authors to make business organizations aware of the effect of organization learning activities in Taiwan and the job satisfaction of employee.

McAdam and McCreedy (1999) highlight an increasing interest in the area of knowledge management within organisations and academia, because of the emergent nature of the field there is a lack of classification of suitable knowledge management models to use in conducting further research, literature evaluation and organisational applications. They discuss a wide spectrum of views from mechanistic to more socially orientated of knowledge management and innovation: KM model classifications are namely knowledge category models, intellectual capital models and socially constructed models. They suggest a modified KM model to act as a useful guide for further research and organisational application, inspired to a holistic approach to scientific and socially constructed knowledge, assuming the need for both emancipatory and business benefits from KM. The model represents KM as a highly recursive process, rather than sequential.

Martins and Terblanche (2003) present a specific model showing the determinants of organisational culture which influence creativity and innovation. Starting from a literature review of Schein (2010) perspective to a holistic approach in describing organisational culture, authors describe the relationship between creativity, innovation and culture is discussed in this context. Against the background of this model, the determinants of organisational culture were identified. The determinants are strategy, structure, support mechanisms, behaviour that encourages innovation, and open communication. The influence of each determinant on creativity and innovation is discussed. Values, norms and beliefs that play a role in creativity and innovation can either support or inhibit creativity and innovation depending on how they influence individual and group behaviour.

According to this approach, creativity is becoming a topic of ever-increasing interest to organizational managers. Thus, there is a need for a greater understanding of the dynamics between the personal and contextual factors responsible for creative performance in work settings. In particular, there is a need to identify the role of leadership for creativity. Until now, creativity studies have examined leadership and employee characteristics from a single-domain perspective. Data from 191 R&D employees of a large chemical company were used to test a multidomain, interactionist creativity model of employee characteristics, leader characteristics, and Leader-Member Exchange (LMX). Results suggest that employee intrinsic motivation and cognitive style, LMX, the interactions between employee intrinsic motivation and leader intrinsic motivation, and between LMX and employee cognitive style relate to employee creative performance as measured by supervisor ratings, invention disclosure forms, or research reports. Implications for practicing managers and research on leadership and creativity are discussed (Tierney et al., 1999).

Creative and habitual actions represent competing behavioral options that may be simultaneously influenced by multiple domains of social action. This article integrates psychological and sociological descriptions of creativity and conformity to present a theory of individual creative action within organizational settings composed of intertwined group, organizational, institutional, and market domains. This theory contributes to the innovation literature by illustrating how intentional action and evolutionary processes that legitimize action interact to facilitate creativity and innovation (Ford, 1991)

Crant (2000) highlights that many practitioner-oriented publications argue that managers should be more proactive on the job, and that proactive behavior is an increasingly important component of job performance for innovation. Organizational research on the antecedents and consequences of proactive behavior has appeared in several different literatures and has taken different approaches toward defining, measuring, and understanding proactivity. In this article, I review a diverse set of literatures that directly address proactive behavior in organizational contexts. I describe four constructs related to proactive behavior: proactive personality, personal initiative, role breadth self-efficacy, and taking charge. Next, I review six research domains that have explicitly addressed proactive behaviors: socialization, feedback seeking, issue selling, innovation, career management, and certain kinds of stress management.

Scott and Bruce (1994) integrate a number of streams of research on the antecedents of innovation to develop and test a model of individual innovative behavior. Hypothesizing that leadership, individual problem-solving style, and work group relations affect innovative behavior directly and indirectly through their influence on perceptions of the climate for innovation, they use structural equation analysis to test the parameters of the proposed model simultaneously and also explored the moderating effect of task characteristics. The model explained approximately 37 percent of the variance in innovative behavior. Task type moderated the relationship between leader role expectations and innovative behavior.

Pierce and Delbecq (1977) focus on innovation as the initiation, adoption and implementation of new ideas or activity in an organizational setting, and reviewed in terms of organization context, structure, and member attitudes. A series of propositions and three predictive models are derived and presented as directions for future research and theory construction.

8.4. Organization learning for innovation: managerial implications and final remarks

The digital era, Innovation 4.0, significantly contributes to develop many challenges that individuals and organizations must face, in any contexts and roles and functions.

Thanks to a deep review of the literature, it is clear that knowledge consists in one of the most important resource for organizations especially in the digital era, where the presence of information, data and knowledge makes a great and significant difference for achieving successful goals. Today, in fact, managers and scholars talk about "innovation and knowledge war" focusing more and more their attention on knowledge creation and transferring through learning processes.

In the digital era, the contribution of learning process, especially organizational learning, becomes more relevant.

Thus, we can observe this phenomenon adopting twofold perspective. First, although the benefits and side effects of learning processes, mostly organizational learning, are still unclear, it has been recognized the importance to stimulate and promote the development of organizational process for creating and transferring knowledge, so that the innovation can be stimulated and shared at the same time. But, for a long time all the scholars and managers have recognized the bidirectional organizational process existing between "knowledge-organizational learning-innovation".

Second, although in the past "knowledge" has been considered as the key driver for the success of any firms, and with knowledge the development of organizational learning, nowadays, it is not enough. Innovation represents the "new key driver" for the success by achieving most challenging goals. In this new digital era, the way to work is dramatically changed, as the way to develop specific strategies or policies for managers, more than past, everything needs to be analyzed and known in advance, but it is not easy because in one very turbolent world nothing can be considered completely known. In this perspective, everything starts with "innovation" and never stops by going beyond the same innovation. We observe one new circular organizational process for facing the very complex challenges "innovation-organizational learning-innovation", where innovation can be interpreted as knowledge, as special and competitive knowledge.

Otherwise, the competency traps might occur because "prior innovative successes reinforce established routines even as the technological frontier shifts to new areas" (Sorensen & Stuart, 2000). As the experience and skills of firms grow, so do the same firms and their competences become prisoners of the innovation process, in terms of being less able to assimilate and exploit new information. Accumulation of knowledge through experience, or learning-by-doing, might lead to failing-by-knowing. This "myopia of learning" (levinthal & March, 1993) might have very relevant implications, such as the replacement of technological leaders by start-ups (Abernathy & Utterback, 1978).

Considering the link between innovating and learning, especially organizational learning, we have to consider these two concepts together adopting a broader point of view without barriers or specific directions.

On the one hand, as already outlined, "as for innovation, learning may occur at the individual, group, organization and industry levels. As new outputs, innovations may come from new knowledge as well as from the combination of existing knowledge to create architectural innovations" (Henderson & Clark, 1990), utilizing combinative capabilities (Kogut & Zander, 1992). Radical and incremental

Innovations, radical or incremental, correspond to high or low degrees of new knowledge (Dewar & Dutton, 1986), making low or high organizational transformation.

Thus, as some previous studies evidenced there is not need to see and talk about the difference between learning and innovating/innovation, also in the Industry 4.0. As already shown, learning means "integrating new knowledge or mixing existing knowledge in different ways, learning leads to newness, and thus to innovation. Innovation will be the by-product of a learning organization". As a consequence "a learning organization is an innovative organization".

We recognize that numerous contributions in the literature significantly participate for trying to understand knowledge and learning adopting various and different epistemological and conceptual perspectives.

Thanks to our study, several features can be outlined, that is the nature of organizational learning as a process involving individual, group, organizational and inter-organizational levels. Learning process includes three stages, that is acquisition, communication and exploitation of knowledge. Otherwise, each stage presents different difficulties depending also on the typologies or dimensions of knowledge, e.g. tacit compared to explicit knowledge, and the influence of firm strategy.

It's possible to support a positive relationship between organizational learning and innovation. If one firm is able to acquire new knowledge and articulate in more effective ways the existing knowledge, this firm should be good at providing innovations (product or process). But, at the same time, innovations, especially in terms of adopting new technologies and ways to work and make organizational processes, might push and stimulate firms to activate more effective and efficient organizational learning process for creating new knowledge and improving the existing one. Furthermore, the better the organizational learning process is, the greater the capacity to develop radical innovations (product or process) will be.

Thus, a successful learning organization leads to the capacity to innovate (Burns & Stalker, 1961), which is the ability of the organization in adopting or implementing new ideas, processes, or products successfully (Hurley & Hutt, 1998).

Of course, organizational learning needs to be in line as well as the innovation with the strategy and the environment of the firm. In any organizations, because of innovation, of the new challenge to face related to Industry 4.0, learning more or faster isn't the best solution, because it does not imply that you learn what you need to perform better than your competitors. One firm could be learning oriented, that is able and with awareness to learn but this doesn't mean that the firm is a learning organization, instead it is only one firm with poor processes that lead to learning, that is organizational learning.

Thus, many questions still remain without adequate replies regarding the bridges between knowledge and organizational learning, organizational learning and the learning organization, the learning organization and innovation, and innovation and performance. Specifically, the constituents, determinants, variables or effective techniques, for making organizational learning successful for fotering innovation and viceversa, are still unexplored .

Organizational earning is then necessary in order to master innovation, especially the new technologies, where a trial and error process takes place.

In summary, in the Industry 4.0 we cannot replace traditional and classical frameworks or concepts like knowledge management and organizational learning, but we need to reread the conclusions of past studies adopting a more opened approach where any barriers or pre-conceptualizations are over. There is still the need to deeply investigate the link between organizational learning and innovation and viceversa focusing the attention on the main determinants and techniques more competitive and useful.

References

Argyris, C., & Schön, D. (1978). Organizational learning: A theory of action perspective, Reading, Mass: Addison Wesley.

Butera F., (1990). Il castello e la rete: Impresa, Organizzazione e Professioni nell'Europa degli anni '90, Franco Angeli, Milano.

Campanini L. (1998). Competenze, apprendimento e teorie d'impresa, Economia e Politica Industriale, 98.

Davenport TH, Jarvenpaa SL, Beers MC (1996). Improving knowledge work processes. In: *Sloan Management Review*, pp. 53-65.

Di Bernardo B., Le dimensioni dell'impresa: scala, scopo, varietà Le dimensioni dell'impresa: scala, scopo, varietà, Hoepli, 1997.

Goktürk, S., Bozoğlu, O. and Gün.avdı, G. (2017). "Error management practices interacting with national and organizational culture: the case of two state university departments in Turkey", The Learning Organization, Vol. 24 No. 4, pp. 245-256.

Hillon, Y.C. and Boje, D.M. (2017). "The dialectical development of 'storytelling' learning organizations: a case study of a public research university", The Learning Organization, Vol. 24 No. 4, pp. 226-235.

Huber, G. (1990) A theory of the effect of advanced information technologies on organizational design, intelligence, and decision-making. *Academy of Management Review*, 15 (1), 47-71.

Nonaka, I. The Knowledge Creating Company. *Harvard Business Review*, 69, 96-104, 1991.

Nonaka, I.; Takeuchi, H. (1995). The knowledge creating company: how Japanese companies create the dynamics of innovation, Oxford University Press, New York.

Poell, R. and Van Der Kroght, F. (2017). "Why is organizing human resource development so problematic? Perspectives from the learning-network theory (Part II)", The Learning Organization, Vol. 24 No. 4, pp. 215-225.

Polanyi M., The Tacit Dimension, London: Routledge & Kegan Paul, 1966.

Rullani E. (1994). Il valore della conoscenza in *Economia e Politica Industriale*, Vol. 82.

Rupčić, N. (2017). "Managing people and learning – major challenge for modern managers", The Learning Organization, Vol. 24 Issue: 4, pp. 257-261, https://doi.org/10.1108/TLO-02-2017-0014.

Sasaki, Y. (2017). "A note on systems intelligence in knowledge management", The Learning Organization, Vol. 24 No. 4, pp. 236-244.

Simonin, B. (2017). "N-Loop learning: part II – an empirical investigation", The Learning Organization, Vol. 24 No. 4, pp. 202-214.

Weick KE. (1979). The Social Psychology of Organizing, second edition, New York, NY: McGraw-Hill.

Chapter 9

THE DIGITAL TRANSFORMATION OF LEARNING. IMPLICATIONS FOR ORGANIZATIONAL TRAINING

Roberta Virtuani-Alessandro Bottazzi

SUMMARY: Introduction. – 9.1. Trends driving the change of organizations toward a digital transformation. – 9.2. The employee learning experience. – 9.3. The role of managers and company training. – 9.4. The value of different ways of learning for and at work. – 9.5. Digital workplace solutions supporting the learning process. – 9.6. Case study: How Cisco Services up-skilled 14,400 employees and transformed into a consultative, solutions-selling organization. – 9.7. Case study: Digital transformation of training in ENEL. From "Training" to "Open Power Learning". – 9.8. Conclusion. – References.

Introduction

The digital transformation that a growing number of companies are currently undergoing is powered by technology, but the results of its application depend almost entirely on people, on their capacity to understand what is happening and on their ability to adapt to changes brought about by the need to integrate, use, connect and work with digital machines. Speed, storage, cost of hardware and networks are constantly evolving, confirming Moore's Law (cost of core technology decreases, while performance increases at an exponential rate). This means that it has now become affordable to adopt technologies that used to be too expensive and/or less powerful. The current technology price-performance level makes it possible to incorporate these technologies to solve current business problems in ways that were not possible before.

ICT (Information and Communication Technologies) can elaborate and transmit such a big amount of data through robotics, cloud computing technologies, artificial intelligence, big data and analytics, augmentation, 3D printing and IoT (Internet of Things), just to mention a few. Businesses now deal with these technologies on a daily basis and try to keep up with them. Moreover, an incredible number of devices are connected and connect everything (from smartphones and tablets to Internet of Everything devices). These technologies are able to monitor, track and collect data and information on things, people and businesses (Iansiti M., Lakhani K.R.

2014). Advanced data analytics and cloud computing can support these critical new technologies and remain crucial for digital business innovation. "*Data* in the 21st Century is like *Oil* in the 18th Century: an immensely, untapped valuable asset" (Wired, Toonders J. 2014). Digital transformation is being accelerated by the explosive growth of data and connected devices. Analytics and data science can definitely drive business competitiveness (DalleMule L., Davenport T.H., 2017).

The process will never stop. To remain competitive and in many cases to survive technology shifts, new business models and changing market demand, companies need to constantly change and innovate their technological architecture. They especially need to rethink their strategy, business model, organizational structure, processes, workforce, culture and partner relationships. Digital transformation affects every aspect of the organizations' value chain. Companies have to optimize and transform it to define new value propositions. Organizations and workflows are changing due to the connection frameworks between physical and smart virtual objects. The organization becomes a data-centric platform able to offer solutions centred on customized individual needs (Puthiyamadam T., 2017).

To keep up with technological change and to achieve results from the transformation process, human capital is essential. The innovation process needs to be supported by new competencies and by a different organizational and social culture (Ala-Mutka K., 2011). Organizations require the right knowledge, skills and experience to drive transformation and sustain competitive advantages. According to many sources the biggest challenge for digital transformation is not the technology itself, but the people. The biggest challenge employers will face over the next years is the shortage of qualified talent and a skill gap that continues to widen. Technology rapidly evolves and organizations' projects change. The rate of acceleration is so swift that it is hard for talent and knowledge to keep up. The contribution of the HR function and the training department for talent development can be large. In the evolving workplace new approaches and practices are necessary to support learning, as well as a flexible mindset to embrace organizational change and a culture for digital change. (Ruél H., Bondarouk T. Looise J.K., 2004)

Digitization can generate new growth opportunities for businesses and the general economy/society as a whole, not just in the short but also in the long term; nonetheless it is a complex, risky and costly process.

The chapter will focus first on the digital transformation that training departments are facing. This involves modifying their processes, work methods and technologies. Then it will deal with the managerial activities that training departments are adopting to align people's skills, culture and mindset. They have to develop the individual and organizational learning structure which prepares employees for an ongoing change (Hunt C.S., 2014).

The chapter will also analyze two case studies: Cisco and Enel. They are both big companies with 70,000 and 60,000 employees respectively. Cisco is a company working in the ICT industry. Enel works in the energy industry. Both have already digitized a large part of their production and distribution processes over the years. Our purpose is to consider how their digital transformation is expanding to HR processes, in particular to training. We aim to highlight their way of managing the innovation process brought about and driven by digitization and all the new ICT such as big data, analytics, augmentation and Internet of Everything in a connected world.

9.1. Trends driving the change of organizations toward a digital transformation

We will highlight a few trends that are challenging organizations concerning people management to understand the impact that digital transformation can have on people and to think about the leading role that HR and training departments can have in managing them. These trends can have a great influence in shaping the future of businesses from a strategic and organizational point of view. They are recognized as forces leading the evolution of the market place.

a) **Experience economics and personalization**: selling products and services is no longer the only factor in the equation. Customers look for an experience. The customer journey can be designed to define how the customers interact with the company and what value they perceive and receive (Pine II B.J., Gilmore J.H., 2011). Customers need a personalized contact to receive what they need, just when they need it. Companies are realizing the incredible importance of their own people towards the company's success. That's why they are designing the employee journey to strengthen the relationship with them, by offering customized ways of working, wellness and work-life balance. New opportunities are now also coming from smart working, a widespread practice that is changing the way work is organized. It drives Human Resources practices to adapt to the new environment.

In the past people had to adapt to the technologies implemented by the company. Today, technology is adapting to the people and to their behaviour. It is the new frontier of digital experience. The distance between human and machines needs to be increasingly user friendly in order to reduce the distance between them and humans. This will allow better interaction.

b) **Process re-engineering**: the way processes are automated has changed with digitization (Attaran M., 2004). The integration of technologies such as sensors, IoT, cloud computing, big data analytics and artificial intelligence in enterprise systems, is making possible to simplify and accelerate processes. They can be monitored and their efficiency improved with the great advantage of being able to predict possible malfunctions without stopping the operation line, thus reducing operating costs (Baird Z., Buolamwini J., Fallows J., Ng Andrew, 2017).

c) **Becoming digital**: The vast majority of business leaders believe in the importance of digital business. Approximately 85% of 3,500 executive interviewed agree that "being a digital business is important for the success of my company" (Kane C.G. et al., 2017). Digital change is continuous and ongoing. Companies compete in an increasingly digital environment. The capabilities that can help companies to find the right solution to respond to their market changes are part of an organizational model like adhocracy (Bodega D., 1997). Adhocracy differs from the burocratic and meritocratic organizational models currently more used. In a model like adhocracy companies find an answer for the flexibility and agility they need to keep up with the fast market changes (Mintzberg H., 1983). Surveyed companies claiming to be "mature" in their process of digital transformation and adaptation have the characteristics of an adhocratic form. This is the most appropriate configuration to make innovation not marginal and to solve complex problems in a cooperative way.

Becoming a mature digital business is not a quick process. The entire business needs to be rethought to adapt to the increasingly changing digital market environments. Companies are trying to take advantage of digital technologies to improve and sometimes maintain their market position. Digitization requires companies to do business differently, not simply by adding to existing processes and practices. Companies change according to the way customers, employees, partners and competitors are using digital technologies. The alignment to changes concerns strategy, organizational structure, talent and culture (Birkinshaw J., Ridderstrale J., 2015). Some main changes are about gaining the attention of the board of directors, with executives that understand the power and limits of information. They should also understand that a team-based organizational structure goes beyond a traditional structure based on command and control systems that may impede the agility to operate. It is essential to simplify the hierarchical management structures to make decisions, decentralize power and support horizontal cooperation using reciprocal adaptation (Senge P.M., 2006). Developing the internal work force and building a supportive culture that embraces collaboration, risk-taking and experimentation are pillars for digital transformation (Rigby D.K., Sutherland J., Takeuchi H., 2016). One of the aspects of the digital culture is in fact the mindset toward innovation. It underlines the importance of trial-and-error experimentation aimed at impacting the core business. The cultural base is the tolerance of failures and the ability to learn from them. Continuous learning and collaboration through cross-functional teams working across organizational boundaries, hence breaking down functional silos, require new skills such as empathy, problem solving, curiosity and adaptability to being a team player (Van Laar E., Van Deursen A.J., Van Dijk J.A, De Haan j., 2017). Collaboration can move beyond the organization itself to involve the other actors of the company's ecosystem.

d) **Creation of ecosystems**: companies are more often integrating the main business functions with 3rd-party platforms, such as technology companies, startups and universities, to develop new ideas. They are not collaborating by using traditional partnerships, but they are using these relationships to define a strategic role in the new digital ecosystems. What is happening in this process is the design of a new value chain able to transform companies, products and the market itself. Today, businesses are not only creating new products or services, they are inventing new digital markets whose rules are still under definition. Businesses are making a critical and significant contribution.

To avoid disruption and to remain competitive, the workforce needs to adapt to these changes too; it has to be able to deal with new market trends and to be comfortable in the new digital environment. The ability of a company is highly dependent on the ability of its employees to be self-organized in often unknown situations and to find creative solutions. The HR department and the training team are called upon to sustain these efforts. In this way they contribute to organizational change and strategically partecipate in the transformation of work and of the whole company. This helps to achieve business aims of productivity increase, growth and value to strengthen its competitive position. HR teams play a role in shaping culture, the great driver of all business changes. However the first step is to work on the gap between aspirations and reality. The road ahead and the direction are already mapped out, even if future developments are uncertain and depend on how companies will move in the digital market.

9.2. The employee learning experience

When a company is transitioning to the digital world, effects on its workforce are far-reaching. Employees and executives might leave the company if they feel they don't have opportunities to develop the required digital skills. Digitally advanced companies can have a strong appeal to attract and develop digital talent. Digital skills and experience acquired can be helpful for achieving career growth ambitions.

Table 1. Employees are more likely to leave if they do not have the opportunities to develop their digital skills.

Percentage who plan to leave their company in one year or less given digital trends

3%	2%	7%	Company provides opportunities to develop in a digital environment
CIO	VP/ Director	Sales Staff	
29%	31%		Company does not provide opportunities to develop in a digital environment
		43%	

Source: 6th Annual Survey MIT Sloan Management Review, Deloitte University Press, 2017

In Tab. 1 the answers based on a global survey of more than 3500 managers and executives show the high percentages of CIO (29%), VP/Directors (31%) and Sales Staff (43%) prepared to leave the company in one year or less if it does not provide opportunities to develop in a digital environment. On the other hand, the percentages when companies provide development opportunities in a digital environment are very low, 3%, 2% and 7% respectively (Kane G.C. et al., 2017). This data shows that digital education and investment in digital talent is very important for creating a dynamic workplace. This leads to a continuous renewal based on innovation, collaboration and an open culture to create a sustainable competitive advantage in a digitized environment. On the other hand, digital education is also necessary for a process of never-ending learning that allows employees to maintain and strengthen their employability in case of future job changes or career advancements. There is no longer such a thing as a job for life. More and more people will be moving from job to job[1]. Workpla-

---

[1] The gig economy: transforming the workplace, EY, http://www.ey.com/gl/en/ services/people-advisory-services/the-gig-economy-transforming-the-workforce.

ces where employees can continuously learn, gain digital experience and grow, may become environments where workers like spending time.

Some companies make learning a priority also for the partners of their ecosystems. It is a win-win process where everyone can benefit. Environments stimulating learning are more likely to retain talent.

Putting people first, at the center of change, is considered the new leadership imperative for creating the future workforce. This is the challenge. This imperative has been recurrent through the years but has never completely materialized. Digitization, pushing companies toward new ways of working, is a challenge but also an opportunity to change the work relationships inside the organization (Murawski M., Bick M., 2017).

Continuous learning is another aspect characterizing the employee learning experience. New technologies, the Internet and the wide spread of connected devices allow self-paced learning. The learner can learn any time, on any advice and from anywhere, whether they are travelling or at home. This highlights the importance of asynchronous learning. Learning is part of the job and not something separate. Learning and knowledge sharing can foster a culture of continuous learning and innovation (Younger J. 2016).

Analysis on the way employees learn (Albano R., Fabbri T.M., 2010) showed that the aspect that stands out for high performers, is their self sufficiency[2]. They are autonomous, making their own choices about what to learn, how to learn it and when to learn it. An example of self sufficient workers is the growing contingent workforce "as a provisional group of workers who work for an organization on a non-permanent basis. These contingent workers, or giggers, are also known as freelancers, independent professionals, temporary contract workers, independent contractors or consultants". EY shows in its research that two out of five organizations expect to increase their use of the contingent workforce by 2020 (Hart J. 2017). For the contingent workforce and non, the new approach consists in the responsibility they need to take for driving their own development, thinking about the skills they need to develop now and in the future (Billet S., Choy S., 2013).

Following the evolution of the employee learning experience, a relevant role is played by the way they relate to the Internet. In fact, their new learning habits are largely based on the Internet, and on making a significant use of mobile devices, such as smartphones and tablets[3] (Bondarouk T. Parry E. & Furtmueller E., 2017).

---

[2] In a knowledge economy corporate learning is necessary to survive, Karl Mehta, Techcrunch, 30 October 2016 https://techcrunch.com/2016/10/30/in-a-knowledge-eco nomy-corporate-learning-is-necessary-to-survive/.

[3] Mary Meeker's Internet Trends 2016 Report shows that the average global mobile user now has around 33 apps installed in their device, 12 of which are used daily whilst 80% of their time is spent on 3 apps.

The social and collaborative side is another aspect that characterizes the way employees learn. They interact through posts and blogs and learn from a diverse range of people, colleagues, industry thought leaders, practitioners, analysts and many others.

When accessing content, individuals prefer it to be short and very visual. For example YouTube videos, screencasts and infographics are very popular. They prefer quick demonstrations or illustrations rather then long textual documents.

A significant aspect is that people no longer see learning as a separate activity but an integral part of working and living. In fact they don't use dedicated learning tools, but make use of the same tools for learning as for work and play (Malcom J., Hodkinson P., Colley H., 2003).

Many employees' web-learning habits are based on social networking. It connects individuals to professional networks, online communities, professional events, knowledge flows and to external resources in general, and courses (Hart, 2017). This is an optimal method to stay up to date with what is happening in their profession or industry.

Professional learning however includes many others activities and methodologies. A large part of learning takes place by carrying out the daily work. Interaction with other colleagues and teams can be extremely relevant sources of knowledge. For instance, answering common questions, can be an occasion for knowledge and experience sharing that will translate into more skilled and resourceful employees.

9.3. The role of managers and company training

An important point of reference is the employee's manager. Managers play an important role in helping their employees to find solutions to enhance their skills and knowledge. They can provide guidance, advice, feedback and support.

In today's workplace, being effective at developing employees is a required skill for managers. If a manager is effective in developing employees, their performance can be improved up to 25-27% (Corporate Leadership Council)[4]. In respect to a non-effective manager, an effective manager can achieve relevant results also in the following areas: employee retention, if the employee reports directly to the manager (+39.7%), employee satisfaction (+37.2%), organizational commitment (+29.4%) and employee adaptability (+8.3%). The three experiential learning items that improve em-

---

[4] Corporate Leadership Council/Learning and Development Roundtable/ Employee Development Survey cited by www.slideshare.net/charlesjennings/the-702010-framework.

ployees' performance more than "teaching new skills" are: a) explain performance evaluation standards, b) ensure projects provide learning, c) provide experiences that develop. Managers can be considered coaches for their employees, if they are sensitive to their development needs. Therefore the use of coaching and mentoring has also become more and more common.

Learning for and at work includes company training as well, whether it is with participation in the classroom or a blend of classroom and e-learning (De Oliveira P.C., De Almeida Cunha C.J.C., Nakayama M.H., 2016).

From the analysis of the employees' habits and according to their learning paths, it emerges that the employees' learning can be on three levels: self-organized, organized by their manager or by the learning and development department. Each individual has his/her own learning path, each one different from the other. During their career, they can be exposed to one, two, or a mix of the three ways. The learning experience through training in classroom or blended with e-learning is defined as a formal experience. Learning while doing the job is defined as an informal one (London M., Hall M.J., 2011) (Comacchio A., Scapolan AC, 2004).

9.4. The value of different ways of learning for and at work

According to Hart's 5th Annual Learning in the Workplace Survey, 5000 individuals in 63 countries worldwide were asked to assess (on a 4 points Likert scale from not important to essential) the importance of the following ten different ways of learning for and at work:

- Company training and e-learning
- Self-directed study of external courses
- Internal company documents
- Job aids
- Knowledge sharing within your team
- General conversations and meetings with people
- Personal and professional networks and communities
- External blogs and news feeds
- Content curated by external sources
- Web search for resources (e.g. using Google).

With a fairly consistent scoring pattern over the years, the main results show that the followings are the top-rated ways individuals learn at work:

- Knowledge sharing (88% find it VI or Essential)
- Searching the Web (80% find it VI or Essential)
- Conversations and meetings (79% find it VI or Essential)
- Professional Networking (75% find it VI or Essential)

The results of the survey are shown in Tab. 2.

Table 2. Value of Different Ways of learning for Individuals.

Rank	Activity	Not important %	Quite important %	Very important %	Essential %	VIP + Essential %
1	Knowledge sharing within your own team	2	10	30	**58**	88
2	Web search for resources (e.g. Google)	2	17	32	**48**	80
3	General conversations and meetings	2	19	39	**40**	79
4	Personal & professionnal networks & communities	3	22	39	**36**	75
5	External blogs and news feeds	12	30	**36**	22	58
6	Content curated from external sources	9	34	**37**	20	57
7	Self-directed study of external courses	13	**36**	34	17	51
8	Internal company documents	13	**38**	31	18	49
9	Internal job aids	18	**36**	31	15	46
10	Company training and e-learning	23	**39**	21	17	38

Source: Hart J. (2017), 5th Annual Learning in the Workplace Survey.

As we can see in Table 2 employees do not consider company training and e-learning very important. In fact we find them in the last place. Just 38% found them VI or Essential (Hart J., 2017). Traditional teaching methods are under scrutiny, new methods are arising, which are better suited to the new context and help to achieve valuable outcomes. (Za S., Spagnoletti P., North-Samardzic A., 2014) New practices and methods are necessary to support learning, and both organizations and individuals need to be aware and be prepared for the coming evolution of the workplace. A special attention is given to the young generation of employees more acquainted to new technologies use. (Baird D.E., Fisher M., 2005). Companies are experimenting and introducing forms of the so called "reverse mentoring". Young generations can give an important contribute to the digital transformation process (Bissola R., Imperatori B., 2013).

9.5. Digital workplace solutions supporting the learning process

The aim of companies in their process of digital transformation is to have digital workplace solutions that can help to build a smarter, more agile and productive workforce, actively contributing to the demand of continuous innovation and with the requested expertise to enable transformation projects. New technologies are now supporting the learning process to meet employees' and companies' needs. There are many different kinds of new tools that adopt an holistic approach. They are based on four pillars: learning, knowledge, collaboration, people. Through their technology as Cloud SaaS (Software as a Service) they allow learners to collaborate, connect and share knowledge safely and securely behind firewalls.

Table 3. LMS Features.
The Collaborative Knowledge Learning Management System

Features
Personalized, digital learning experience
Formal and informal learning opportunities
Training Catalog
Learning plans and reporting
Learning communities
Knowledge Center
Catalog management
Automated registration and roster administration
Resource management
SCORM – and AICC – compliant courses
Training delivered anytime, anywhere, on any device
Built-in learning management system analytics
Third-party learning content partners
Mobility
Unified collaboration and communication tools

Source: CISCO, 2017.

These tools allow employees to manage training, talent development and learning by integrating the three aspects of formal, informal and social learning within the process of digital transformation. They offer a blend of collaborative learning and formal training, learning plans and reporting. Employees need to access their own knowledge strengths and weaknesses. With this information they can customize learning paths that mutually support career development and organizational goals. The same goes for the company which accesses and addresses organizational knowledge strengths and weaknesses for individuals, teams and departments. The tools support learning communities, knowledge centres which provide access to enterprise-wide best practice. These tools also make learning easy and simple for mobile and remote employees, with training delivered any time, anywhere, on any advice, with built-in learning management system analytics.

There is a wide availability of learning and collaboration platforms. Companies can choose the one that best suits their needs. The adoption of these platforms, as for any kind of new software application, needs time to be implemented and used. Implementing the new learning platforms leads to big changes that needs to be carefully managed to obtain the advantages of this solution. Some critical issues must be consider carefully in order to achieve a favourable implementation. They include "commitment from top management, reengineering of the existing processes, integration of the learning platform with other business information systems, selection and management of consultants and employees, and training of employees within the new system"(Bingi P., Sharma M.K., Godla J.K.,1999). In particular it can take a lot of time to transfer knowledge to employees even if these platforms are supposed to be as easy and friendly as possible. Their interfaces try to imitate the same style as websites used by employees in their free time. These platforms are continuously updated to follow new technological advances. This requires employees to be flexible and fast when the platform changes.

Other critical issues concern high investments made by companies for technological systems and in general for formal and informal training activities. The return of these investments is not certain. Training is considered to be useless if it cannot be translated into performance. This is known as the transfer of training. The following aspects are equally important: evaluation of the return on investment and of how much is actually transferred from what is taught in training programs to the job. Through training transfer, employees should put trained knowledge and skills back into the job (Burke L.A., Hutchins H.M., 2007).

9.6. Case study: How Cisco Services up-skilled 14,400 employees and transformed into a consultative, solutions-selling organization

Cisco

Cisco Systems, headquartered in San Jose, California, was founded in 1984 by a small group of computer scientists from Stanford University. Since the company's inception, Cisco engineers have been leaders in the development of Internet Protocol (IP)-based networking technologies. Today, with more than 71,000 employees and operating in more than 65 countries, this tradition of innovation continues with industry-leading products and solutions in the company's core development areas of routing and switching, as well as in advanced technologies such as home networking, IP telephony, optical networking, security, storage area networking, and wireless technology. In addition to its products, Cisco provides a broad range of service offerings, including technical support and advanced services, to provide the highest levels of enterprise-grade security, data center software, cloud performance and reliability.

Learning@Cisco

Learning@Cisco addresses the need for Cisco technical talent worldwide by providing the educational resources, training, certifications, social networks and communities, knowledge systems and consulting services that accelerate productivity, opportunity, and growth. Through educational expertise, Learning@Cisco drives the talent development needed to evolve the workforce of today to meet the demands of tomorrow.

Need to re-skill in the Digital Transformation

For organizations that act now, digitalization is a huge business opportunity. First-to-market leaders can capture mind share and market share in ways that were unthinkable previously. To move ahead of the curve and prepare its workforce for the digital future, Cisco decided in 2013 to shift its Services organization to a consultative, solutions-selling model. To support this transformational play, Services would need to re-skill 14,000-plus employees for new positions supporting the evolved Services strategy.

By transitioning to the new consultative-style approach, leaders believed that Services employees could acquire the transformational capabilities and expertise needed to support customers transiting to digital. From a first-mover position, Cisco could gain a competitive advantage, by innovating new business models to creating additional value for new Internet of Everything (IoE) solutions. Moreover, employees could use their new skills to redefine the customer experience.

To align around this project, Edzard Overbeek, who formerly served as senior vice president of Services, convened a steering team of Human Resources, Learning & Development, and Learning@Cisco leaders to define the transformation vision, strategy, and journey. To understand the challenges before them, the steering team commissioned an independent Human Resources assessment of the business unit. The resulting assessment identified a number of gaps and opportunities. Most notably, two-thirds of Services employees needed new skills to shift to the newly prescribed selling motion. Additionally, nearly half of Services employees lacked access to critical learning paths to develop the transformational skills and capabilities needed to support the project. It quickly became apparent to executive leaders that a whole new approach to learning and talent development would be necessary for Services to achieve its desired business outcomes. With new end goals in mind, Services embarked on building a new social learning platform called Career Connection.

Career Connection and the Cisco Collaborative Knowledge

After months of meetings, surveys, interviews, user testing, employee participation, and executive input, the Career Connection internal proof-of-concept pilot went live in 2014. The platform, which was purposefully designed to scale content, context, and community across the enterprise, offered employees a social, collaborative environment to learn and grow within.

To drive adoption, Career Connection was designed and developed so that Services employees were the beneficiaries of crucial tools and technology that empowered them to take charge of their own careers and learning and development. To cultivate collaboration and knowledge-sharing across functions, employees could connect with peers, experts, and mentors to learn and share information in real time. They could also acquire knowledge and specialized skills through interactive discussion forums, blogs, and online training. To support transformational capabilities development, employees, Services leaders, Human Resources, and Learning & Development teams worked together to create Career Playbooks. By providing prescriptive guidance on job skills and training, employees could better prepare for current and future job roles that aligned with their career and development goals.

Unlike Cisco Collaborative Knowledge, Career Connection initially focused primarily on formal and informal learning: Career Universe, Learning Plan, Community, and the Training Catalog. **Career Universe** contained Career Playbooks, organized by job families, and skills-based capabilities. **Learning Plan** scheduled and tracked learning and development and progress toward career goals. **Community** connected peers, mentors, and experts so they could learn, encourage, and help one another on assignments and projects. The **Training Catalog** standardized learning and development across Services, providing every employee with new opportunities to learn and grow.

The dynamic nature of Career Connection meant that learning was enabled through a *rich blend of formal and informal learning* opportunities, including discussion threads, blogs, and even crowdsourcing. In addition to enabling Cisco Services to reskill 14,400 employees quickly and cost-effectively, Career Connection offered many tangible business benefits:

- Engaged employees in business transformation of Services
- Increased collaboration and communication among peers, experts, and executives.
- Improved employee engagement, participation, and satisfaction.
- Standardized and democratized learning and development across the Services organization.

Product Validation

Once deployed, it quickly became apparent that Career Connection had the right blend of learning and collaboration for Cisco Services. Early field trial results demonstrated that employees not only liked the platform, they supported its mission:

- 8 out of 10 employees agreed or strongly agreed they had a better sense of Services business transformation, and consequently were more engaged on Services business topics. They also felt empowered to share professional knowledge with peers as a result of Career Connection.
- 9 out of 10 employees agreed or strongly agreed that learning about the organization's strategic direction from leaders (directly via blogs and discussion threads) was important to engagement and career development.
- 3 out of 4 employees agreed or strongly agreed that being able to share information through discussion forums was important to their learning and development.
- 8 out of 10 employees agreed or strongly agreed that being able to access job roles and requisites in Career Universe better enabled them to meet their aspirational career goals.
- 8 out of 10 employees agreed or strongly agreed that the information in their Career Playbook enabled them to more effectively create their professional development plan.

- 8 out of 10 employees agreed or strongly agreed that Career Connection was useful and informative in planning career goals.

With such positive feedback, Learning@Cisco executives began asking: Could Cisco customers benefit from a similar platform to transform their own companies? To determine if there was an unmet need in the marketplace, Learning@Cisco connected with over 150 customers to discuss their challenges. Armed with customer interest and a proof-of-concept pilot validated by 14,400 Cisco Services employees, Career Connection quickly evolved from an internal learning offering into a fully integrated, cloud-based knowledge and learning digital workplace solution called **Cisco Collaborative Knowledge**.

According to Michael Carter, former vice president of human resources for Cisco Services and an original sponsor of Career Connection, to achieve the agility required for today's workforce, talent must be empowered to define, grow, and redefine their careers. "Career Connection grew out of an in-house pilot that connected the evolving needs of the business with the skills and capabilities in the workforce. It made the business strategy relevant to how employees want to come together to connect, develop, and transform", he says.

Kathy Bries, a senior director and general manager for Learning@Cisco who led the development and marketing of Cisco Collaborative Knowledge, concurs. "Today's organizations need to inspire and energize their employees to learn, relearn, and unlearn time and again. They also need to provide them with the digital tools and technology needed to support their careers and the organization. Cisco accomplished this with Career Connection, and now our customers can build a smarter, more agile and productive workforce with Cisco Collaborative Knowledge.

From Career Connection to Cisco Collaborative Knowledge Today

Designed to optimize knowledge-sharing and collaborative learning, Cisco Collaborative Knowledge can empower everyone within an organization with the digital tools and technology needed to access experts, learning, and knowledge in real time-anytime, anywhere. By combining the best of Career Connection with crucial technologies to streamline communication and business results, Cisco Collaborative Knowledge evolved into a digital workplace solution.

Launched in April 2015, Cisco Collaborative Knowledge integrates best-in-class consumer and business applications – secure knowledge sharing, expert identification, collaboration, continuous learning, social networking, and analytics – into one complete and end-to-end knowledge-exchange solution.

Powered by five knowledge and learning S-modules – Mobile Knowledge, Expert Discovery, Knowledge Center, Social Communities, and the Learning Management System, Cisco Collaborative Knowledge can provide every employee with the tools and capabilities they need to reimagine the customer and employee experience. Following are highlights of the modules that constitute Cisco Collaborative Knowledge:

- **Mobile Knowledge**: Makes knowledge portable and shareable. With it, everyone can capture, share, and manage content anytime, anywhere with a laptop, tablet, or smartphone.
- **Expert Discovery**: Provides just-in-time access to expert resources using Cisco WebEx® and Jabber® technology. Workers can identify and locate resources and connect safely inside the firewall to share ideas, exchange knowledge, or solve business challenges in real time.
- **Knowledge Center**: Centralizes and preserves institutional knowledge and best practices from across the organization in an enterprisewide library.
- **Social Communities**: Fosters real-time learning, problem solving, and innovation through social communities, discussion forums, blogs, and crowdsourcing.
- **Learning Management System**: Supports formal, prescribed, and informal learning and development through a centralized learning management system. Students can track their progress and take assessments, and instructors can leverage the system to prescribe learning.

Incorporating industry-leading Cisco innovation, including Cisco WebEx and Jabber collaboration tools and Visual Knowledge Mapping and Analytics Technology, Cisco Collaborative Knowledge can help every organization build a smarter, more agile, and more productive digital workplace for today and tomorrow.

One Solution: Multiple Functions

Because of its comprehensive feature set, Cisco Collaborative Knowledge can enable many outcomes across different job functions and industries. To drive digital disruption in the automotive industry, one Cisco manufacturing customer is engaging with universities and thought leaders on the platform, sharing information and research to reimagine consumer automotive safety. Another organization is scaling science, technology, engineering, and mathematics (STEM) education globally so that students have access to experts and mentors. In doing so, they are preparing the next generation of scientists and engineers to handle critical global challenges.

Additionally, with Cisco Collaborative Knowledge, the organization can:

- Mobilize its workforce with knowledge, speed, and flexibility to create a more agile and engaged organization. For example, with Cisco Collaborative Knowledge, mobile sales professionals who engage with new prospects can quickly access learning modules about a particular product, solution, or market – right as they need it. Through knowledge that is available and shareable via a mobile platform, everyone can quickly access valuable resources to reinvent the way they work, learn, collaborate, and innovate together.
- Tap into the collective knowledge of the entire organization to innovate and transform the customer and employee experience. With Cisco Collaborative Knowledge, employees have instant access to experts, enterprisewide repositories of collective knowledge and social learning, and collaboration tools that enable them to innovate in the moment.

From Learning Certifications to Education-as-a-Service Software

As a result of its commitment to education, Cisco has expended significant resources on advancing education and learning innovation globally. As a business unit, Learning@Cisco is focused on the development of educational, knowledge-sharing, and learning-based solutions that meet the demands of the new digital economy. To that end, Cisco Collaborative Knowledge supports Learning@Cisco's commitment to develop collaborative, virtualized, and accessible education that accelerates overall workforce performance as it removes barriers to learning.

To help customers solve their most pressing business challenges, Learning@Cisco developed Education as a Service (EdaaS) to reinvent the delivery of knowledge and learning. Cisco Collaborative Knowledge is the company's first **EdaaS platform** to address the needs of the digital workplace and reflects Learning@Cisco's drive to develop collaborative, virtualized and accessible education, delivered in real time. Since its introduction, Cisco Collaborative Knowledge, has received 11 industry awards.

9.7. Case study: Digital transformation of training in ENEL. From "Training" to "Open Power Learning"

Enel

Enel is a multinational energy group that has developed over the years to become one of the world's leading integrated electricity and gas operators. It was founded as an Italian monopolist and in recent years it has become a partly private international group which has recently undergone a profound transformation on a corporate, strategic, cultural and organizational level.

"Enel Group works in 29 countries across 4 continents, generating energy with a net installed capacity of around 83 GW and distributing electricity and gas across a network spanning about 2.1 million km. With around 64 million end users around the world, the group has the biggest customer base among our European competitors, and it is one of Europe's leading energy companies by installed capacity and reported EBITDA[5].

The "Open Power" vision and Enel's cultural identity

In January 2016 Enel announced its new global corporate identity at a group level. It will help it to adapt to the ongoing changes within the group and follow and anticipate the rapid evolution of the energy sector, which Enel is driving. This identity can be summed up in the expression "Open Power" "meaning a modern, open, flexible and responsive utility company, ready to lead the energy transition" This is the vision that Enel shares with all its stakeholders. It highlights the relevance and essentially of continuous investments on new technologies and an open participation through every connection with the opportunity to face the big challenges that already tackle us in a fast moving and complex world. "Openness as a key element of the Group's strategic and operational approach" shapes Enel's mission through Open Power that means "opening energy access to more people; opening the world of energy to new technologies; opening new ways for people to manage energy; opening new uses of energy; and opening more partnerships".

Open power requires much more than being simple power generators and distributors. The new mission fully embodies the innovative, sustainable, multidimensional and open nature of the Enel Group. "By 2030, approximately 30% of the planet's energy demand will be covered by green energy. We are committed to renewable energy sources, such as hydro, wind, solar, geothermal, biomass and cogeneration plants, and together with our partners we are developing new environmentally-friendly technologies. We are aiming to go further: by 2050, we want to become an entirely carbon-neutral company". With this new identity, Enel wants to affirm its new image of a modern, open, flexible, responsive utility that can drive the energy transition.

---

[5] https://www.enel.com/en/aboutus/a201608-vision.html.

According to this view digitization plays a key role. Enel is an highly digitized company that is "working on smarter, data-driven ways to analyse energy consumption in real time, distribute energy more efficiently and enable entirely new services for people. These smart grids only deliver electricity when and where it is needed – reducing costs and waste while helping to protect the environment." Enel has embarked on the road to digital development and anticipated the era of smart technologies by designing and installing the first electronic counters already in 2001 [6].

Enel is in a strategic and valuable strong position according to the vision of Open Power as a general connotation.

Enel has been given a system of values that relate to trust, innovation, responsibility and proactivity. In this framework of values, starting from openness, the themes of transformation and digitization are an integral part of the strategic change that Enel has undergone over the years and that allow it to support innovation.

The organizational matrix structure [7]

To govern this complexity, open power, internationalization and the needs of the business, in 2014 Enel adopted an organizational matrix structure. The matrix has five Global Divisions as global business lines (Infrastructure and Networks, Generation, Trading, Renewable Energy and Upstream Gas) which cross with the four countries of the Group (Italy, Spain, South America and Eastern Europe). Functions and Holding Functions complete the matrix. There are two service levels: Information and Communication Technology and Group-level Procurement. The holding company will continue to manage the Group's governance processes, which have been symplified compared to the past.

Even before starting a digital transformation investment project, Enel adopted an organization that can support its development and innovation plans.

During 2017 the Global E-Solutions Business Line, was established with the mission of: • managing the portfolio of solutions, as well as growing the customer base both in existing and new countries, in accordance with security, safety and environmental guidelines and regulations, maximizing customer value and operational efficiency, sharing with Countries the growth and profitability targets; • innovating and developing all solutions by managing the entire lifecycle, from ideation to technological develop-

---

[6] https://www.enel.com/it/storie/a201609lanostrastoriailnostrofuturo.html.

[7] https://www.enel.com/it/media/news/d201411-una-matrice-globale-per-le-nuove-sfide-della-energia.html.

ment, from testing to commercialization, sales, operations and post-sales activities, leveraging on best practices; • scouting new technologies and developing new business models and revenue streams, both in existing and new countries also through equity transactions.

The Digital Ambassadors and the Digital Customer Journey Program

Enel has been working on the topic of digital transformation since the beginning of 2016. In 2017 it established the Digital Customer Journey Program within Country Italy. The aim of the program is to redesign the end-to-end customer journey and experience through the digitization of core business processes, capabilities and overall ecosystem. Within the Enel Group, eleven Digital Managers have been identified and more will be identified in the near future. They report to the division they work for and to the Head of the Digital Enabler unit.

These Digital Managers are real digital ambassadors, awareness-raising activists on digitization issues. In this way Enel has been equipped with organizational structures to support the digitization process with dedicated features on the part of customer experience. There are Digital Managers inside the holding functions such as Administration, Finance and Control or HR and Organization business line divisions like Global Renewable Energies or Global Thermal Generation, in country division like Italy and Iberia.

From "Training" to "Open Power Learning": the global governance of training

The Global Training and Recruiting Department is a global governance structure at a holding level. It deals with policies, strategy, processes and projects world-wide

It relates to all the training units world-wide for the different countries and for the different business lines. They are working on the employee experience with individuals that are becoming more and more autonomous in their training choices and development.

Enel's global training department is currently making a significant investment in the spread of knowledge on digital transformation to create the culture and mind-set of digital change. It is a change management approach.

The Global and Holding Training offer deals with the very transversal issues of the company's citizenship. They talk about values, training for managerial roles, ethics and language training. Language training is a topic spread across countries at all levels of business. Employees should speak

English, Spanish and Italian as the main languages in the company. The Training Department tries to represent the organizational matrix also in the learning models. Training activities at a holding level cross with the different lines of business and the different countries. Every business area has its vertical training, its professional family with scholarships and academies. Every business/country line designs, implements and offers their own employees training dealing with the trade theme. On the one hand, there is the content provided by the holding world that represents the themes of values, Enel's culture and linguistics. On the other hand, the country or business lines offer topics that concern trade. In their governance model the Training Department takes into account the whole person as a citizen of Enel.

In Enel's training architecture technical training is steered by the business lines. Strategies for technical training are created on a global level and are then developed by each country. The situation is different for behavioural training. For example leadership courses are decided and managed centrally and concern top management levels. Courses for intermediate-level management are planned and delivered in the different countries. The Global Training Department in Enel also manages global campaigns or local ones in each country. The three levels of behavioural training, (global, local and concerning campaigns) overlap in many cases.

While until yesterday, the unit manager decided on the software or sales techniques courses, today the employee knows which skills are required and knows that these are the things he/she will have to do.

1. **The training governance model, digitization and the digital transformation process.** The training governance model intersects with the facilitation that digitization brings. Digitization does not change the model they have in mind and that is what they want to continue with. Digitization helps them achieve it more and more by making the person central so that he/she is aware of his/her learning path. The governance model will be facilitated through the digital tools. They are implemented to support the ability to change the culture of participation and responsibility of individuals in their learning path. The training department has been working on the project for at least a year with experiments and small pilots.

2. **Experimentation and pilot projects to support innovation as an agile enterprise.** Aiming at the participation of people in the choice of their priorities, the Training Department is experimenting tools and models on small numbers with an agile approach to verify if the tool could be adopted in Enel Group. At the beginning of 2017, they esperimented MOOC (Massive Open Online Course) on language

training project: Italian, Spanish and English. Countries, cultures and professions differ from each other and they need to consider this aspect. They are adopting blended tools that can combine classroom and online courses. In May 2017 the Training Department experimented a pilot project on 20,000 employees in Italy as a self-management experience for their training path. They could choose the course they considered useful to strengthen behaviour or capacities consistent with organizational demands and expectations. They could choose from a catalog of 20 courses on soft skills congruent with the 4 values of the corporate identity linked to the performance appraisal process: trust, innovation, responsibility and proactivity. This proposal was disruptive, because they changed how HR is perceived. The new decision logic aims at spreading self-awareness and responsibility. Responsibility is one of the four above mentioned values. The Training Department is working a lot on this, together with participation and autonomy. The meaning of the project "A Course for You" is to create a new mind-set. 9,000 employees have applied to follow the course. In this way the project focused on the individual, giving him/her the chance to choose without interference from his/her superior or from the HR Department.

The adoption of a Learning Management System (LMS)

In support of these goals Enel has activated a business process outsourcing system and has invested in an important Learning Management System. It's not just a technology choice, but part of a more complex digital strategy Enel has adopted.

The adoption of a Learning Management System platform on Cloud is an important project that will be completed in December 2017. The project will be open to all the 29 countries where Enel works. In Italy, the Training Department currently uses a personalised platform purchased over ten years ago. At the time, it was a cutting-edge product but today it no longer possesses the functions of the ever-evolving Cloud platforms, also from a graphics point of view. Moreover, it did not have the features necessary for extending it to other countries. A learning platform also creates a sense of belonging and engagement that brings together all the countries, in a project with common lines of development. The adoption of the LMS gives all the players the feeling that they are making big progress compared to the different applications that support training in the different countries. Having an LMS platform that channels all the information is a clear advantage and justifies Enel's decision to make such an investment.

On people management today, the Training Department's focus is to work on a platform that gives user a different way of understanding their own learning and training experience. Employees want to be protagonists. The global training department knows that the challenge is not just to launch homogeneous catalogs rather than online training activities. It is a more difficult challenge. The challenge is to offer people a different way to make them feel protagonists of their learning path. It is very interesting to make people independent and owners of their experience. The project will be supported by the introduction of the Learning Management System platform on 1ˢᵗ December 2017. It will be open to all employees according to the vision of Open Learning. The employees will have direct access to the platform. Attending the course, doing tests, making assessment: everything will be decided by the user. However, if an employee wants to take a classroom course he can do so by applying to the HR.

The platform will help the training managers in the various countries. This is the only tool that can be used to socialize and to have training tools and training processes in common. Today they have very different models. They do not want to overlap with local specifics and cultures, but they want a standard process and a government. On one hand, this platform will help in the process of government, on the other hand it gives employees very powerful functions. People will face this cultural passage of direct participation. Through the platform, employees can share best practices and socialize also through mobile tools and all kinds of devices.

1. **The orientation architecture within the LMS.** The Training Department designed an orientation architecture within the LMS. The employees who enter the LMS should not feel lost in a tide of content. They need to know that there is an architecture that can guide them towards the right training for the job they need to do today and tomorrow, at any stage of the professional life cycle: as a newcomer, as an expert or who is near retirement. By using the data on users' records the Training Department can suggest what courses have been followed by people with the same role, profile, and the same profession. The Training Department is studying how to design the user interface to guarantee that each person can choose his/her learning path. The aim is to point out the possible paths according to the clusters that emerge. The system will show the users' profiles, which will be updated with flexibility and continuity according to the use of the learning system. Training becomes part of the total reward as a benefit. An annual budget of virtual credits will be created individually and at the unit level in a "passport" containing all the courses attended. People can monitor their training. This

can also create engagement because the process is very transparent.Online contents can be created inside Enel (for instance Enel talks, video-tutorials, reverse mentoring, emotional learning). There will be the possibility to ask colleagues: "who can help me?" both colleagues receiving rewards. Enel's employees can organize courses directly. They can suggest a course and collect a number of participants to enable it to take place. The aim is to help employees develop and grow while adding value to all the training. All the steps of the training process will be open and shared: 1) needs analysis with direct listening, 2) delivery with content to share, 3) assessment with a system of "like", sharing and forum community. The new model: is user centric, enhances internal and external resources, with an interface that selects and guides the content choice

2. **The survey on people digital transformation and the "My Training Path" project.** In September 2017 a corporate wide survey on people digital transformation was launched to listen to the voice of employees and define the employee journey they need to be developed. This global survey had an excellent redemption of more than 25,000 respondents with more than 40,000 helpful comments for designing the employee journey. They could identify three employee journeys starting from an initial 30. The aim of the survey is to detect the kind of digitization people need. From the analysis emerged indications that led to a project called "My Training Path". The project involves the possibility for people to be active protagonists of their training experience. The "My Training Path" is one of the employee journeys considered.

The "My Training Path" project is managed by the Training Department with the help of the other HR Departments and other colleagues, for example from ICT. The method they are using is very innovative because the model is agile, fast, multidisciplinary, with an ongoing experimentation with pilot projects

Digital Change Management: a world-wide project for managers. Turning agile in reality

To spread the culture of digitalization and a mindset oriented to change all Enel's managers are involved in a series of workshops in Rome, Madrid and Bogotà. Digitization culture influence the way of thinking and of managing processes and people. The digital mindset in Enel is focused on the conviction that digital transformation must be strongly supported by a change in company's culture and in the way of working. The speed of change is increasing and many managers in Enel are ready with ideas, capacities and processes needed by this cultural transformation. This transformation will involve all the people that works in the Enel Group. The transformation is not only centered on assets and on the approach to their customers. It deeply concern the way of working of their people through their processes. Becoming digital is a concrete change in their way of working. To work in a different way it is necessary to change the cultural mindset. Enel's aim is to find the way to be agile in its complex world. It is important how people work in team and how they try to follow models and connect them with values in an agile perspective.

9.8. Conclusion

To keep up with technological change and to achieve results from the digital transformation process, human capital is essential. Organizations require the right knowledge, skills and experience to drive transformation and sustain a competitive advantage. Technology rapidly evolves and organizations' projects change. The rate of acceleration is so swift that it is hard for talent and knowledge to keep up. The result of our analysis highlights that to prepare the workforce for the digital future it is paramount building the right culture and mind-set at a company level first. Digitization is the new way of doing business and requires a new corporate identity. Both the case studies show this identity change towards a service culture in Cisco and towards "Open Power" in Enel, at a strategic and operational level. Both companies are committed to on-going innovation, flexibility and agility. Another aspect that emerges is the importance to change the organizational structure: Cisco transformed the Service Division with 14,400 employees into a consultative, dynamic, solutions-selling organization; Enel adopted a organizational matrix structure to govern its complexity linked to its large internationalization process. Moreover, eleven Digital Managers have been identified within the Enel Group as Digital Ambassadors. They are awareness-raising activists on digitization issues as part of the Digital Customer Journey Program. The digital transformation of training is framed by this wide process of transformation at a corporate level. The main guidelines are focused on the employee experience to make individuals more and more autonomous in their training choices and development. In Cisco, employees are empowered to take charge of their own careers, learning and development and prepared for current and future job roles by creating their professional development path. Enel has launched the "My Training Path" project to change how HR is perceived. The new decision logic aims to spread self-awareness and responsibility among employees. They can manage their learning and development under the guidance of all the training organizational structures, from a corporate level to country and business line levels. Given this cultural and organizational framework, in both cases, the changes are made possible by digitization with the adoption of advanced, powerful and ever-evolving cloud learning management systems. The Cisco Collaborative Knowledge platform is also open to Cisco's customers. In Enel, the Learning Management System will be extended to the 29 countries where Enel works. It is a common infrastructure and architecture that makes people feel protagonists of their own learning path and owners of their learning experience. These platforms offer the employees the digital tools and technology needed to access the learning and knowledge of their peers as well as experts. Sharing information and knowledge can be done in real time, at any time and anywhere. For Cisco, for instance, employees have instant access to experts, enterprise-wide repositories of collective knowledge and social learning and collaboration tools. The aim is to develop collaborative, virtualized and accessible education delivered in real time, in order to advance education and learning innovation.

In both cases, Cisco and Enel, the digital transformation of training, learning and knowledge sharing is taking place successfully. Two aspects remain open for further investigation and research; on the one hand how employees can accept the implementation of new and continually updated technological systems. On the other hand how Training Departments can evaluate the return of their investment and how effective the new model is on employees' learning and on corporate performance.

References

Ala-Mutka K. (2016). *Mapping Digital Competence: Towards a Conceptual Understanding*, European Commission – IPTS, Luxembourg, Publications Office of the European Union.

Albano R., Fabbri T.M. (2010). Competenze per l'apprendimento organizzativo. Un approccio simoniano. *Rassegna Italiana di Sociologia*, 2, 255-282.

Attaran M. (2004). Exploring the relationship between IT and business process reengineering, *Information and Management*, vol.41(5), 585-596.

Baird D.E., Fisher M., (2005). Neomillenial User Experience Design Strategies: Utilizing Social Networking Media to Support *"Always On"* Learning Styles, *Journal Educational Technology Systems*, vol.34(1), 5-32.

Baird Z., Buolamwini J., Fallows J. Ng A., (2017). The evolution of employment and skills in the age of AI, *McKinsey Quarterly*, August.

Billet S., Choy S., (2013). Learning through Work: Emerging Perspectives and New Challenges, *Journal of Workplace Learning*, vol.25(4), 264-276.

Bingi P., Sharma M.K., Godla J.K. (1999). Critical Issue Affecting an ERP Implementation, *Information Systems Management*, vol.16(3), 7-14.

Birkinshaw J., Ridderstrale J., (2015). Adhocracy for an Agile Age, *McKinsey Quarterly*, December.

Bissola R., Imperatori B. (2013). Enhancing the Relationship between Generation Y and the HR Department through e-HR, *HRZone*, Nov., 47-50.

Bodega D. (1997). *Le architetture organizzative. L'adhocrazia. Manuale di Organizzazione aziendale*. A cura di Costa G. e Nacamulli R.C.D., *Manuale di Organizzazione Aziendale. La progettazione organizzativa*. Utet Libreria, vol.2, 536-574.

Bondarouk T., Parry E. & Furtmueller E. (2017). Electronic HRM: Four Decades of Research on Adoption and Consequences, *The International Journal of Human Resource Management*, vol. 28(1), 98-131.

Bondarouk T., Ruël H. J. M., Parry E., (2017). *Electronic HRM in the Smart Era*, Emerald Publishing UK.

Burke, L. A. & Hutchins, H.M. (2007). Training Transfer: An Integrative Literature Review. *Human Resource Development Review*, 6, 263-296.

Comacchio A., Scapolan AC, (2004). The Adoption Process of Corporate e-Learning in Italy, *Education &Training*, 46, 6/7.

Corporate leadership Council/ Learning and Development Roundtable – Employee's Development Survey cited in: www.slideshare.net/charlesjennings/the-702010-framework.

DalleMule L., Davenport T.H., (2017). What's your Data Strategy?, *Harvard Business Review*, May-June.

De Oliveira P.C., De Almeida Cunha C.J.C., Nakayama M.K., (2016). Learning Management Systems and E-Learning Management: an Integrative Review and Research Agenda, *Journal of Information Systems and Technology Management*, vol.13(2) May-Aug, 157-180.

Hunt C.S. (2014). Managing Human Capital in the Digital Era, *People & Strategy*, vol. 37(2), 36-41.

Hart J. (2017). *Learning in the Modern Workplace*, Centre for Learning and Performance Technologies.

Iansiti M., Lakhani K.R., (2014). Digital Ubiquity: How Connections, Sensors and Data are Revolutionizing Business, *Harvard Business Review*, Nov.

Kane G.C. et al. (2017). Achieving Digital Maturity, Adapting your Company to a Changing World, 6th Annual Survey, *MIT Sloan Management Review*, Deloitte University Press.

London M., Hall M.J., (2011). Unlocking the value of Web 2.0 Technologies for training and development: the shift from instructor-controlled, adaptive learning to learner driven, generative learning. *Human Resource Management*, vol.50(6), Nov-Dec, 757-775.

Malcom J., Hodkinson P., Colley H. (2003). The Interrelationships between Informal and Formal Learning, *Journal of Workplace Learning*, vol.15(7/8), 313-318.

Mintzberg H. (1983). *Structure in Five. Designing Effective Organizations*, Prentice Hall, Englewood Cliffs.

Murawski M., Bick M. (2017). Digital Competences of the workforce – A Research topic? , *Business Process Management Journal*, vol.23(3), 721-734.

Pine II B.J., Gilmore J.H. (2011). *The Experience Economy: Work is Theatre & Every Business a Stage*. HBR Press, Boston Massachusetts.

Puthiyamadam T. (2017). How the Meaning of Digital Transformation Has Evolved, *HBR.org*, Digital Article.

Rigby D.K., Sutherland J., Takeuchi H., (2016). *Harvard Business Review*, May

Ruël H., Bondarouk T., Looise J.K. (2004). E-HRM: Innovation or Irritation. An Explorative Empirical Study in Five Large Companies on Web-based HRM, *Management revue. The International Review of Management Studies*, vol.15(3), 364-381.

Senge, P.M. *The Fifth Discipline: The Art and Practice of the Learning Organization*. Doubleday Business, New York, 1990, revised 2006.

Toonders J. https://www.wired.com/insights/2014/07/data-new-oil-digital-economy/

Van Laar E., Van Deursen A.J.A.M.,Van Dijk J., De Haan J., (2017). The relation between 21st – Century skills and digital skills: a systematic literature review, *Computers in Human Behavior*, March, 72, 577-588.

Younger J. (2016). How Learning and Development are becoming more agile, *HBR.org*, Digital Article, 11 October.

Za S., Spagnoletti P., North-Samardzic A., (2014). Organizational Learning as an emerging process: the generative role of digital tools in informal learning practices. *British Journal of Educational Technology*, vol.45(6), 1023-1035.

Chapter 10

SOCIAL MEDIA STRATEGY WITHIN ORGANIZATIONAL COMMUNICATION: MAJOR OPEN ISSUES AND CHALLENGES

Francesca Di Virgilio-Mónica Valderrama Santomé-Alba López Bolás

SUMMARY: 10.1. Introduction. – 10.2. Social media definitions and research topics. – 10.3. Social media practice and user behavior. – 10.4. Social media strategy within organizational communication. – 10.5. Social media security and the impact on the organizational communication: some scientific enquiries. – 10.5.1. Various attacks on social media. – 10.6. Future research directions. – 10.7. Conclusion. – References.

10.1. Introduction

In recent years there is an increasing usage of web 2.0 technologies from a group and managerial point of view (Di Virgilio, 2018a; Gaál et al. 2015; Usman, & Oyefolahan, 2014; Yassin, et al. 2013).

Web technologies have enabled people to create and share what they have in mind with others around the world. Web technologies cover a wide set of publishing tools and social networking that enable users to combine or render content in new and novel form. The simple reason is that web tools are new social web that enable collaboration, contribution, and interactions (Eijkman, 2011; Di Virgilio, 2018a).

As a consequence, the availability of user-generated contents is growing rapidly, due to the new and easy tools provided by these technologies, which people are able to make use of social media tools in order to increase range and richness of their networks, gather information and nowadays, increasingly organizations are finding ways of integrating social media into their business processes (Gaál et al., 2014).

The capability of managing information becomes a core competence of the firm in creating competitive long term strategies. Since social media websites are powerful tools used to expand one's network and help in connecting with acquaintances and strangers (Chang et al., 2015), as the proliferation and the use of social media apps improve, firms have a great opportunity to determine consumers' requirements and needs by involving consumers in panel questionnaires and interviews. A broad variety of social media tools enable firms to connect with a wide range of potential and existing customers (Briones, et al., 2011; Chang et al., 2015; Wu, 2016; Bianchi & Andrews, 2015; Curran & Lennon, 2011; Di Virgilio & Antonelli, 2018), to post contents, share ideas, learn and fulfill social needs (Ferreira, et al., 2014). In particular, a growing number of companies recognize that social media provide a means to communicate and change the business model while creating new opportunities (Kim & Ko, 2012; Sashi, 2012, Wu, 2016; Chang et al., 2015; Culnan et al., 2010).

In particular, there is urgency for studies with a strong theoretical foundation that might offer a last in guidance within a phenomenon that evolves dramatically on a daily basis. More specifically, the extant research on social media has been placing its focus on how large-size companies or incumbents in the one hand, and users or customers on the other hand, adopt and use social media (Aral et al., 2013). Therefore, the literature has been dealing with the investigation of antecedents, moderators, mediators and outcomes of social media adoption, as well as its impacts on the organizational and individual level (Ngai et al., 2015; Ghezzi et al., 2016).

In this regards, two missing links emerge. The first, the social media phenomenon arose as an applied paradigm for communication and networking among individuals, with a limited or fuzzy theorization backing it (Ngai et al., 2015; Ghezzi et al., 2016). The second, relatively little attention has been paid to new platforms, new scenes, and new applications of social media, practical application problems have been derived that are related to security control mechanism and individual privacy protection (Zhang, 2015; Di Virgilio, 2018b). Considering the emergence of trust and even risk into security issues, the investigation of social media security would be more sophisticated and challenging than ever before, as combined with explosive social users, as well as their various identifications, roles, groups and corresponding behaviors. Therefore, security of the fundamental platforms is important to various aspects of social media strategy in order to establish a credible, safe, and lasting social platform (Zhang, 2015; Di Virgilio, 2018b).

In this scenario, we organized the chapter in different parts. In the first part we make a contribution to the body of literature by examining the definitions and functionalities of social media platforms and the major open issues. In the second part, we analyze the outcomes of the applications of social media on the individual and organizational levels and then we investigate the crucial role of security to play in social media strategy. Finally we identify three scientific inquiries which are the results of the literature review. We close the chapter by discussing future research directions for this work. This approach introduces a new framework applicable both as a tool for enhancing the understanding the role of social media mechanisms for organizational communication, and as a useful guide to future research on social media innovation and social media strategy as a whole.

By identifying and discussing the main application domains, the chapter will shed first light on the current and future streams of innovation in social media, thus pointing at future research directions while providing practitioners with guidelines on the innovation paths they should follow to integrate or complement their social media efforts.

10.2. Social media definitions and research topics

The literature defines social media as a variety of broad definitions, such as "collaborative online applications and technologies which enable and encourage participation, conversation, openness, creation and socialization amongst a community of users" (Bowley, 2009, p. 15), web-based tools and practices enabling participation and collaboration based on individuals' activities (Storey et al., 2010). Surowiecki (2005) defined that social media is to make use of the "wisdom of the crowd". Group of people are better at problem solving, fostering decision making than the individuals alone, a group of Internet-based applications that build on the ideological and technological foundations of Web 2.0 technology, and that allow the creation and exchange of user-generated content (Bianchi & Andrews, 2015; Chang et al., 2015; Kaplan & Haenlein, 2010).

Several studies, (Vuori, 2011; Jalonen, 2014; Bonson and Flores, 2011) characterises social media by considering the extent to which they support communication (social media provides new tools to share, store and publish contents, discuss and express opinions and influence); collaboration (social media enables collective content creation and edition without location and time constraints), connecting (social media offers new ways of networking with other people, socializing oneself into the community), completing (social media tools are used to complete content by describing, adding or filtering information, tagging contents, and showing a connection between contents and combining social media tools are developed for mixing and matching contents) and combination of pre-existing web services that allow a certain user within a platform to use another application, in a specific window, without the need to get out of the initial website. Tab. 1 represents an analysis of these aspects with technologies and tools.

Table 1. Five C (Jalonen, 2014).

Five C	Technologies	Tools
Communication	Blogs	Blogger
	microblogs	Twitter
	Video sharing	YouTube
	Presentation sharing	Slide Share
	Instant messaging service	Skype
Collaboration	Wikis	Wikipedia
	Groupware/shared workspaces	Google Docs
Connecting	Social networking services	Facebook LinkedIn
Completing	Visual bookmarking tool	Pinterest
	News aggregator	Digg
Combining	Mash-ups	Google Maps

Social media have changed the classic business dynamics. Through more efficient communication means, such as blogs (like Blogger), video sharing (like YouTube), presentation sharing (like SlideShare), social networking service (like Facebook, LinkedIn), instant messaging service (like Skype) and groupware (like Google Docs) - foster a more socially connected platform (Anderson, 2007; Curran & Lennon, 2011), social media facilitate promotion among dispersed individuals with seemingly, marginal concerns (Rodriguez, et al., 2012), they foster mutual enrichment through conversation, exchange, and participation (Whelan et al., 2011) and they reduce transaction and coordination costs. In addition, social media platforms allow sales people to coordinate internal value-creating functions and deliver superior value in customer relationships (Bharadwaj, 2000; Kaplan & Haenlien, 2009). In doing so, they represent an important marketing strategy in which organizations build relationships with customers (Agnihotri et al., 2012; Culnan et al., 2010). Social media also capture the attention of managers. A recent global survey of managers has found that almost half of the buyers pay attention to social media's role when involved in the buying process (Agnihotri, et al., 2012). Kaplan and Haenlein (2011) and Sashi (2012) define social media marketing as electronic-word-of-mouth and as a sort of marketing message of a firm, brand, or product. Despite buyers' strong enthusiasm, many firms remain skeptical about embracing social media to assist the marketing function (Ferreira et al., 2014; Sashi, 2012; Bruhn et al., 2012).

Several research has been conducted about using social media and Web 2.0 in the workplace for sharing knowledge (Di Virgilio, 2018a). Paroutis and Saleh (2009) investigated the key determinants of knowledge sharing and collaboration using Web 2.0 technologies by exploring the reasons for and barriers to employees' active participation in its various platforms within a large multinational firm. Their study identifies the key determinants of knowledge sharing and collaboration using Web 2.0 technologies by exploring the reasons for and barriers to employees' active participation in its various platforms within a large multinational firm. Using insights from both users and non-users of Web 2.0, the following four key determinants were identified: history, outcome expectations, perceived organizational support and trust. Dumbrell and Steele (2014) presented an informal knowledge management framework based on the system capabilities present in social media technologies as well as the requirements of older adult users. The system capabilities distinctive to social media technologies are: public peer-to-peer sharing, content evaluation amongst peers, and the "push" nature of these systems. Behringer and Sassenberg (2015) studied the relation between importance of knowledge exchange, deficits in knowledge exchange, perceived usefulness of social media for knowledge exchange, as well as social media experience on the one hand and the intention to use knowledge exchange technology on the other hand. The results showed that the interplay between the importance and deficits concerning knowledge exchange, perceived usefulness of social media for knowledge exchange, and experience in social media use jointly affected the intention to apply social media for knowledge exchange after their implementation.

Another study (Sigalaa & Chalkiti, 2015) investigates the relation between social media use and employee creativity by adopting a knowledge management approach in order to consider the influence of social networks and interactions on individuals' creativity. Their findings highlight the need to shift focus from identifying and managing creative individuals (micro level) and/or organizational contexts (macro level) to creating and managing creative social networks (meso level). The use of social media for externalizing, disseminating and discussing information with others within various social networks as well as for combining and generating shared (new) knowledge can further trigger, enrich and expand the employees' individual cognitive abilities and provide them with stimuli for generating and (co)-creating more and newer ideas/knowledge.

Another interesting categorization is the one base on social media functionalities.

Kietzman et al. (2011) divided social media's features and functionalities into seven blocks:

1. Identity: is the extent to which users reveal themselves by adjusting data privacy control or using tools for self-promotion;
2. Reputation: it is the extent to which users can identify the social standing of others in social media settings;
3. Relationship: is about the relations between users; two or more users may have something in common that connect them, like the same friends or favorite music;
4. Presence: is about giving possibility to check whether other users are available, e.g. willing to talk or not;
5. Sharing: represents the extent to which users exchange, distribute, and receive content; as a whole, it is a measure of how "social" users or customers are;
6. Conversation: it is the extent to which users communicate with each other and implies different communication formats and protocols for both users who wish to use specific social media tools and firms who seek to host and track such conversations;
7. Groups: represent the extent to which users are ordered or form communities defining membership rules and protocols to be followed in the various communication activities. Utilized individually or together, these blocks can help mangers making sense of the social media ecology, and better understanding both their audience as well as their engagement needs (Kietzmanet al., 2011).

From this viewpoint, researchers have explored possible applications as well as business impacts on companies. The various contributions can be grouped into two main research streams. A first stream is labelled as social recruitment, which discusses the potential role social media might play as a recruitment tool to support the human resource department (Doherty, 2010).This possibly promising area is still under-investigated in the innovation management and information systems research. A second stream focuses on the analysis, management and prediction of social media users' behavior (Ansari et al., 2011; Tan et al., 2011; Stieglitz & Dang-Xuan, 2013) as well as on social media related content that a company might deliver through or extract from social platforms (Kaplan& Haenlein, 2010; Kietzman et al., 2011).

A recent literature review (Ngai et al., 2015; Ghezzi et al., 2016; Di Virgilio, 2018a) concluded that social media covers a wide range of research topics, cross cutting three major research theories, namely: personal behavior theories, social behavior theories and mass communication theories, which in turn may be split into thirty-one different sub-streams of research, the most widely referred to being: technology acceptance, social capital theory, social identity theory, social influence theory, uses and gratifications theory, personal traits theory, theory of planned behavior, social cognitive theory, expectation and disconfirmation paradigm, social exchange theory and social network analysis.

10.3. Social media practice and user behavior

In the last years, several authors (Enders, et al., 2008; Kietzman, et al., 2011) remarked how companies have paradigmatically changed the way they are organized and managed, as well as how they compete. The broad social media practice embeds a number of new tools and approaches that have the potential to support or enhance these strategic, organizational and managerial modifications (Ngai et al., 2015), to innovate their business models and managerial practices (He et al., 2013; Luo et al., 2013, Ghezzi et al., 2016).

Ngai et al. (2015) hence develop the causal-chain framework for social media research which identifies the inter-relationships of different research dimensions and constructs linking to causes and results of users' behavior in the adoption of social media. Antecedents of users' behavior refer to social factors (e.g., social capital), users' attributes (e.g., user personality) and organizational attributes (e.g., marketing orientation). Users' behavior is also mediated by platform attributes (e.g., tool integrity), social factors (e.g., social influence) and users' attributes (e.g., user behavior), while it is moderated by user characteristics (e.g., user personality) and social factors (e.g. social influence). Out-comes affect both the personal context (e.g. user intention) and the organizational context (e.g., customer relationship). Such framework helps shedding light on the multifaceted impacts of social media both at individual and organizational levels.

When discussing the outcomes and impacts of the above mentioned applications of social media, the extant literature focuses on the organizational and the individual levels (Ngai et al., 2015; Ghezzi et al., 2016).

At the individual level, social media offer the opportunity to break communication barriers and help people expanding their social circles. However, notwithstanding these positive impacts, possible drawbacks may be associated to the use of these tools and instruments, such as: the decrease of real life interactions and the subsequent impoverishment of actual experience as social media replace other face-to-face, less-mediated communication channels (Hanna et al., 2011).

The negative effects of social media usage, like the so called "social overload" determined by an excessive use of and reliance on technological tools, thus leading to social exhaustion or the intention to discontinue social media use (Maier et al., 2015).

The risk that a wrong usage of social media could bring tensions among the employees within a company, where a bad reputational impact may lead to distrust on colleagues and bosses (Kumar & Devi, 2014).

An excessive reliance on social media-related information may create perception biases, as a person could base his thoughts only on the basis of social media reputation, avoiding the real knowledge of colleagues' strengths and weaknesses (Nagendra, 2014).

In particular employees communicate in social media and contribute to the company's image and reputation (Julich, 2012). The role of internal communication expands in the direction of getting feedback from within the organization. Classic communication, through traditional channels, no longer satisfies the needs of employees, nor does it create the feeling of belonging to a group. The external public perceives the employees as true ambassadors of the company and thus feedback takes on a major role in building its reputation (Badea, 2014). Wahlroos (2010) examines the role of benefits, costs, and experience with social media in relation to individual factors to share knowledge among employees using social media. The outcome of the research shows that benefits and experience with social media have a significant impact on personal factors while the influence of costs was not supported by the study.

Positive results can be achieved only through proper training and control of those users and employees who are in charge to use companies' social media platforms or to gather customer related information (Kaplan & Haenlein, 2010; Martini, et al., 2013).

The challenge for organizations is whether they will make their structures flexible and harmonized so as to successfully integrate social media into the communication policy.

10.4. Social media strategy within organizational communication

At the organization level, social media allow people to connect, share information, and participate in all business processes. In order to position social media within communication, we must first highlight their particularities. Specialists in the field (Kaplan & Haenlein, 2010; Badea, 2014) believe that social media represent a group of Internet-based applications which rely on ideological and technological principles of Web 2.0 and allow the creation and exchange of user-generated content. The term "Web 2.0" was generated by O'Reilly (2005). It refers to technologies that allow individuals to interactively participate with information and with other individuals, and to build networks based on mutual personal or professional interest. Web 2.0 facilitates social networking therefore is also referred to as the social media.

In this context, the issue of positioning social media within the communication strategy is being raised. Many specialists place the use of the new media within the application mechanism of public relations. These aim primarily to transmit information in order to facilitate communication and mutual understanding among various institutions and various audience types. The new breakthroughs and technical applications create new opportunities for public relations experts. Thus, modern communication techniques can reach to increasingly larger audiences much faster (Badea, 2014).

Thus communication will address not only the consuming mass and potential or existing customers, but also a large and diversified mass of audiences: employees, shareholders, partners, channels, analysts, investors, suppliers, public administrators (Public Affairs and lobby), non-profit organizations (social political engagement), geographical community, mass-media (online and offline) etc. Tudor (2013) places social media alongside public relations within the integrated organizational communication elements.

At the same time, the new communication technologies bring along, beside their numerous advantages, unexpected challenges as well, therefore the preparation of online messages should involve a much more elaborated and applied creative work than for traditional media (Badea, 2014).

The question is, if social media should be used by all companies and, on the other, if the organizations which use them should adopt proactive strategies for this environment. It is obvious that not all companies use social media, at least for product promotion. If target audiences are not Internet users, then this attempt is futile (for example, rural aging population). The company addressing these audiences must see, however, if social media are somehow necessary for brand or internal communication. It should also be taken into account whether the organization is prepared for social media implementation and which are the potential barriers that can block this attempt. Moreover, the resources required for implementation shall be considered and it shall be established whether the goals of social media communication should be enclosed in the general goals of organizational communication.

Social media strategy implementation and results should be followed by the top management because these channels are not just a means of communication but also one of relating to customers (Badea, 2014).

Performance indicators for social media are set from the beginning, when the strategy in the field is being built, depending on the company communication and business goals: reputation, brand associations, turnover. The following can be mentioned (Botezatu, 2012):

- qualitative indicators: degree of community involvement, relevance of general conversations, quality of the content published;
- quantitative indicators: number of fans/followers/members, number of shares generated by them (likes, comments, tweets, retweets, shares, mentions, referrals etc.);

In a similar approach, Tudor (2013) shows the steps to pursue in creating an online communication strategy, as follows: setting goals, short-term; medium-term; long-term; choosing the mix of communication channels, establishing work policies; making the editorial plan; implementing; continuous monitoring.

Internally, social media can contribute to a number of organizational dimensions: improvement of communication processes, community development, facilitation of information flow, promotion of values and consolidation of organizational culture, stimulation of creativity, even of collective intelligence, under optimum conditions (Badea, 2014).

Social media adoption constraints emerge as difficult to counteract limits, whether we speak about hesitation (users do not know how to use social media and find difficulties in adopting the technology), incertitude (the user has opinions regarding the low potential of the communication means) or conditions of reduced adaptability of the organizational environment and the list could go on depending on the social-economic and cultural background in which the organization operates (Ciochina, 2013).

Risks may appear following the use of social media (Zhang, 2015; Zhang, & Gupta, 2016), they are related to information security, to how employees are supervised, the way resources are granted, time management, how organizational culture and online identity manifest themselves and to the implementation and management of the new technologies (the lack of knowledge and understanding of social media).

10.5. Social media security and the impact on the organizational communication: some scientific enquiries

The never ending security breaches over social media have entitled the organizations to safeguard the information that is shared over the network.

Any violation to security hinders directly with economic growth of the organization (Zhang, 2015; Zhang, & Gupta, 2016). The social media can be analyzed by studying the behavior of its users, which might be an individual or group. The Internet users need to be well informed about the threats that are faced by their personal and financial information. They should be able to behave securely and use reliable security measures at their aid. The behavior depends on their actual realization and their experience over the social media.

Another factor that affects the users' perception is whether or not they consider and carefully go through the security notices and direction issued at various social networking sites. Although, now it seems that regular reports of privacy and security attacks on the news have made the users more considerate about their behavior. The business organizations are also making more efforts in protecting their consumers' private information because any harm will lead to loss of consumer trust.

In order to study social media strategy and privacy formation is to investigate the perceived control from the users' point of view.

Perceived control here can be defined as the users' realization of their own control over their information. It is considered to be an efficient tool for the prediction of user behavior, better than actual control.

The concept of perceived control stems from presumption that user has supremacy over the social network habitat (Hoadley et al., 2010; Lee, 2012). Perceived control can be:

- behavioral, which refers to users' tendency to adapt according to circumstance;
- decisional, which refers to ability of the user to successfully obtain the desired outcome out of circumstances based on his/her actions and conclusion;
- cognitive, which notifies whether or not the user is able to understand the circumstances.

We can also refer perceived control as the amount of control users assumes that he/she is having however, it is not actually there. Actual control however, is generally taken into consideration while performing hypothetical interpretations. It determines the degree of true hold that user possess over the network.

Perceived control is defined as an emissary of actual control. It plays a very prominent role in relieving the privacy and trust issues of the user. Hajli and Lin (2016) studied the role of perception control and risks on user behavior. They stated that the increase in the degree of perceived control affects the user behavior positively and leads to increased information sharing whereas any perceived privacy vulnerability have a negative effect on user behavior. Vladlena and collegues (2015), analyzed user behavior over social media based on their attention to security notices and features. They stated that user who use social media more frequently are more likely to observe such notices. However, the users having previous experiences are less likely to observe these notices. Similarly, the victims of online fraud are more likely to pay attention to security notices (Vladlena et al., 2015; Mohamed & Ahmad, 2012; Zhang, & Gupta, 2016).

However, in this study we ask three important scientific questions regarding the role of security on social media strategy within organizational communication. Hence we posit that:

1) Security affects the perceived control of the social media platforms as supporting tool for organizational communication?
2) Which mechanism carries the effects of security on social media strategy?
3) Security has a direct influence on the trust toward the social media platforms?

10.5.1. Various attacks on social media

The various types of social media platforms invite a variety of attacks towards them, which tend to steal users' identity or threaten then privacy and trust over the network (Joshi & Kuo, 2011; Cutillo et al. 2010; Zhang, 2015; Zhang & Gupta, 2016). In this paragraph, we present the some attacks which are prominent over the social media these days (see Tab. 2):

Table 2. Various attacks and impact on user (Zhang & Gupta, 2016).

Attacks	Impact on user
Identity theft	This refers to the real time impersonation of legitimate user, the attacker takes control the target profile and is able to successfully other genuine user that the profile belongs to him. Here the attacker misuses the profile in any way possible which could have severe impact on the user whose identity it was once
Spam attack	Here, the attacker somehow obtains communication details about the user and are able to send spam or junk data. The communication details are not that hard to obtain, they can be extracted by the profiles of the legitimate user. The spam emails send in bulk cause network congestion and cost of sending emails falls mo-

	stly upon the service providers and sometimes on the user.
Malware attacks	They are becoming very common among social networking sites these. The attackers send malware injected scripts to the legitimate user. On clicking the malicious URL a malware might be installed on the attackers devices or it can lead to a fake website which attempts to steal some personal information from the target user.
Sybil attacks	Fake profiles are the foundation for Sybil attacks, which can be harm the proper functioning of the social media platform, they can be used for the distribution of junk information or even malware over the network. To prevent these attacks the authentication mechanisms while user registration should be stronger.
Social phishing	It refers to the attack where the attacker aims to obtain sensitive information from a target user via some fake website which appears to be real or by impersonating someone the target is acquainted with. These attacks can be significantly reduced if the users are aware and should examine the data they receive carefully beforehand.
Impersonation	Here the aim of the attacker is to create fake profile in order to successfully impersonate a real-world person. This attack highly depend on the authentication techniques that are faced by the users while registration to make new account. These attacks can do serious damage to the target which is being impersonated.
Hijacking	It refers to acquiring control over someone else's profile. The attacker is successful in hijacking a legitimate profile if they are able to crack login password of the account. Weak passwords are thus a poor choice as they increase the threat of hijacking such passwords can be obtained by dictionary attacks. Strong passwords and changing them frequently is good practice.
Fake requests	The attacker sends fake request with their own profile, so as to enlarge their network. If the users accept fake request it gives the attacker more privileges and they are able to more information from the victim profiles. The prevention of fake requests is not possible, thus, the user should be more responsible over the social media.

Image retrieval and analysis	The attacker here uses various face and image recognition software to find more information about the target and its linked profiles. It not only affects the target but also his/her friends and family. This attacks aims to gather images videos etc. from the target.

In earlier studies, Barbara and colleagues (2011) pointed out that an enhanced access control system for social networks is the first step for addressing the security and privacy problems of online networking.

With regard to the personal information disclosure and privacy protection of social media users, Fogues and colleagues (2015) represented that given the explosive increase of users in the last few years, the current beneficial services of Social Networking Service (SNS), like Facebook and Twitter, are being overshadowed because of the existence of a privacy hazard while providing convenience and rich experiences to social users. Therefore, they listed all privacy hazards that may potentially affect the privacy threat of SNSs users, together with the requirements of privacy mechanism to realize the restraint of threats. They further described and analyzed the current solutions that can cover the range and degree of important needs. Viejo and colleagues (2016) indicates that the big data released on social media platforms contains sensitive personal information that can be collected and utilized by external entities for profit. However, the current solutions mainly adopt strict access control means for protection, but do not support users to know which content are sensitive and confidential. Furthermore, current solutions require social media operators to participate to realize the control mechanism; therefore these solutions may not be practical.

10.6. Future research directions

From a research perspective, this chapter sets a broad agenda for future research. Given the nascent nature of the study phenomenon, there are many exciting opportunities for new research. This study has also aimed to contribute to the management and organizational disciplines in two principal and differentiated but related ways.

First, future studies should compare firms that use this approach of social media tools with those that do not and determine the impact on organizational communication. At a larger scale a comparison could be made between a firm that uses this approach and one that does not in terms of the impact on job satisfaction, employee loyalty, and development of new idea.

The issue of how to effectively design and deploy security in this approach is the second future research direction. It has become clear that security offers many opportunities for firms to interact with their groups along the entire organizational structures and communication flows.

Future research could analyse and develop training system for employees and companies to gather data from the security with respect to variables governing the dynamics within individual or group. Using the determinants interpretation of social media, and guided by the theoretical approaches from related research in business and management, this chapter provides an analytical approach to explore the organizational communication investigating the influence of social media tools and security on organizational structures and communication flows. Our study shows that there are some important potential applications of social media strategy in the study of organizational communication, with an outline of the major theoretical approaches to these applications.

Furthermore, companies have to clearly identify what information and knowledge is to be kept confidential and what is to be shared and made available to others. Such practices as crowd-sourcing and open innovation practices have demonstrated the value of sharing information that has previously been considered to be confidential. In this study, social media emerges a new perspective (Di Virgilio, 2018a). Enormous information can be shared using powerful tools to a world in which the social factors play an essential role. In our new accelerated world, numerous technologies have been developed to support social capital connections (social networking services like Facebook, LinkedIn) and to communicate in a more effective way (instant messaging services like Skype, Viber).

For organizations that ensure value of organizational communication, integrating social media tools into their daily business life is essential to enable for the employees an easy access; and offer trainings to inexperienced users. The social media can be analyzed by studying the behavior of its' users, which might be an individual or organization. The Internet users need to be well-informed about the threats that are faced by their personal and financial information. They should be able to behave securely and use reliable security measures at their aid. The direction is significantly theoretical meaningful for realizing secure interaction, sharing and digital rights management of social media content, continuously improving platform security. It has also better applicable vision and practical application value for healthy, normal and rapid development of digital media content industry. Building and strengthening trustworthiness will provide awareness and guarantee of safety to users.

Practitioners can use this study to evaluate the role of social media strategy within organizational communication and better target future interventions towards security most likely to benefit. From a better understanding of the determinants, a company will have greater understanding of the true needs and expectations of human resources.

10.7. Conclusion

In this chapter highlights the numerous opportunities exist using social media tools in action in business organization, communication between employees can be encouraged to support problem solving: if organization needs an expert for a specific task, a post can be placed on a blog and likely receive a response from another employee or search on LinkedIn to find a person, who can help.

Discuss professional problems: with a group of people who are active practitioners in a particular area, professional communities can be useful because they are neutral and can provide a way to share best practices, ask questions of and provide support for each other outside the organization. Reduce time and money through integrated system: using a new technology, the calendar, but not because of the calendar function, but organizing and sharing events, meetings, making appointment in a shorter time (instead of phone calls or sending lots of e-mails). The great challenge for the future is the development of organizational structures and processes that are flexible enough to meet the communicative demands in the era of social media.

This chapter has shown how users are stimulated through social media use and how internal and external communication can thus be highlighted. The study has also presented several social media strategies and illustrated some of the constraints and risks which organizations that use this modern communication method are subject to.

Nowadays it's very difficult to evaluate the role of security on social media strategies because no one is able to learn and valuate security's dynamics and understand how to help organizational communication. Anyway, considering that social media is global, cross-cultural research on the organizational communication effect would be an interesting issue.

Several managerial implications can also be utilized. It is recommended for management to support introducing social media technologies, establish the terms and conditions of usage, communicate the benefits and provide the necessary trainings.

References

Agnihotri, R., Kothandaraman, P., Kashyap, R., & Singh, R. (2012). Bringing "social" into sales: The impact of salespeople's social media use on service behaviors and value creation. *Journal of Personal Selling & Sales Management, 22*(3), 333-348.

Anderson, P. (2007). What is Web 2.0? Ideas, technologies and implications for education, JISC reports, [Online], Available: http://www.jisc.ac.uk/media/documents/techwatch/tsw0701b.p.

Ansari, A., Koenigsberg, O., & Stahl, F. (2011). Modeling multiple relationships in social Networks. *Journal of Marketing Research*, *48*(4), 713-728.

Aral, S., Dellarocas, C., & Godes, D. (2013). Social media and business transformation: a framework for research. *Information Systems Research*, *24*(1), 3-13.

Badea, M. (2014). Social Media and Organizational Communication. *Social and Behavioral Sciences, 149*, 70-75

Barbara, C., Elena, F. & Raymond, H. (2011). Semantic web-based social network access control. *Computer Security*, *30*(2), 108-115.

Behringer, N. & Sassenberg, K. (2015). Introducing social media for knowledge management: Determinants of employees' intentions to adopt new tools. *Computers in Human Behavior*, *48*, 290-296.

Bharadwaj, A.S. (2000). A resource-based perspective on information technology capability and firm performance: An empirical investigation. *MIS Quarterly*, *24*(1), 169-196.

Bianchi, C., & Andrews, L. (2015). Investigating marketing managers' perspectives on social media in Chile. *Journal of Business Research*, *68*(12), 2552–2559.

Bonson, E. & Flores, F. (2011). Social media and corporate dialogue: the response of the global financial institutions. *Online Information Review*, *35* (1), 34-49.

Botezatu, A. (2012). Cum sa iti faci strategia de social media. Startups.ro. Retrieved from http://www.startups.ro/tutoriale/cum-sa-iti-facistrategia-de-social-media

Bowley, R. C. (2009). A comparative case study: Examining the organizational use of social networking sites. Thesis, The University of Waikato, Hamilton, [Online], Available: http://researchcommons.waikato.ac.nz/bitstream/handle/10289/3590/thesis.pdf?sequence=1&isAllowed=y.

Briones, R.L., Kuch, B., Liu, B.F., & Jin, Y. (2011). Keeping up with the digital age: How the American Red Cross uses social media to build relationships. *Public Relations Review*, *37*(1), 37–43.

Bruhn, M., Schoenmueller, V., & Schafer, D.B. (2012). Are social media replacing traditional media in terms of brand equity creation? *Management Research Review*, *35*(9), 770–790.

Chang, Y., Yu, H., & Lu, H. (2015). Persuasive messages, popularity cohesion, and message diffusion in social media marketing. *Journal of Business Research*, *68*(4), 777-782.

Chih-Wen Wu, (2016). The performance impact of social media in the chain store industry. *Journal of Business Research*, *69*, 5310-5316.

Ciochina, R. (2013). Social media si comunicarea interna: pasi marunti, nesiguri. Organizational Learning RO. Retrieved from -http://organizationslearning. wordpress.com/2013/12/21/social-media-si-comunicarea-interna-pasi-marunti-nesiguri

Culnan, M., McHugh, P., & Zubillaga, J. (2010). How large U.S. companies can use twitter and other social media to gain business value. *MIS Quarterly Executive, 9*(4), 243-259.

Curran, J., & Lennon, R. (2011). Participating in the conversation: Exploring usage of social media. *Academy of Marketing Studies Journal, 15*(1), 21-38.

Cutillo, L.A., Manulis, M. & Strufe, T. (2010). Security and privacy in online social networks. In: *Handbook of Social Network, Technologies and Applications.* Springer.

Di Virgilio, F. (Ed.) (2018a). *Social Media for Knowledge Management Applications in Modern Organizations.* Pennsylvania, USA: IGI Global.

Di Virgilio, F. (2018b). Exploring determinants of knowledge sharing: the role of social media in business organizations. Overview and new direction. In Di Virgilio, F. (Ed.), *Social Media for Knowledge Management Applications in Modern Organizations.* Pennsylvania, USA: IGI Global (pp. 1-30).

Di Virgilio, F. & Antonelli, G. (2018). Consumer behavior, trust and electronic word-of-mouth communication: toward a model of understanding of consumer's purchase intentions online. In Di Virgilio, F. (Ed.), *Social Media for Knowledge Management Applications in Modern Organizations*, Pennsylvania, USA: IGI Global (pp. 58-80).

Doherty, R. (2010). Getting social with recruitment. *Strategic HR Review, 9*(6),11–15.

Dumbrell, D. & Steele, R. (2014). Social Media Technologies for Achieving Knowledge Management Amongst Older Adult Communities. *Procedia Social and Behavioral Sciences, 147,* 229-236.

Eijkman, H. (2011). Dancing with Post modernity: Web 2.0+ as a New Epistemic Learning Space. Pennsylvania, USA: IGI Global (pp. 343-346).

Enders, A., Hungenberg, H., Denker, H.P., & Mauch, S. (2008). The long tail of socialnetworking: revenue models of social networking sites. *European Management Journal, 26*(3), 199-211.

Ferreira, J.B., da Rocha, A., & Ferreira da Silva, J. (2014). Impacts of technology readiness on emotions and cognition in Brazil. *Journal of Business Research, 67*(5), 865-873.

Fogues, R., Such, J.M. & Espinosa, A. (2015). Open challenges in relationship-based privacy mechanisms for social network services. *International Journal Human Computer Interaction, 31* (5), 350-370.

Gaál Z., Szabó L., Obermayer-Kovács, N. & Csepregi A. (2015). Exploring the role of social media in knowledge sharing. *The Electronic Journal of Knowledge Management, 13* (3), 185-197.

Ghezzi, A., Gastaldi, L., Lettieri, E. Martini, A. & Corso, M. (2016). A role for startups in unleashing the disruptive power of social media. *International Journal of Information Management, 36,* 1152-1159.

Hanna, R., Rohm, A., & Crittenden, V.L. (2011). We're all connected: the power of the social media ecosystem. *Business Horizons*, *54*(3), 265-273.

He, W., Zha, S., & Ling, L. (2013). Social media competitive analysis and text mining: a case study in the pizza industry. *International Journal of Information Management*, *33*(3), 464-472.

Hoadley, C.M., Xu, H. & Lee, J.J. (2010). Privacy as information access and illusory control: The case of the facebook news feed privacy outcry. *Electronic Commercial Research Applications*, *9*, 50-60.

Jalonen, H. (2014). Social media and emotions in organisational knowledge creation. Conference Proceedings, Federated Conference on Computer Science and Information Systems, Warsaw, (pp. 1371-1379).

Joshi, P. & Kuo, C.C. (2011). Security and privacy in online social networks: A survey, in: Proceedings of IEEE International Conference on Multimedia and Expo, ICME, Barcelona, Spain.

Julich, T. (2012). BMV Group: Social Media-un canal de comunicare, dar cu alte reguli de joc (traducere din original: Ein Kommunikationskanal, aber mit anderen Spielregeln. KommunikationsManager, 2012). PR Romania. Retrieved from http://www.prromania.ro/articole/pr-20/1385-thorsten-julich-bmw-group-social-media-un-canal-de-comunicare-dar-cu-alte-reguli-de-joc.html

Kaplan, A.M., & Haenlein, M. (2010). Users of the world, unite! The challenges and opportunities of social media. *Business Horizons*, *53*(1), 59-68.

Kaplan, A.M., & Haenlein, M. (2009). Consumers, companies, and virtual social worlds: A qualitative analysis of Second Life. *Advances in Consumer Research*, *36*(1), 873-874.

Kietzman, J.H., Hermkens, K., McCarthy, I.P., & Silvestre, B.S. (2011). Social media? Get serious! Understanding the functional building blocks of social media. *Business Horizons*, *54*(3), 241-251.

Kim, A. J., & Ko, E. (2012). Do social media marketing activities enhance customer equity? An empirical study of luxury fashion brand. *Journal of Business Research*, *65*(10), 1480-1486.

Kumar, K.V., & Devi, V.R. (2014). Social media in financial services a theoretical perspective. *Procedia Economics and Finance*, *11*, 306-313.

Lee, J. (2012). Components of medical service users' dissatisfaction: A perceived control perspective. *International Journal Management Marketing Research*, *5*, 53-63.

Luo, X., Zhang, J., & Duan, W. (2013). Social media and firm equity value. *Information Systems Research*, *24*(1), 146-163.

Maier, C., Laumer, S., Eckhardt, A., & Weitzel, T. (2015). Giving too much socialsupport: social overload on social networking sites. *European Journal of Information Systems*, *24*(5), 447-464.

Martini, A., Massa, S., & Testa, S. (2013). The Firm, the platform and the customer: a 'double mangle' interpretation of social media for innovation. *Information & Organization*, *23*(3), 198-213.

Mohamed, N. & Ahmad, I.H. (2012). Information privacy concerns, antecedents and privacy measure use in social networking sites: Evidence from Malaysia. *Computer Human Behavior, 28* (6), 2366-2375.

N. Hajli, X. Lin, (2016). Exploring the security of information sharing on social networking sites: The role of perceived control of information. *Journal Business Ethics, 133* (1) 111-123.

Nagendra, A. (2014). Paradigm shift in hr practices on employee life cycle due to influence of social media. *Procedia Economics and Finance, 11*, 197-207.

Ngai, E.W., Tao, S.S., & Moon, K.K. (2015). Social media research: theories, constructs, and conceptual frameworks. *International Journal of Information Management, 35*(1), 33-44.

O'Reilly, T. (2005). What is Web 2.0? Design patterns and business models for the next generation of software, [Online], Available: http://www.oreilly.com/pub/a/web2/archive/what-is-web-20.html.

Paroutis, A., & Al Saleh, A. (2009). Determinants of knowledge sharing using Web 2.0 technologies. *Journal of Knowledge Management, 13*(4), 52-63.

Rodriguez, M., Peterson, R.M., & Krishnan, V. (2012). Social media's influence on business-to-business sales performance. *Journal of Personal Selling & Sales Management, 32*(2), 365-378.

Sashi, C.M. (2012). Customer engagement, buyer–seller relationships, and social media. *Management Decision, 50*(2), 253-272.

Sigalaa, M. & Chalkiti, K. (2015). Knowledge management, social media and employee creativity. *International Journal of Hospitality Management, 45*, 44-58.

Stieglitz, S., & Dang-Xuan, L. (2013). Emotions and information diffusion in social media: sentiment of microblogs and sharing behavior. *Journal of Management Information Systems, 29*(4), 217-248.

Storey, M.A., Treude, C., Deursen, A. & Cheng, L.T. (2010). The Impact of Social Media on Software Engineering Practices and Tools. FoSER '10 Proceedings of the FSE/SDP workshop on Future of software engineering research New York: ACM, (pp 359-364).

Surowiecki, J. (Ed.) (2005). *The Wisdom of the Crowds*. Anchor Books, New York.

Tan, C., Lee, L., Tang, J., Jiang, L., Zhou, M., & Li, P. (2011). User-level sentiment analysis incorporating social networks. In Proceedings of the 17th ACM SIGKDD international conference on Knowledge discovery and data mining (pp.1397-1405).

Tudor, D. (2013). Impactul social media asupra relatiilor publice. [Power Point Presentation]. Retrieved from http://www.slideshare.net/denisatudor/curs-impactul-social-media-asupra-rp.

Usman, S., H. & Oyefolahan, O. (2014). Determinants of Knowledge Sharing Using Web Technologies among Students in Higher Education. *Journal of Knowledge Management, Economics and Information Technology, IV* (2).

Viejo, A. & Sánchez, D. (2015). Enforcing transparent access to private content in social networks by means of automatic sanitization. *Expert Systems with Application, 42*(23), 9366-9378.

Vladlena, B., Saridakis, G.& Tennakoon, H. (2015). The role of security notices and online consumer behaviour: An empirical study of social networking users. *International Journal Human Computer Study*, *80*, 36-44.

Vuori, V. (2011). Social Media Changing the Competitive Intelligence Process: Elicitation of Employees' Competitive Knowledge. Academic Dissertation, [Online], Available: http://dspace.cc.tut.fi/dpub/bitstream/handle/123456789/20724/vuori.pdf.

Wahlroos, J. K. (2010). Social Media as a Form of Organizational Knowledge Sharing. A Case Study on Employee Participation. Wärtsilä. Helsinki: unpublished thesis of the University of Helsinki.https://helda.helsinki.fi/bitstream/handle/10138/24624/Thesis.Johanna.Wahlroos.pdf?sequence=1.

Whelan, E., Parise, S., De Valk, J., & Aalbers, R. (2011). Creating employee networks that deliver open innovation. *MIT Sloan Management Review*, *53*(1), 37-44.

Yassin, F., Salim, J. & Sahari, N. (2013). The Influence of Organizational Factors on Knowledge Sharing Using ICT among Teachers. *Procedia Technology*, *11*, 272-280.

Zhang, Z.Y. (2015). Security, trust and risk in multimedia social networks. *Computer Journal*, *58*(4), 515-517.

Zhang, Z. & Gupta, B.B. (2016). Social media security and trustworthiness: Overview and new direction. Future Generation Computer Systems (in press), http://dx.doi.org/10.1016/j.future.2016.10.007.

Part IV

COMPETENCIES AND ROLES

Chapter 11

DIGITAL REVOLUTION EQUALS DIGITAL COMPETENCIES? WHAT WE EXPECT FOR WORKERS' COMPETENCIES IN INDUSTRY 4.0

Martina Gianecchini-Caterina Muzzi-Diego Campagnolo

SUMMARY: 11.1. Introduction. – 11.2. Industry 4.0: jobs, workers and skills. – 11.3. Implications for stakeholders. – 11.4. Conclusion. – References.

11.1. Introduction

The three industrial revolutions of the past were all triggered by technical innovations: the introduction of water- and steam-powered mechanical manufacturing at the end of the 18th century, the electrification that led to mass production at the beginning of the 20th century and introduction of automation in manufacturing in the 1970s. The upcoming industrial revolution will be triggered by the Internet, which allows communication between humans as well as machines throughout large networks.

In factories, computerized systems allow communication between humans, machines and products alike. These systems (also referred to as cyberphysical systems) can interact with one another using standard Internet-based protocols and analyze data to predict failure, configure themselves, and adapt to changes. In smart factories, intelligent and customized products comprise the knowledge of their manufacturing process and consumer application and independently lead their way through the supply-chain (Brettel, Friederichsen, Keller and Rosenberg, 2014).

Such environment is not futuristic but is turning into reality in an increasing number of large and even small firms.

The rise of new digital industrial technology, also known as Industry 4.0, is likely to have breakthrough effects in a variety of areas including revenue growth, productivity, investments and employment (Bughin, Lund and Remes, 2016; Rußmann et al., 2015).

As far as employment is concerned, estimates indicate that a number of jobs will be substituted by technology because repetitive and standardized, while new jobs are more likely to be created in such fields as analytics, mechatronics and software development to name a few. The balance between the number of substituted jobs and the number of new jobs it is still an open debate, instead it is largely ascertained that the digital revolution will be competence destroying.

For example, recent research conducted by McKinsey show that digital transformation has the potential, at least with regard to its technical feasibility, to transform entire sectors. Such transformation goes beyond routine manufacturing and involves also those industries characterized by a substantial share of knowledge work such as healthcare and finance (Chui, Manyika and Miremadi, 2016). Hence, up-skilling or re-skilling employees will become fundamental activities for companies and institutions both on technical and soft skills. Indeed, as digitalization will replace more routine or repetitive tasks, it allows employees to focus more on tasks that utilize creativity and emotion (Chui, Manyika and Miremadi, 2015).

In this chapter we are aimed at studying whether the Italian University system is adapting its offer to accommodate the requirements of Industry 4.0.

The chapter proceeds as follows. In the next paragraph we present the main technologies that characterize the so called Industry 4.0. Then we discuss the implications for stakeholders and, in particular, how the Italian University system is responding to the challenges posed by such revolution. Next, we conclude the paper and derive some policy implications.

11.2. Industry 4.0: jobs, workers and skills

Industry 4.0 has been initially proposed as a technological radical change powered by nine foundational technology advances (Rüßmann et al., 2015): big data and analytics, autonomous robots, simulations, horizontal and vertical system integration, Internet of Things, cybersecurity, the cloud, additive manufacturing, augmented reality. The foundation of the concept in the technological realm produced an initial interest of the topic in terms of the design of smart factories (e.g. Shrouf, Ordieres and Miragliotta, 2014) where physical objects are seamlessly integrated into the information network where they can become active participants in business processes, communicate information about their status, surrounding environment, production processes, maintenance schedule and even more.

However, right after the technological hype, scholars started to focus their attention on the impact of Industry 4.0 on work and workers. In particular, a first group of studies analyze if and to what extent new technologies may substitute workers (e.g. Frey and Osborne, 2013; Chui, Manyika, and Miremadi, 2015 and 2016). These studies analyzed the susceptibility of jobs to automation or computerization, on the base of their job descriptions, suggesting different scenarios in terms of disappearance of human-executed jobs. Interestingly, all these studies agree in identifying a set of competencies (e.g. managing others, creativity, stakeholder interaction) that cannot be executed by machines. A second group of studies (e.g. Arntz, Gregory and Zierahn, 2016) aimed at identifying the characteristics of the workers that would be most affected by the increasing work automation. These studies suggest that older and less educated workers suffer a higher risk of being displaced by the machines. Finally, a third group of studies (e.g. De Smet, Lund and Schaninger, 2016) illustrate the change in the set of competencies required to workers in order remain competitive in the automated labour market. One of the most complete studies produced so far (World Economic Forum, 2016) ranks the most required skills for workers in 2015 and 2020. Interestingly, among the top 10 skills for the 2020 (i.e. complex problem solving, critical thinking, creativity, people management, coordinating with others, emotional intelligence, decision making, service orientation, negotiation, cognitive flexibility) only two of them are "new" if compared with the ones listed for the 2015 (i.e. complex problem solving, coordinating with others, people management, critical thinking, negotiation, quality control, service orientation, decision making, active listening, creativity). This analysis weakens the dramatic scenarios painted by the analyses on the disappearance of jobs and workers, suggesting instead that the technologies related with Industry 4.0 implies for workers a "reshuffle" and redefinition of their existing skills.

Artificial Intelligence (AI) – AI encompasses a range of technologies that learn over time as they are exposed to more data. It includes speech recognition, natural language processing, semantic technology, biometrics, machine and deep learning, swarm intelligence, and chatbots or voice bots (Capgemini, 2017). AI has a broad range of applications in different organizational functions, such as information technology, operations and manufacturing, supply chain management, and customer-facing activities. Generating business value from AI is directly connected to effective training of AI algorithms. Many current AI applications start with one or more "naked" algorithms that become intelligent only upon being trained (predominantly on company-specific data). Successful training depends on having well-developed information systems that can pull together relevant training data (Ransbotham, Kiron, Gerbert and Reeves, 2017).

Adopting AI broadly across the enterprise will likely place a premium on soft skills and organizational flexibility that enable new forms of collaboration, including project teams composed of humans and machines. However, if we assume that AI can execute operations on data with a higher accuracy than humans, one may wonder what is the role of individuals in front of a developed AI system. We suggest that whether AI represents an effective way of elaborating information and solving problems, individuals still play a role in defining the problems, namely framing the contextual conditions for the AI to work. Indeed, problem definition, i.e. how one sees the problem, has the most profound effect on where one ends up (Kühberger, 1998). The initial representation of a problem may be the most crucial single factor governing the likelihood of problem solution. What may appear as a formidable problem in one representation may be solved immediately in another format. A mere change of representation may by itself provide a solution. Whether a problem is solved or not, and how long the solution will take depend a great deal upon the initial representation (Posner, 1973). The problem definition ramifies throughout the problem-solving process in many ways, such as embodying preconceptions and assumptions that underpin how one approaches the problem, and guiding the strategies and actions taken to address the problem.

Horizontal and vertical system integration – As the complexity of products and processes increase, collaboration gains importance. Within a collaborative network, risks can be balanced and combined resources can expand the range of market opportunities. Hence, companies in collaborative networks can adapt to volatile markets and shortened product lifecycles with high agility. In contrast to the many benefits, the decoupling and spatial separation of production processes has drastically increased the need for coordination (Brettel, Friederichsen, Keller and Rosenberg, 2014): companies and their employees have to communicate with various departments across company boundaries very efficiently. As illustrated by Bughin, Lund and Remes (2016), companies with high adoption rates for digital tools expect workflows to become more project- than function-based and that teams in the future will organize themselves.

These changes in the organization of corporate activities and collaborations between companies call for the capability to cooperate in inter-organizational teams that are geographically dispersed and multi-functional. Virtual teams are defined as "work arrangements where team members are geographically dispersed, have limited face-to-face contact, and work interdependently through the use of electronic communication media to achieve common goals" (Dulebohn and Hoch, 2017: 569). While initially it was assumed that competencies and behaviors needed to collaborate in virtual teams were the same as co-located teams, today it is widely recognized that virtual teams require appropriate skills and behaviors to deal with the lack of face-to-face contact among team members (Gibson and Cohen, 2003). These include communication skills, depth of understanding in collaborative technology, ability to influence and facilitate team members engagement, an appreciation for cultural diversity, and an ability to influence and build trust and relationships with their geographical dispersed team members. Furthermore, virtual collaborations between people belonging to different companies are hindered by the reduced willingness to share information with other companies (e.g. suppliers, partners).

Simulation and augmented reality – In the engineering phase of many products, simulations of materials and production processes are already used, but in the future, simulations will be used more extensively in plant operations as well (Rüßmann et al., 2015). These simulations will leverage real-time data to mirror the physical world in a virtual model, which can include machines, products, and humans. Similarly, augmented reality provides workers with real-time information to improve decision-making and work procedures, such as selecting parts in a warehouse and sending repair instructions over mobile devices.

Both these technologies require individuals and organizations to be responsive and adaptable to changes in the environment. As a consequence, we can consider "agility" as a key characteristic for the future workers. The characteristics of an agile workforce have been examined by a variety of authors. Plonka (1997) identifies the attributes of agile employees as: attitudes towards learning and self-development; problem solving ability; being comfortable with change, new ideas, and new technologies; ability to generate innovative ideas; accepting new responsibilities. According to Breu and colleagues (2002) agile workforce should be responsive and fast to face the changing environment, and for this purpose, it should be constantly updated with the new skills required by the circumstances and empowered for a quick and independent decision-making. Dyer and Shafer (2003) first identify the behaviors of an agile workforce, as being proactive, adaptive and generative. Being proactive means searching and exploiting new opportunities that contribute to the success of the firm, and approaching in a creative and new way opportunities and threats. Being adaptive involves quickly moving from role to role and simultaneously assuming more than one role focusing on task accomplishment. Being generative means to learn, by exploiting as much as possible the competencies in a role, and to educate, by sharing information within the organization.

11.3. Implications for stakeholders

In late 2016 the Italian Government launched the "Industry 4.0 national plan" (the so-called Piano Calenda by the surname of the Ministry of Economic Development that proposed it) by illustrating a set of targets, tools and measures to be implemented and reached by 2020 in accordance with the EC "Digitizing European Industrial Strategy". The plan was developed by a steering committee that included representatives from six Ministries, the Presidency of the Council of Ministries, some of the major Italian Universities, Unions, the "Cassa Depositi e Prestiti" institution, public research centers and the association of Italian employers "Confindustria". Plan's major aims are supporting innovative investments and developing digital skills. In order to get the first of them, the plan proposes a set of infrastructural and financial measures to foster digitalization and to make easier and cheaper investing in digital technologies; while skills development would be pursued by involving the educational system as a whole, introducing digital classes at primary and secondary schools, fostering connections between undergraduate students and firms, activating specific curricula in professional schools and financing Industry 4.0 research clusters and Ph.Ds. Together with these interventions, the plan also includes the creation of Competence Centers (CCs) and Digital Innovation Hubs (DIHs).

Figure 1. Excerpt from "Industry 4.0 National Plan".

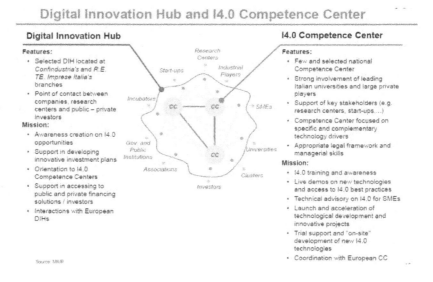

Source: MIUR – Italian Ministry of Education and Research (2016).

Figure 1 shows the basic features and the mission of CCs and DIHs within Italian Industry 4.0 National Plan. It clearly emerges the strategic view of strengthening the collaboration among all stakeholders that could be considered as key-players in the digitalization framework. In line with the Triple Helix Model developed by Etzkovitz and Leydersdorff (2000), specific actions in the skills development proposition are not merely focused on digital technologies diffusion, as deterministic approaches would suggest (Webster, 2014); they are instead oriented to create and support a co-evolving system aimed to enhance and foster innovation under a multidimensional perspective.

However, the sources of innovation in a Triple Helix configuration are not expected to be stable, because "they generate puzzles for participants, analysts, and policymakers to solve. This network of relations generates a reflexive sub-dynamic of intentions, strategies, and projects that adds surplus value by reorganizing and harmonizing continuously the underlying infrastructure in order to achieve at least an approximation of the goals" (Etzkovitz and Leydersdorff, 2000, pp. 112-113). Investing on skills is thus an uncertain investment and outcomes are unpredictable. This issue is more relevant when dealing with skills that are not merely technical ones. Technical skills could be, until a certain point, standardized by introducing specific knowledge in the educational system whereas soft skills and competencies are embedded in human beings, depend on personality traits and are expected to change over people's life (Heckman and Kautz, 2012). This is the reason why strategies aimed in developing such kind of skills are focused on actions directed to create the fertile ground for knowledge flows across helix's stakeholders and to improve actors' own awareness about skills needs.

In general terms, thus, the skills area of the Italian Industry 4.0 plan seems to be built in an interesting and promising way. Unfortunately, as it always happens when bureaucracy, politics and business are involved, plan's development is encountering a set of obstacles that are delaying its implementation.

It is worthy to admit that one of the main bundles of obstacles is due to the innate stickiness of the public sector: dozens of laws are needed in order to make the plan working, and then several administrative regulations have to be published in order to make the laws applicable in practice to various sectors. Laws and decrees have to be approved by the Italian Court of Accountancy in order to verify their financial sustainability and internal coherency. This step, that is an important guarantee of the applicability of laws, could imply the need of a complete or partial revision of the laws and their decrees, so the lead time for having operative indications tend to be quite long. It happens, in the specific case, to the set of norms and decrees that deal with CCs creation: in autumn 2017 they lay at the Court since several months and a relevant pack of the plan could not be implemented at the moment.

DIHs are having, instead, a broad diffusion and several Italian regions have already created them and are filling them in by contents and concrete actions.

Getting back to obstacles in plan's implementation, another relevant bundle depends on the lack of specific competencies in the educational system by teachers and professors: new courses and schools-firms collaborations have to be sustained by skilled actors and the Italian system is still missing them. This is the reason why intensive courses for teachers started all along the peninsula and the contents vary from technical (in other words, technological) to methodological (how to use digital technologies at school) ones.

Another major challenge is offered by lobbyist behaviors that so frequently occurs when public funds are involved: the different stakeholders involved in the plan pursue well defined objectives and making them dialoguing around a common issue is definitely more difficult that writing it down, even if several examples of good practices are arising.

In this chapter we are interested in verifying to what extent a key-player of the Triple Helix, the University, is ready to respond to the call of Industry 4.0 challenge, by supplying high quality and complete sets of competencies to students. The completeness of competencies directly relates to the need of crucial soft skills by firms, together with technological ones, highlighted in previous paragraphs, and this is the reason why we are investigating what kind of courses Italian Universities are delivering over the last couple of years that could have a direct impact on competencies requested by the Fourth Industrial Revolution. We analyzed the contents of different kinds of courses: bachelor's degrees, masters of sciences degrees and first and second levels masters [1], provided by the major Italian universities grouped by dimension (i.e. number of students). Censis (Center for Studies on Social Investments) publishes each year a ranking of Italian universities according to several criteria (internationalization, communication, grants, services), and provides an aggregate overall index for each university, by distinguishing among public, private and polytechnic universities and by splitting them, according to the number of students enrolled, in: mega, big, medium and small-sized institutions.

For our analysis, we considered the first 10 universities for each category (some category includes less than 10 members) in 2017 Censis' ranking and we got a sample of 55 institutions out of the total 97 Italian

---

[1] First and second level postgraduate Master and Specialization Courses (First and second level masters, hereafter) are short courses that, by law, have to deliver at least 60 ECTS in a variable duration from one to two years. They respectively corresponds to the 7th and the 8th levels in the European Qualifications Framework even if they aren't equivalent to any other European degree. Organized by universities, they provide participants with an official recognition of the educational qualification. In order to get access to First level masters, students need bachelor's degree while a MSc degree is needed to get access to Second Level Masters.

universities including public, private and telematics ones.

We went into each university's website and looked at educational offers. We selected a list of degrees or masters according to a set of keywords, namely; "digital", "data", "intelligence", "innovation", "cyber", "analyst" and combinations of them. We got a list of 42 courses including bachelor's degrees, MSc degrees and first and second level masters activated in 20 universities. We then looked at the date of foundation of each degree and master and excluded those that were older than 4 years. In this way we could exclude all the courses that have been activated several years ago in specific degrees, like Informatics or Informatics Engineering, because they have always been a part of that discipline's base of knowledge, but are not directly related to the advent of Industry 4.0, even if the contents fit with it. After this selection we got at the final number of 27 courses, divided as shown in Table 1.

Table 1. Distribution of courses by typology.

Bachelor's Degrees	2
MSc Degrees	11
First level Masters	8
Second level Masters	6

The following round of investigation implied a closer look into each course's program and department of belonging, in order to understand how the different disciplines are blended into each course and what the courses' prevalent imprint is. With respect to this last aspect, that is usually specified only for bachelor's and MSc degrees, the majority of the courses are rooted into Engineering, Informatics and Statistics Departments (8 out of 11) while the other 3 are activated in Economics and Management Departments. In these latter cases managerial, financial and accounting contents are given together with courses of informatics, statistics and mathematics.

Also, first and second level masters have a strong technological and statistical vocation and management and business contents could be considered as residual, even if some exceptions exist: three of them were opened by Management Departments and managerial contents are quite strong. Only one first level master, organized by sociologists and a design school, explicitly recalls, also in the title, to "soft skills" for the digital transformation.

As far as the dimension of universities where these courses are activated is concerned, a strong concentration could be highlighted. More than 74%

of all the courses we found are in 13 mega and big universities, both public and private ones. Only one second level master is active in a small private university while the other small ones do not have any course.

The above-mentioned analyses could stimulate several considerations about Italian higher education system in the Industry 4.0 framework. First of all, evidences show that the Fourth Industrial Revolution has carried on a strong intensification of technological and statistical courses in order to deal with some of the major digital challenges cited in the above paragraphs, such as Artificial Intelligence and IoT. The main driver for the higher educational spiral of the Italian Helix could thus be individuated in the technological innovation. However poor or little attention is given to the organizational side of innovation that deals with soft skills, social interactions and the organization of work in general. This situation could lead, in the short run, to a significant lack of soft-skilled young workers and it could be detrimental for the economic system as a whole, as organizational performance risk to decrease, or to increase with lower marginal rates, than expected.

Secondly, we could ask ourselves whether Italian Universities, and Management Departments more specifically, are conscious of this lack of expertise they are contributing to create.

Even assuming that they are, the Italian University system is showing here all its weaknesses in term of inner rigidity and slow times of reaction to the innovation-driven needs. On one side we see a sort of institutional myopia (Buckland, 2009) in making strategic plans and correctly interpreting market dynamics; on the other side, the system shows all the criticisms of big bureaucratic institutions in changing processes, specifically in changing the educational offer. These changes are not easy for several reasons and a relevant part of them lies on the strict criteria that the Ministry of Education and Research imposes to universities for opening new courses. Specific parameters in terms of number of students enrolled and number of structured professors have to be respected, and this could be one of the reasons for the lack of courses activated by small-sized universities. They could be, under an organizational point of view, more flexible than bigger ones, but they do not have numbers. It is easier to launch First and Second Level Masters, but still a basin of prospect participants has to be individuated and also partnerships with companies are needed. A last set of problems could rely upon the difficulty in multidisciplinary dialogue within universities. Different departments are not used to collaborate for teaching reasons, and several universities do not even have the complementarity of internal skills to develop integrated and complete courses. Under this perspective, small universities are again penalized because they could be composed by few departments and the needed knowledge could not be internally available.

11.4. Conclusion

In this chapter we analyzed the impacts of the Industry 4.0 on work and workers, specifically focusing on the competences that will be at the center of the digital transformation of firms and institutions.

First, we presented the main technological innovations included in the so called Industry 4.0. Second, we analyzed for some of them what could be the possible effects at the individual and organization level. Our analysis showed that the digital transformation will require an increasing number of "agile" workers who must approach in a new and creative way the emergent job opportunities.

In the second part of the chapter we tried to establish a link between such competences and how the Italian education system at the University level is reacting to prepare the workers of the future. Our analysis shows that a substantial mismatch exist between what are the main competences required by Industry 4.0 and the current graduate and undergraduate programs of the majority of the University, as only a limited number of them seems to be adapting their programs accordingly.

References

Arntz, M., Gregory, T., & Zierahn, U. (2016). The risk of automation for jobs in OECD countries: A comparative analysis. OECD Social, *Employment, and Migration Working Papers*, 189, 1-42.

Brettel, M., Friederichsen, N., Keller, M., & Rosenberg, M. (2014). How virtualization, decentralization and network building change the manufacturing landscape: An industry 4.0 perspective. *International Journal of Mechanical, Industrial Science and Engineering*, 8(1), 37-44.

Breu, K., Hemingway, C.J., Strathern, M., & Bridger, D. (2002). Workforce agility: the new employee strategy for the knowledge economy. *Journal of Information Technology*, 17(1), 21-31.

Buckland, R. (2009). Private and public sector models for strategies in universities. *British Journal of Management*, 20(4), 524-536.

Bughin, J., Lund, S., & Remes, J. (2016). Rethinking work in the digital age. *McKinsey Quarterly*, October, 1-6.

Capgemini. (2017). *Turning AI into concrete value: the successful implementers' toolkit*. Research report (downloadable at https://www.capgemini.com/consulting/resources/ai-the-successful-implementers-toolkit/).

Chui, M., Manyika, J., & Miremadi, M. (2016). Where machines could replace humans – and where they can't (yet). *McKinsey Quarterly*, July, 1-12.

Chui, M., Manyika, J., & Miremadi, M. (2015). Four fundamentals of workplace automation. *McKinsey Quarterly*, November, 1-9.

De Smet, A., Lund, S., & Schaninger, W. (2016). Organizing for the future. *McKinsey Quarterly*, January, 1-14.

Dulebohn, J.H., & Hoch, J.E. (2017). Virtual teams in organization. *Human Resource Management Review*, 27(4), 569-574.

Dyer, L., & Shafer, R.A. (2003). *Dynamic organizations: Achieving marketplace and organizational agility with people*. CAHRS Working Paper Series, 27.

Etzkowitz, H., & Leydesdorff, L. (2000). The dynamics of innovation: from National Systems and "Mode 2" to a Triple Helix of university–industry–government relations. *Research Policy*, 29(2), 109-123.

Frey, C.B., & Osborne, M.A. (2013). *The future of employment. How susceptible are jobs to computerisation*. Working paper – Oxford Martin School (downloadable at http://www.oxfordmartin.ox.ac.uk/downloads/academic/future-of-employment.pdf).

Gibson, C.B., & Cohen, S.G. (2003). Virtual teams that work: Creating conditions for virtual team effectiveness. San Francisco, CA: Jossey-Bass.

Heckman, J.J., & Kautz, T. (2012). Hard evidence on soft skills. Labour economics, 19(4), 451-464.

Kühberger, A. (1998). The influence of framing on risky decisions: A meta-analysis. *Organizational Behavior and Human Decision Processes*, 75(1), 23-55.

Plonka, F.E. (1997). Developing a lean and agile work force. *Human Factors and Ergonomics in Manufacturing & Service Industries*, 7(1), 11-20.

Posner, R.A. (1973). An economic approach to legal procedure and judicial administration. *The Journal of Legal Studies*, 2(2), 399-458.

Ransbotham, S., Kiron, D., Gerbert, P. & Reeves, M. (2017). *Reshaping Business With Artificial Intelligence*. Research report (downloadable at -http://sloanreview.mit.edu/projects/reshaping-business-with-artificial-intelligence/).

Rüßmann, M., Lorenz, M., Gerbert, P., Waldner, M., Justus, J., Engel, P., & Harnisch, M. (2015). *Industry 4.0: The future of productivity and growth in manufacturing industries*. Boston Consulting Group, Reseach report (downloadable at http://www.inovasyon.org/pdf/bcg.perspectives_Industry.4.0_2015.pdf)

Shrouf, F., Ordieres, J., & Miragliotta, G. (2014). Smart factories in Industry 4.0: A review of the concept and of energy management approached in production based on the Internet of Things paradigm. In *Proceedings of the IEEE/IEEM International Conference* (pp. 697-701)

Webster, F. (2014). *Theories of the information society*. Routledge.

World Economic Forum. (2016). *The future of jobs: Employment, skills and workforce strategy for the fourth industrial revolution*. Research Report (downloadable at https://www.weforum.org/reports/the-future-of-jobs).

Chapter 12

DIGITALIZATION AND HR ANALYTICS: A BIG GAME FOR AN HR MANAGER

Tommaso Fabbri-Anna Chiara Scapolan

SUMMARY: 12.1. Introduction. – 12.2. The digitalization of the enterprise: an organizational perspective. – 12.3. The digitalization of HRM. – 12.4. The transformation of HRM in the digital enterprise. – 12.4.1. HR as a managerial function: the design of the digital workplace. – 12.4.2. HR as a set of practices: data-driven HRM. – 12.5. Implications for practice and research. – References.

12.1. Introduction

The phenomenon addressed in this contribution, whatever the expression one chooses to indicate it, is the digital transformation of working processes, understood as the upgrading, or the "augmentation" of socio-technical relationships – those among men, between man and machine, and among machines – both internal and external – that is, inside and between organizations (topologically understood) – enabled by the latest generation of information and communication technologies (ICTs). A privileged perspective for the observation of such a phenomenon is that of the enterprise information systems: digitalization (of machineries, semi-products, products, services, technical actions, etc.) comes with the "datafication" of production and work in its making and consequently provides new sources of data, to be integrated with existing information systems and databases into valuable datalakes in support of managerial decision making.

Given this, the implications of digital transformation at the HR level are twofold. First and most immediate, HR activities and processes themselves can be upgraded to the new technologies (digitalization of HRM). Second and more disruptive on contemporary practices, is the more or less radical transformation of HRM as a consequence of the digitalization of working processes.

As a result the chapter is structured as follows: section 2 introduces to the digitalization of the enterprise from a strictly organizational perspective, section 3 discusses briefly the digitalization of HRM processes and section 4 illustrates our hypotheses on the transformation of HRM in the digital enterprise, both as managerial function (par.4.1) and as set of practices (par. 4.2). In the last section some implications for practice and research are discussed.

12.2. The digitalization of the enterprise: an organizational perspective

When we talk about digitalization we talk about ICTs. From an organizational standpoint, every single work process can be described as an information processing process: the more information – both as input-to and output-of the work process – is made explicit (vs tacit), hence formalized and distributed or made available, the more the work process is liable to digitalization, which in turn allows for automation. In this respect, we can see a difference between service processes and manufacturing processes: service processes, such as clerical work, are in essence mainly immaterial and digitalization, as a requisite for automation, is easier. This is why management, professional support, clerical support are the types of jobs where, at present, according to the recent ILO/Eurofound Report (2017), digital work is most diffused. But, the rise of Industry 4.0 promises increasing digitalization also of manufacturing processes and, potentially, the digitalization of blue collar work, which in turn might eventually pave the way to the substitution of workers with robots and algorithms (e.g. Chui, Manyika and Miremadi, 2016). From an organizational standpoint communication is the raw material of coordination which, in turn, is the essence of organized action: "Where media are primitive – March and Simon claimed back in 1958 – coordination system is primitive" (March & Simon, 1958). Consequently, digitalization is mainly the transformation of coordination processes and tools enabled by new generation ICTs. More precisely, the most advanced ICTs bring unprecedented (communication and) coordination power: in space, because they allow for the substitution of physical proximity with powerful remote communication and coordination tools, and in time, because they allow for augmented synchronous and asynchronous coordination options.

As a result, digitalization can be described as an organizational transformation process characterized by the substitution of analog rules (therefore to some extent tacit and informal) for decision and action with digital rules (therefore explicit and formalized) for decision and action. In a digitally transformed enterprise actions and decisions at every level are increasingly performed in a digital mode: using digital information, within digital workflows that are hosted in digital "spaces", which are accessible anytime and anywhere via digital mobile devices.

Digital infrastructure (channels and artifacts) increasingly innervate organizational processes, dissolving work spatial and temporal coordinates, making communication more efficient and coordination more sophisticated and powerful. In sum, digital transformation represents an upgrading of the information processing capacity of organizations, allowing them to manage more complexity, both adaptively and pro-actively, and therefore to be more competitive; again with March and Simon (1958): "The more the efficiency of the communication in the organization, the higher the "tolerance for interdependence".

Having pointed out the organizational meaning of digital technologies, now we turn to the famous "computer paradox" in order to better specify the relationship we believe to exist between organization and technology. In spite of traditional economic theory claim that technical progress *per se* makes work more productive, the famous economist Robert Solow, who had significantly contributed to that economic theory, said that "You can see the computer age everywhere but in the productivity statistics" (Solow, 1987). His intention was to underline the fact that productivity gains exhibited a downward trend in spite of large-scale and continued investment into computerization and automation. Today, consistent with non-deterministic approaches to technology, an idea seems to be gaining legitimation even among the technological apologists such as Brynjolfsson and McAfee (2014), according to whom, in order to untap the potential of new ICTs not only the organizational system needs to be receptive but also incoming technologies need to be embedded into the specific organizational context and its requirements. Valenduc and Vendramin (2016) exempt us from digging into organization theory again in order to make the point: "Productivity gains are a corollary of the organizational changes facilitated by technological innovations rather than the technologies themselves, and will be achieved only by companies which adopt new forms of work organization at the same time as the new technologies".

12.3. The digitalization of HRM

The digitalization of HRM processes is not a new phenomenon. Indeed, the awareness and acceptance of information systems in HR practice have developed since the '80s and '90s, when the first automation of payroll and data administration have taken place (i.e. information human resource systems – IHRS and employee self-service systems –ESS). However, we have witnessed a rapid growth and an increasing interrelatedness between information and communication technology and HRM only in the following years, mostly due to the development of Internet (van den Heuvel and

Bondarouk, 2017). The term e-HRM appeared during the 2000s; since then, together with the most popular administrative applications, there has been an increasing use of e-recruiting (e.g. job boards and career portals, corporate web recruiting), e-training (by means of intranets and management learning systems) and e-performance management systems (meaning both electronic tracking of employees performance but above all electronic feedback). More recently, the development of interactive technologies (e.g. Web 2.0, social media, virtual reality) have opened up new opportunities for personalizing recruitment and selection practices and thus increasing the overall effectiveness of e-recruiting (e.g. Stone et al., 2015). Applications such as virtual job fairs, virtual job and organization previews, and electronic interviews are increasingly used to develop interaction between job applicants and organizational members. Social networks, such as Linkedin, are employed not only for scanning individual profiles, identifying talented employees and contacting them about job openings but also for implementing proactive employer branding strategies. The same technologies, along with digital practices such as gamification, knowledge repositories and crowdsourcing are transforming e-traning processes, increasing interpersonal interaction and communication among trainees thus fostering social learning. In a similar vein, cloud versions of videoconferencing and internal social media (e.g. wikis, microblogs, chat rooms) may increase the social interaction between supervisors and subordinates and the richness of vertical communication, reducing social distances and improving computerized feedback processes. Moreover, enterprise social software can be used to feed multi-source e-performance appraisal systems gathering feedback from group members as well as customers. Finally, the most advanced new technologies (included handheld electronic devices and wearable technologies used in production and service delivery) enhance electronic performance measurement opportunities, tracking and recording employees behaviors and outcomes on an ongoing basis, thus favoring datified performance appraisal and management processes. As van den Heuvel and Bondarouk (2017, p.128) recently asserted, sentiments, emotions, interactions and relationships are also eligible for datafication, pursuant to the widespread self-reporting on social media.

A common feature of new generation HR software and applications, which identifies both the existing ones and those to come and will exploit the informative value of new data streams, is clearly identified by Bersin (2015): "originally conceived as systems to help HR managers administer people practices, [HR software and applications] are now really designed to help line managers and employees manage themselves". The line manager not only is where people management "occurs", but also enjoys decentered people management digital tools that make the HR manager redundant. Therefore, a consequence of the digitalization of HR processes might be the crisis of the traditional HR manager's role as organizational development expert capable at training and helping people professionals and the associated crowding out of basic, functional HR competencies. In Bersin (2015) terms, "Human resources professionals, as the stewards and experts in people processes and change practices in the organization, must reinvent [them]selves to stay relevant, valued, and strategic in the organization of the future". We discuss the how's of the Chief Human Resource Officer role reconfiguration (as digital workplace architect and data-driven manager) in the following sections.

12.4. The transformation of HRM in the digital enterprise

Given the organizational virtue of ICTs outlined in section 2, we now collapse our understanding of digitalization with respect to people management into what we hypothesize are the main implication for HRM, as a managerial function and as a set of practices.

12.4.1 HR as a managerial function: the design of the digital workplace

The brief argument that follows is hypothetical, and relies on what we have specified in section 2 about the organizational significance of digital transformation and about the non-deterministic relationship we claim to exist between (information and communication) technology and organization.

To the extent that work is carried out inside digital environments, the management of "decision making premises" (March & Simon, 1958) is achieved through the design of the company's digital architecture and content. To the extent that work becomes more and more digitalizes (*digital workplace*), the designer and content manager of the company's digital environments becomes a new operation manager.

If the two preceding claims are somehow plausible – and we suggest empirical exploration – digital technologies are essentially an "organizational" phenomeno and the competences needed for the management of a company digital transformation are essentially "organizational" skills. Therefore the Chief Human Resource Officer appears to be top positioned to drive the digital transformation. Although still too often in charge of the digital transformation budget, the Chief Information Officer doesn't seem fit to the task, because of his/her function-and-feature way of thinking about technology, nor does the Chief Communication Officer, often in charge of some company's digital layer (e.g.: the intranet) but generally with no "organizational" competences.

12.4.2. HR as a set of practices: data-driven HRM

Conceivably, digital workplaces as sketched out in the previous sections could be able to provide a large amount of information and data regarding (digital) workers' emotions, behaviors and performance, fostering enormous opportunities for generating HR big data and thus developing HR analytics.

The term 'Big data' is employed to identify data that is large in volume, high in velocity, diverse in variety, exhaustive in scope, fine-grained in resolution, relational in nature and, at the same time, flexible (Scholz, 2017). In accordance with consultants, big data is anything too large for being captured, stored, managed and analyzed by traditional database tools, since it ranges from "a few dozen terabytes to multiple petabytes"' (Manyika et al., 2011: 1). Hover, academics have recently moved the emphasis "from the size of the data to its smartness, i.e. the extent to which it is able to provide the material to conduct fine-grained analysis that successfully explains and predicts behavior and outcomes" (Angrave et al., 20016: 2). Such a definition goes beyond data collected and managed by HRIS embracing the idea of HR analytics.

According to Angrave and collegues (2016), "analytics is the discipline, which has developed at the intersection of engineering, computer science, decision-making and quantitative methods to organise, analyse and make sense of the increasing amounts of data being generated by contemporary societies" (p. 1). Related to HR, analytics involves both traditional databases and spread-sheet analysis, new forms of database software capable to efficiently store and organize a huge quantity of data, and new (statistical) techniques for representing, understanding and visualizing data (Angrave et al., 2016). Thus, traditional data on job applicants and new-hired employees (e.g. demographic information, education, professional background) and workers' performance (e.g. sales, individual output measure) along with "soft data" (collected, for instance, from performance management systems, training programs, internal surveys) not only are increasingly collected together and stored in cloud-based data warehouses (such as Taleo talent management suite of Oracle or Kenexa HR software of IBM) but they might also been combined with further data coming from digital work tools and spaces. For instance, information extracted from mobile phones, Internet browsing, and other electronic devices (eg. Wearable technologies used in production) along with data derived by e-mails and digital collaborative platforms (e.g. the content of emails, instant digital messages and so on) might be used for mapping social networks, understanding employees' morale and extracting information on what employees do, who and what about they communicate and how they interact (Angrave et al., 2016).

As a result, in parallel with the digitalization of HRM we have briefly discussed in the section 3, opportunities are being created for HR professionals to use the data generated by advanced technologies to support HRM and business solutions, thus contributing to create value from people and positioning HR departments as a fact-based strategic partner of the executive board (Fechyr-Lippens, Schaninger and Tanner, 2015; Ulrich & Dulebohn, 2015).

HR analytics can be implemented at different analytical layers: descriptive, diagnostic, predictive and prescriptive. The descriptive level consists on effectively visualizing large amounts of data which meaning would otherwise be impossible to grasp. The screenshot depicted in figure 1 is taken form a dashboard we have developed for a large Italian bank that allows for real-time investigation of absenteeism throughout 10.000 employees (approximately 3 million records a year), by geographical area, typology of absence, organizational unit, and several other control variables extracted from the company HR databases.

Figure 1. An example of descriptive HR analytics.

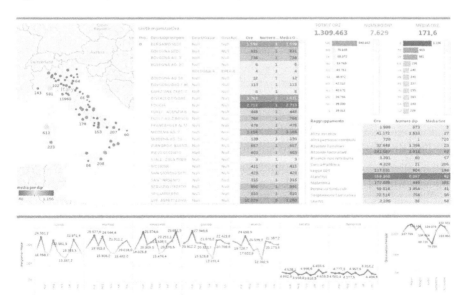

More sophisticated HR analytics applications involve the search, among ad hoc merged company's databases, for casual antecedents of people and/or business dynamics of interest to managers. Rasmussen and Ulrich (2015) provide two interesting examples of sophisticated projects, conducted in an offshore drilling company, which have provided a significant improvement in the business performance. In the first example (reported in the figure 2), HR analytics exploited both qualitative and quantitative data, experience from the business, and leaders' intuition to identify the most relevant performance determinants: they found a strong and significant relationship between leadership quality, crew competence, safety performance, environmental performance, operational outcomes and customer satisfaction.

Figure 2. An example of predictive HR analytics.

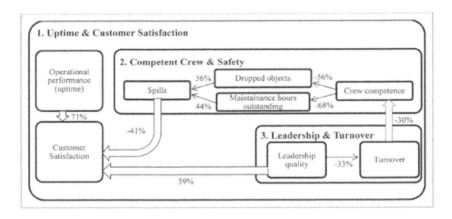

Source: Rasmussen & Ulrich, 2015: 240.

The findings were used to support the following line of reasoning and tell a coherent history: customer satisfaction is about operational performance, but other factors also matter for company success. Specifically, leaders assessed more positively by their subordinates have lower crew turnover, lower turnover is associated with higher crew competence, which in turn is related to better safety performance, fewer spills, and fewer maintenance hours which affects customer satisfaction. Consistently, at the prescriptive level, HR analytics were used to recommend to focus on the training and selection of leaders, the crew's training budget and control, the placement of unit scorecards for monitoring maintenance hours, and communication of the findings throughout the company to all leaders, employees and customers.

In the second example, HR analytics was used to demonstrate the beneficial impact of the company's graduate training program on the business. Data on key outcomes (reported in the table 1) were used to demonstrate that specialist trainees involved in the program exhibited desirable outcomes on compared with their peer-group. These findings triggered a discussion on alternative talent acquisition strategies (i.e. build, buy, borrow) and as a result this graduate training program was doubled in size to sustain the company's growth plans.

Table 1   Outcome of Specialist trainee program compared to peer-group.

KPI	Specialist trainees	Peer group	Difference
Retention after 5 years	63%	60%	3% better retention
Time to develop into Lead Specialist	6.6 years	10.2 years	3.6 years less
Total cost pr. person prior to Lead Specialist position	1,882,500 USD	2,850,000 USD	967,500 USD per trainee
Performance average in Lead Specialist position 2010–11	3.3/3.5	3.2/3.2	+2%/6% performance

Source: Rasmussen & Ulrich, 2015: 240.

Similarly, some leading organizations (e.g. healthcare organizations) have been using advanced HR analytics in talent-management area for not only reducing their employees' rate of attrition but also generating savings in total compensation expenditures while simultaneously improving the engagement and productivity of their staff (Fechyr-Lippens, Schaninger and Tanner, 2015). Again, Sparrow et al. (2015) provide the examples of Tesco, which applied the business analytics developed to understand its customers to better understand also its workforce and of McDonalds, which was able to identify how employees' demographics, management behaviors and staff attitudes interacted to optimize the restaurant performance.

Such examples suggest how HR analytics goes beyond the simple use of advanced statistical methods and might be used to support a storytelling for a (technical) business audience (line managers, top executives, customers), where the story looks at the entire value chain and different stakeholders, suggesting ways for improving or enhancing business results (Rasmussen & Ulrich, 2015).

12.5. Implications for practice and research

Since HR analytics have become increasingly important and represent a "must have" capability for the HR profession (Boston Consulting Group, 2014; CIPD, 2013), the first implication for HR managers is to acquire analytical capabilities and develop an analytical mindset. Unfortunately, many HR professionals went into HR to avoid the quantitative side of business but this is no longer possible (Ulrich & Dulebohn, 2015). Moreover, there are few training courses in HR analytics and most of them are superficial (Rasmussen & Ulrich, 2015). Indeed, such courses should offer not only basic training in statistics and science methodology; they would also include "deploying a diagnostic framework [...], change management and storytelling" (Rasmussen & Ulrich, 2015: 239). In doing so, the pitfall "mean/end inversion" (Angrave et al. 2016, Rasmussen & Ulrich, 2015; Ulrich & Dulebohn, 2015) might be avoided. In fact, the end of HR is creating value and HR analytics are a means to make value happen. Thinking that big data is always better is a wrong idea, since it is not about data, but about data for better informed decision-making. Accordingly to the strategic "outside-in-approach" outlined by Ulrich and Dulebohn (2015), HR analytics should not start with data but with a business problem, with key questions on context, stakeholder, and strategies, such as: "What are the biggest challenges facing our business the next 3-5 years and how can HR support the business on same?" (p: 238)

Thus, data and analytics should be integrated in an overall diagnostic framework where HR analytics go beyond particular HR issues (e.g. training ROI, turnover prediction) and are part of a cross functional business analytics, looking at human resources as elements in the entire value chain.

Consistently, HR professional should "not forget about the (H) of HR" (Rasmussen & Ulrich, 2015: 239), considering that data *per se* does not change anything; HR analytics should be exploited to feed management discussion that can increase decision quality and then promote consistent organizational change.

Since the HR function often lacks the skills, knowledge and insight to ask the right questions of the available big data on business and HR, many scholars (e.g. Angrave et al., 2016; van den Heuvel and Bondarouk, 2017) believe that academics may have an important role to play, contributing at developing effective HR metrics and analytics. More specifically, drawing on their empirical research findings, academics may help HR managers and professionals to ask the right questions, measure what is right and as result develop predictive models which may really orient decisions and actions. From the academic research standpoint, this means that future studies should, first of all, collect big data on the state of HR analytics and their future which might add evidence to the few extant study (eg. CAHRS, 2010; van den Heuvel and Bondarouk, 2017). Moreover, future empirical research should contribute at advancing academic understanding of the relationships between HR (eg. HR activities and employees' behaviors and attitudes, such as individual abilities and job satisfaction) and organizational performance. Sofar such research has been carried out by means of longitudinal quantitative analysis on large-scale and ambitious sample surveys.

More specifically, mainstream research in human resource management use surveys to assess employee attitudes (e.g. satisfaction, engagement, embeddedness) and attitudes are deemed relevant predictors of work behaviors: the more satisfied employees are, the better they perform; the more organizationally embedded, the more they adopt behaviors exceeding task prescriptions (OCBs). However, surveys are expensive, thus "engagement with organizations' own data on HR and performance may allow for more fine-grained and convincing causal analysis without the need for such expensive data collection" (Angrave et al., 2016: 9). For instance, the recent contribution of Shah, Irani & Sharif (2017) investigating the relationship between employee behaviors and attitudes and organizational change readiness represents an interesting example of contextual application for big data within a HR case study setting.

In a similar vein, since surveys are "picture-like", while digital data flows provide "movie-like" representations, a promising interdisciplinary future line of research (which combines knowledge and skills of organizational behavior, computer and data science) is collecting both traditional HR attitudes (by means of surveys) and data generated by companies' digital collaborative and social and applying advanced analytics techniques to investigate the relationship between employees' attitudes and digital work behaviors. If such relationship actually holds, employee attitudes and as a result task performance and also extra-role performance could be better understood and predicted on an on-going basis by collecting and analyzing employees' digital work behaviors. Again, precious insights for informing decisions and actions of people and change management in organizations are potentially enormous.

References

Angrave D., Charlwood A., Kirkpatrick I., Lawrence M., Stuart M. (2016). HR and analytics: why HR is set to fail the big data challenge. *Human Resouce Management Journal*, 26(1). 1-11.

Bersin (2015). HR's Role in the Digital Workplace: A Time for Reinvention. In Ulrich D., Schiemann W.A., Sartain L. *The Rise of HR. Widsom from thought leaders*, Alexandria, VA: HR Certification Institute: 19-23.

Boston Consulting Group (2014). *Creating people advantage*. Boston, MA: The Boston Consulting Group, Inc.

Brynjolfsson E., McAfee A. (2014). The Second Machine Age: Work Progress, and Prosperity in a Time of Brilliant Technologies. New York: W.W. Norton & Company.

CAHRS (2010). *State of HR analytics: Facts and Findings from CAHRS Topical Working Groups*. New York, NY: Center of Advances Human Resource Studies. Cornell University.

Chui M., Manyika J., Miremadi M. (2016). *Where machines could replace humans – and where they can't (yet)*. McKinsey & Company.

CIPD (2013). *Talent Analytics and Big Data – The Challenge for HR*. London: Chartered Institute for Personnel and Development.

Eurofound and the International Labour Office (2017). *Working anytime, anywhere: the effects on the world of work*, Publications Office of the European Union, Luxemburg and the International Labour Office, Geneva.

Fecheyr-Lippens B., Schaninger B., Tanner K. (2015). *Power to the new people analytics*. McKinsey Quarterly, March: 1-2.

Manyika J., Chui M., Brown B., Bughin J., Dobbs R., Roxburgh C., Byers A. (2011). Big data: the next frontier for innovation, competition and productivity. McKinsey & Company.

March J.G., Simon H.A. (1958). *Organizations*, Wiley & Sons, New York.

Rasmussen T., Ulrich D. (2015). Learning from practice: how HR analytics avoids becoming a fad. *Organizational Dynamics*, 44: 3, 236-242.

Scholz T.B. (2017). *Big Data in Organizations and the Role of Human Resource Management. A Complex Systems Theory-Based Conceptualization*. New York: Peter Lang, [2017] Series: Personalmanagement und Organisation, Vol. 5.

Shah N., Irani Z., Sharif A.M. (2017). Big data in an HR context: exploring organizational change readiness, employee attitudes and behaviors. *Journal of Business Research*, 70: 366-378.

Solow R. (1987). *We'd better watch out*. New York Times Book Review, July 12, 1987, p. 36.

Stone D.L., Deadrick D.L., Lukaszewski K.M., Johnson R. (2015). The influence of technology on the future of human resource management. *Human Resource Management Review*, 25: 216-231.

Ulrich D., Dulebohn (2015). Are we there yet? What's next for HR? *Human Resource Management Review*. 25: 188-204.

Valenduc G., Vendramin P. (2016). *Work in the digital economy: sorting the old from the new*. Brussels: ETUI.

van den Heuvel S., Bondarouk T. (2017). The rise (and fall?) of HR analytics: A study into the future application, value, structure, and system support. *Journal of Organizational Effectiveness: People and Performance*, 4(2): 127-148.

Chapter 13

INDUSTRY 4.0 AND THE EMERGING CHALLENGES TO LEADERSHIP

Alessio Paris-Luca Giustiniano

SUMMARY: 13.1. Human dimensions of industry 4.0. – 13.2. The robotic work-force's deep learning. – 13.3. Non replaceable practices human leaders need to foster. – 13.4. Organizational "ambidexterity". – 13.5. Conclusion.

There is some consensus that four industrial revolutions can be associated with new technological waves. Innovations related to steam power, cotton, steel, and railways helped to give us the first industrial revolution of mass production and mechanization. The second was triggered by the introduction of electricity, heavy and mechanical engineering and synthetic chemistry. The third was triggered by innovations in electronics and computers, petrochemicals and aerospace.

What about the fourth[1]? Nanotechnology, bioscience, renewable energies, Artificial Intelligence (AI), cyber-physical systems and others have all brought many disruptive innovations over the last few years creating the so-called "Industry 4.0". Smart manufacturing, product development, logistics and even customers have all been involved in such new "industrial revolution" era[2].

Take GE Aviation which – on one hand – produces engines, also using additive manufacturing technology developed through Avio Aereo[3], and – on the other hand – sells them with the Predix software package, a configurable and open platform that connects those to the aircraft to maximize efficiency and maintenance cycles predictability[4]. Another example is Amazon Web Services where manufacturing gets into the cloud becoming "cloud manufacturing" whose main pro companies may benefit from is to replace up-front capital infrastructure expenses with low variable costs.

---

[1] LISA DE PROPIS – *A forth industrial revolution is powering the rise of smart manufacturing* – World Economic Forum / theConvesation.com 2017.

[2] SARAH STAFFEN, LUISA SCHOENWALD – *Leading in the context of the industrial revolution; the key role of the Leader 4.0* – Capgemini Consulting 2016.

[3] www.avioaero.com.

[4] www.geaviation.com.

Yet, what are the implications of this ever-changing phenomenon for leaders? What are the skills and challenges any manager may need to master and face to encouraging their employees to embrace such changes? How about organization structures and designs?

There is no unique answer, no unique comment; giving the challenges such "hybrid" questions bring to the expert: the fusion of technology and leadership. Therefore, we will try to address our analysis as follows:

a) human dimensions of industry 4.0;
b) the robotic workforce's deep learning;
c) non replaceable practices human leaders need to foster;
d) organizational "ambidexterity".

13.1. Human dimensions of industry 4.0

No doubt, the human dimension of "digital" is challenging as much as the technological one. In particular, there are five "people dimensions" more affected than others in this context. First of all: leadership.

Leaders 4.0 are those who will first move and navigate in this new world. Not only do they need to embrace the above-mentioned disruptive changes, they must encourage their employees to do the same. Indeed, entrepreneurial, agile and visionary sentiments are of paramount importance for the new leaders. Only by thinking entrepreneurially, they can inspire their team to trust new technologies, to heighten each ones' attention on questions regarding data security. Only by accepting this in-depth evolution, they can be part of a real change of thinking which starts from taking apart fears of potential job-losses and layoffs and move people to see and exploit new technologies as an opportunity rather than a risk.

Former CEO of CISCO – John Chambers – predicts that organization that understands this environment can thrive, others whose leaders cannot handle these changes will fail[5].

This requires – overall – a change of strategy where leadership couples with other elements such as:

a) new skills and talents HR departments may recruit, enable and retain;
b) organization structures re-design towards an interdisciplinary and international approach (the so-called "ambidexterity");
c) more flexible work environment where traditional workforce man-

---

[5] Interview with the Telegraph's Business Reporter; appeared on Oxford Leadership thoughts 2016.

agement models adapt to smart machines and hyper-connected teams allow firms to become much faster and agile in making decisions;

d) more flexible work environment where traditional workforce management models adapt to smart machines and hyper-connected teams allow firms to become much faster and agile in making decisions;

e) cross-functional way of working.

13.2. The robotic workforce's deep learning

As mentioned, this new strategy allows leaders and machines to become "colleagues", by working and making decisions together. Humans code software to "teach" machines what to do in any circumstances they need them (e.g.: from making to ... driving a car!). Hence, AI has been always human-trained so far. Deep learning could change this by making machines learning by themselves and decide autonomously.

Indeed, the power of deep learning-based AI systems lies in their ability to automatically detect noticeable features and use them to solve hard recognition problems[6].

Although humans could easily perform such recognition tasks almost unconsciously, it is often difficult for them to explain the exact procedure at a sufficiently detailed level so that it could be programmed into a computer. With deep learning all this has changed. Now, deep learning-based AI systems can figure out the important features for solving difficult problems that were once thought to be solvable exclusively by humans. That assumption could require – on one hand – a faster and more flexible way to change leadership approach and – on the other – a deep dive understanding of what remains human and cannot be replaced by machines.

13.3. Non replaceable practices human leaders need to foster

Thanks to deep learning, AI intelligence will soon be able to do many administrative tasks that consume much of managers' time.

In order to find out what is unreplaceable (so far ...) by machine, a survey[7] on 1,770 managers from 14 countries and interviews of 37 executives

---

[6] DANUSHKA BOLLEGALA – *Robot revolution: rise of the intelligent automated workforce* – theConversation.com 2016.

[7] VEGARD KOLBJØRNSRUD, RICHARD AMICO, ROBERT J. THOMAS – *How Artificial Intelligence will Redefine Management* – Harvard Business Review 2016.

SARAH STAFFEN, LUISA SCHOENWALD – Leading in the context of the industrial revolution; the key role of the Leader 4.0 – Capgemini Consulting 2016.

in charge of digital transformation in their organizations identified the following practices managers need to master.

While most of them considers administrative coordination and control (e.g. shifts of personnel; report writing[8]) to be delegated to AI, leaders should be focused on:

a) the essence of human judgement such as empathy, ethical reflection, creative thinking and capacity to improvise[9];
b) avoiding any "race against the machine" approach by trusting the advice of intelligent systems in making everyday business decisions;
c) creative thinking and curiosity;
d) social skills, networking and coaching to bring together diverse perspective, insights and experiences.

Taking for granted all the above is unmistakably human, the AI could be an opportunity to foster such human people skills.

13.4. Organizational "ambidexterity"

A possible approach to manage, accomplish and take the best out of the disruptive changes industry 4.0 – in general – and AI – in particular – bring to companies is organizations to move from line hierarchy to a network organization. Thus, ensuring long term success and firms' survival. The so-called ambidexterity[10].

In other words – taking the manufacturing industry as example – leaders should:

– (*exploit*) the existing and necessary business with its hierarchical and complex projects' structures, to allow a basic efficiency ... and
– (*explore*) innovative, flexible and agile processes and business models, to address new opportunities. This can be even a start-up where

---

[8] According to the study, this could free up to 54% of time managers can devote to other tasks.

[9] See MIGUEL PINA E CUNHA, JOAO VIEIRA DA CUNHA, AND KEN KAMOCHE, Organizational improvisation: What, when, how and why, *International Journal of Management Reviews* 1, no. 3, 1999: 299-341; MARIA DA GRAÇA BATISTA ET AL., Improvising prescription: evidence from the emergency room, *British Journal of Management* 27, no. 2, 2016: 406-425.

[10] SARAH STAFFEN, LUISA SCHOENWALD – *Leading in the context of the industrial revolution; the key role of the Leader 4.0* – Capgemini Consulting 2016; SEBASTIAN RAISCH, JULIAN BIRKINSHAW, GILBERT PROBST, AND MICHAEL L. TUSHMAN, Organizational ambidexterity: Balancing exploitation and exploration for sustained performance, *Organization Science* 20, No. 4, 2009: 685-695.

leaders adapt themselves to the new technologies and digital environment.

The adaptation of organizational structures towards a more flexible set-up could be a key element to realize Industry 4.0 initiatives and – as far as AI improve – to shape all the company.

13.5. Conclusion

All Industrial Revolutions have had a profound impact on global society. Industry 4.0 and its striving for innovation has no exception to that. Workplaces are experiencing dramatic transformations never seen before. Companies are challenged while recognizing and adapting to these changes.

Even though leaders 4.0 need to transform themselves faster than the corporations they are part of, in light of the complexity of the digital transformations and the indispensable organizational structures, the traditional meaning of "leadership" will not change its meaning. That is because soft skills such coaching, strategic thinking as part of every leader, will remain because they are unreplaceable and 100% human.

Part V
INSTITUTIONS

Chapter 14

E-LEARNING EXPERIENCES IN EUROPEAN UNIVERSITIES: A MULTIPLE CASE STUDY ANALYSIS

Davide Bizjak-Teresa Anna Rita Gentile-Ernesto De Nito-Paolo Canonico

14.1. Introduction

In the contemporary knowledge-based economy there is an increasing demand of higher education delivered by well established Universities. The adoption of e-learning technologies may be seen as a way to react to such demand, coming from students located in a variety of different countries (Al-Qathani and Higgins, 2013; Bell and Federman, 2013). It is thought as the natural outcome of the students' tendency to use more and more electronics sources and references (Yuan and Powell, 2013). But it also relies on learners' self-discipline, and neither does it give the chance to structure study time nor provides the benefit deriving from of face to fact interaction (Banerjee and Duflo, 2014). Furthermore, e-learning systems are praised as being a disruptive innovation that will re-design higher education (Yuan and Powell, 2013); hence considering the Internet and its applications as a "cognitive extension for humanity" (McAuley et al., 2010: 33). The widespread diffusion of e-learning has also been coupled with a debate concerning its efficacy and usefulness in learning processes (Al-Qahtani and Higgins, 2013; Adeola et al., 2013; Carril et al., 2013).

In this chapter we wish to understand how traditional Universities are adopting E-learning technologies. The manuscript will unfold as follows: we begin with an overview of e-learning as a tool in educational process, covering how universities have dealt with it. Then we move to the empirical field, represented by a multiple case study based on four academic institutions, which have adopted different kind of e-learning platforms.

14.2. E-learning tools

E-learning systems provide integrated learning environments using network technologies to design, deploy, select, manage and expand the resources for learning (Asfor Glossary, 2007). Learning environments are provide on digital devices such as a computer or mobile phones or tablets (Clark and Mayer, 2011). The most frequently used forms of tuition and courses provision are: asynchronous self-learning through the use of pre-packaged content available on the delivery platform; synchronous learning through the use of video conferencing and virtual classrooms; collaborative learning through the activities of virtual learning communities.

There are several types of e-learning in universities: blended learning, mobile-learning; cloud computing and Massive Open Online Courses (MOOCs).

Lin and Wang (2012) argue that blended learning combines two teaching methods: face-to-face classroom teaching and e-learning based on web-based teaching platform. According to Al-Qahtani and Higgins (2013), this approach takes advantage of both the structure resulting from the physical presence of the teacher and the more self-directed study implemented through technology.

Mobile-learning (M-learning) is an additional form of e-learning for mobile devices (Simkova et al., 2012), which allows students to engage in learning activities without any spatial or physical constraints (Kukulska-Hulme, 2005). Cochrane and Bateman (2010) argue that the use of mobile wireless devices can support and improve learning contexts and exploit the potential of current and emerging collaboration.

Cloud computing is a network-based computing model, which allows users to have access to on-demand processing and pay-per-view resources (Riahi, 2015). This enables the creation of a new generation of e-learning systems capable of operating on a wide range of hardware devices (Masud and Huang, 2012).

A Massive Open Online Course (MOOC) is an online course with open registration (McAuley et al., 2010), which can be accessed from any location and without the need to meet formal entry requirements (Sinclair et al., 2015). Course participants form a learning network and support the knowledge that comes not only from experts, but also by all members of the same community.

One of the main point of discussion on e-learning is related to its own definition. Therefore, different perspectives on what e-learning should be have been put forward (Sangrà et al, 2012; Moore et al., 2011). It is possible to classify definitions of e-learning under four broad categories: Technology-Driven, Delivery-System-Oriented, Communication-Oriented, Educational-Paradigm Oriented (Sangrà et al., 2012). Despite it is not the objective of this chapter to review the thousands possible definition of e-learning, we can assume that each of this category has been preferred by different scholars and has allowed the scientific and professional community on e-learning to highlight positively or negatively different aspects of the use of this technology in universities. Accordingly, thanks to e-learning there are more chances for users to have access to education (Al-Qahtani and Higgins, 2013) and it is now possible to reach, in a cheaper way, a larger number of students all over the world (Begg et al., 2011), contributing to the knowledge diffusion that is considered the most important role for academic institutions (Starkey and Tempest, 2006).

As to the drawbacks, e-learning systems are typically considered to be closed infrastructures, being often available only to students enrolled at the specific University which is delivering the course (Masud, 2016). E-learning is not always reported useful by students (Ad-Alwan et al., 2013; Oproiu, 2015), maybe due to some competencies requested for the effective use of the learning programme (Parkes et al., 2013). Indeed, there is a lack of attention for the competencies requested both to students (Parkes et al., 2013) and teachers (Carril et al., 2013) to effectively use the e-learning technologies, in order to implement a virtual environment, assessing the competencies, suitable for the different learning delivery. Kurilovas et al. (2014) foster the deployment of the learning object to nurture an increasing adaptive learning based on the students learning style. Moreover, the increasing adoption of e-learning brings about the risk of shaping negatively the relationship between students and teacher. For example, those who attended a Moodle course tend to consider less important the feedback from the teacher. However, students claim that teacher should be more persuasive in suggesting the use of this tool (Oproiu, 2015). In contexts where the presence of an instructor is constant, it may be less easy to use solely asynchronous classroom technologies based on the web. On the contrary, as pointed out by Al-Qahtani and Higgins (2013), the use of blended learning is more effective for students used to a study-in-presence culture, as it provides additional material to learners.

14.3. Methodology

We used a mixed research method (Creswell, 2014): initially we relied on quantitative analysis, and then we moved to a qualitative enquiry, through the construction of a multiple case study and semi-structured interviews.

In the first phase, the analysis was based on the acquisition of documentary information found on internet (Corbetta, 2014). The activities carried out by different universities have been considered through the analysis of their websites. This method has been adopted and compared with others, because it has been considered more convenient in order to obtain quantitative data on European universities in a short time.

The analysis was conducted by examining the websites of the top 100 European universities. The international ranking used was Quacquarelli Symonds, known as QS World University ranking 2015/16. The ranking focused exclusively on the top 100 universities, identified by region, which included the word "Europe" in the "drop-down" list of "QS World University rankings 2015/16". The investigation, in particular, made it possible to verify the presence on university's website of appropriate E-learning platforms. The survey was conducted by entering in the "home page" of each university and search through specific keywords as "E-learning", "MOOCs", "Online Courses" and "Distance Learning".

Once identified the universities under scrutiny, we carried out an empirical enquiry in order:

(a) to select universities to further analyze through a multiple case study: the analysis, in particular, allowed us to ensure that the highest number of universities in the ranking by nationality come from two European countries: United Kingdom and Germany. Only three Italian Universities appear in the ranking; so the third university was chosen by taking into account the presence of a century-old university, with a long historical tradition in Europe and not just teaching methods based on e-learning. The three European universities were identified respectively as: University of Dresden (Germany), Queen's University Belfast - Northern Ireland (United Kingdom) and University of Bologna (Italy). Considering ease of access, the pilot case was built on data from a university not included in the top 100 universities in the QS rankings, i.e. University of Naples Federico II.

(b) to design and conduct semi-structured interviews with E-learning executives of selected universities. Questions were grouped under different labels, relying on the elements identified by Roberts (2004). Strategy identifies all the questions related to the alternative choices that universities may face regarding e-learning. Organization is understood as the way in which they implement the strategies. It involves all questions related to organizational configuration and organizational design, professional figures and technologies. User area includes all the questions connected with the potential users of the service. Context is linked to the general concept of technology and more precisely to the impact that technology has in the organization and the influence of the organization itself. Interviews were adminis-

tered to e-learning services managers. These professional figures are primarily involved in the design and delivery of e-learning services.
(c) to implement a comparative analysis on examined case studies.

We compared the main questions in the different case studies A final synoptic prospectus was prepared to test the similarities or differences (Yin, 2014) between the reality of the examined university primarily in relation with the design of e-learning system.

14.4. Case studies

14.4.1. Pilot-case: University of Naples Federico II (Italy)

Federico II University[1] has a Federica Web-learning service center (Center for Innovation, Experimentation and Dissemination of Multimedia Didactics) active in the area of new multimedia technologies.

Federica-Campus virtual project is an advanced web-learning model for those who cannot attend university in a traditional way.

Federica.it was born in 2007 with the idea of giving free access to the network of academic knowledge, with the offer of the teaching materials of the individual courses and a structured guide to the huge information assets already available. E-learning courses are available in any podcast format at any time, with a variety of content organized in training modules: lessons, images, videos and links.

As a second step, the project has evolved giving birth to another platform called Federica.eu, which currently delivers 75 MOOCs, each lasting from six to eight weeks.

Federica.eu MOOCs are now expanding the audience. Course recipients are no longer only traditional students, but also people in lifelong learning trying to improve their access to the labour market.

14.4.2. Case Study 1: University of Dresden (Germany)

Technical University of Dresden (Technische Universität Dresden - TUD) is a public university founded in 1828, although the current name "Technische Universität" dates back to 1961[2]. There are currently 35,961 registered students; the number of employees is 4,876.

The MedienZentrum (Multimedia Center) is a multimedia infrastructure that aims to digitize learning and teaching (Schoop et al., 2016). Al-

---

[1] http://www.unina.it.
[2] https://tu-dresden.de/tu-dresden/.

most 100 people work at the Media Center. The team is made up of scientists, designers, psychologists, educators and economists.

MedienZentrum supports educators in planning, implementing, and evaluating sustainable e-learning courses. In addition to providing support to users for the OPAL Learning Platform (OnLine Platform for Academic Learning and Teaching), this also includes consultation and guidance for educators in multimedia teaching courses as well as the planning and provision of training courses and workshops.

This university, in fact, has a website for the management of e-learning courses, where students and teachers can access prior registration. The content of courses offered in e-learning is not freely available, but is only available for registered users on the platform.

E-learning courses are provided, alongside those held in frontal mode, at the school of Humanities and Social Sciences (faculties of Languages, Literature and Cultural Studies; Education; Economics and Business) and at the school of Civil and Environmental Engineering, faculty of Civil Engineering.

14.4.3. Case Study 2: Queen's University Belfast (United Kingdom)

Belfast University (Queen's University Belfast), founded by Royal Charter in 1845, and since 1908 an autonomous body, is one of the most important universities in the United Kingdom[3].

According to QS Quacquarelli Symonds, the number of students enrolled at Queen's University is about 17,820, including 5,606 international students. Professionals in the university are well 1,728 (academic year 2016/2017). There are 77 graduate courses and 138 postgraduate courses. A Center for Educational Development offers counseling and a range of professional development activities and support for major educational study, learning, teaching and assessment programs, student engagement, and progression.

This structure is also in charge of the provision of e-learning service, largely implemented through blended learning.

In addition, a dedicated Center for Computer Training and Development Services has been set up to provide advice on the implementation of learning and teaching technology.

Before the beginning of any online teaching activity, the centre organizes an introductory course specific to the use of e-learning systems. Through the use of the FutureLearn platform, MOOCs are also provided.

E-learning courses are provided in areas related to humanities, social sciences, Engineering and Physical Sciences, and Life Sciences.

---

[3] http://www.qub.ac.uk/.

14.4.4. Case Study 3: University of Bologna (Italy)

The University of Bologna[4] has very ancient origins dating back to 1088. Students enrolled during the academic year 2015/2016 were 84,724. The total number of university staff is 5,856, including 2,819 teaching staff and no. 3,037 technical-administrative staff. Vocational training plays a key role. In 2015, 6,673 training hours were delivered. Starting from 2016, there are also continuous training sessions for newly recruited teaching staff. The Information Systems and Applications Area (CeSIA) has the purpose of designing, implementing, and managing the IT services of the University. Within this area, the e-learning sector has a major role to play in satisfying the demand for e-learning services at the University and providing the necessary support for those who provide training activities through online teaching (blended learning).

There are courses in blended-learning mode within the 11 schools i.e. in the school of Agriculture and Veterinary Medicine; Economics, Management and Statistics; Pharmacy, Biotechnology and Motor Science; Law; Engineering and Architecture; Letters and Cultural Heritage; Languages and Literature, Translation and Interpretation; Medicine and Surgery; Psychology and Education Sciences; Political Science.

14.5. Results and discussion

The online courses provided at the Universities under scrutiny are intended not only for students enrolled, but are also open to free lance participants, free of charge. Learning activities are provided in different way (see figure 1): with restricted access to members only (32%); with free access through MOOCs (22%); both restricted and free access (46%).

Figure 1. Access to e-learning services/MOOCs in the top 100 European universities.

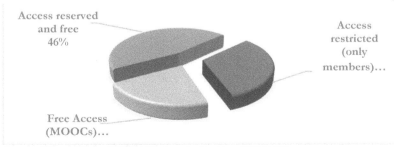

Source: Adapted from QS World University Rankings® 2015/16.

---

[4] http://www.unibo.it.

We have also conducted interviews with managers of E-learning services of four Universities: (Pilot-case) University of Naples Federico II (Italy); University 1: University of Dresden (Germany), University 2: Queen's University Belfast (United Kingdom), and, University 3: University of Bologna (Italy) (See Table 1).

Table 1: Summary of the Interviews conducted within four European universities.

Area	Synthetic content Question	Pilote-case: University of Naples Federico II – Italy	Case Study 1: University of Dresden – Germany	Case Study 2: Queen's University Belfast – UK	Case Study 3: University of Bologna – Italy
Strategy	1.Motivating the adoption of e-learning courses in universities.	Need to innovate their teaching methods	Need to innovate their teaching methods	Opportunities to offer students/ users service at any time.	Opportunities to offer students/ users service at any time.
	2.Presence of teaching forms in blended learning mode.	Adopting blended learning models.	Adopting blended learning models.	Adopting blended learning models.	Adopting blended learning models.
	3.Assessing the costs and benefits (ROI) from the investment in e-learning.	No cost/benefit analysis of e-learning training activities.	No cost/benefit analysis of e-learning training activities.	No cost/benefit analysis of e-learning training activities.	No cost/benefit analysis of e-learning training activities.
Organization	1.Choosing a course in e-learning and professional figures involved.	Assistance from course managers in carrying out educational activities in e-learning	The professionals involved in this project come from different fields.	The professionals involved in this project come from different fields.	The design is carried out independently by the teachers and there is only the coaching by a technician using the platform.
	2.Technologies adopted Cloud Computing.	Using Cloud Computing on Federica.eu Platform	No-existence of Cloud Computing.	Using Cloud Computing	No-existence of Cloud Computing.
	3.Technologies adopted: Mobile Learning.	Using Mobile Learning.	Using Mobile Learning.	Using Mobile Learning.	No-existence of Mobile Learning.

Area	Synthetic content Question	Pilote-case: University of Naples Federico II – Italy	Case Study 1: University of Dresden – Germany	Case Study 2: Queen's University Belfast – UK	Case Study 3: University of Bologna – Italy
Users	The number of students likely to follow these courses in e-learning.	Existence of precise data.	Lack of reliable data	Lack of reliable data	Lack of reliable data
	2. Category of user interested in following these courses (worker, off-site, off-course or other).	Difficulty setting out who "is" the student most typically interested in following these courses.	Worker and off-shore students prefer such teaching methods.	Retired, career workers, graduates or master students.	Difficulty setting out who "is" the student most typically interested in following these courses.
	3. Types of services offered to users/students in synchronous, asynchronous and collaborative form.	Provision of e-learning services in asynchronous form, without collaborative and synchronous forms.	Provision of e-learning services in asynchronous form, without collaborative and synchronous forms.	Adopting teaching methods both in synchronous, asynchronous form and also encouraging activities in a collaborative form.	The main use of the asynchronous system and only in specific cases is synchronous and collaborative forms, through forums and discussions.
Context	1. The main factors affecting the increase/decrease in the use of e-learning teaching methods in universities.	Increased use of such technologies due to institutional actors' policies, but also the tendency to use the different ways of delivering training.	Increased use of such technologies as a result of the ease with which students can use online digital devices anytime, and can share educational materials more easily with others.	Increased use of such technologies due to the development that the technological factor has gained in recent years in the university context.	Increased use of such technologies due to the development that the technological factor has gained in recent years in the university context.
	2. The use of such technologies worsens or improves learners' learning.	Learning would depend on how learners use e-learning.	Inadequate statistical data to make a difference with traditional teaching methods.	Using technology could adversely affect learning.	Technology would improve students' learning

(i) In the section related to the "strategic" aspect of e-learning, respondents focused on two different issues. Those from the University of Naples Federico II and the University of Dresden emphasized the internal need of the organization to innovate its teaching modalities. Those from Queen's University Belfast and University of Bologna have instead streamlined the opportunity to offer students/users service at all times to facilitate working and off-shore students. With reference to the other question on the existence of forms of teaching in blended learning mode, all those interviewed confirmed the existence in their institutions of blended learning models. With reference to the further question about the cost and benefit assessment (ROI) resulting from the e-learning investment, responses were identical, as no cost/benefit analysis was carried out in the four universities concerned of e-learning training activities.

(ii) In the section related to the "organizational" aspects, the following elements emerged. Interviewees at the University of Naples on the question of choosing the e-learning course said that there is an appropriate professional figure, the "Manager of the Course" who contacts the teacher for instructions on preparing and posting the slides. The director of the University of Bologna has shown that teachers play the major part of the project independently, although there is a technician to manage the platform. About this question, the Dresden University agent pointed out that the professionals involved at this stage come from different areas. The interviewee at Queen's University in Belfast pointed out that the project is subject to the approval of the faculty executive committee, and the involvement of professional staff such as Educational and Graphic Designer, marketing team, technical support and coordinator of the academic module.

(iii) In the section related to "Users" three issues arise. The first is related to the number of students who attend these courses through e-learning. There are no reliable data on this question at the universities of Dresden, Bologna and Belfast. Only at University of Naples it is possible to track the number of subscribers for the federica.eu platform that corresponds to 10,000-12,000 students and "Federica Web Learning (Federica.unina)" visited by over 500,000 users per month. Answers were different with reference to the second question about the category of users most interested in attending these courses (student, off-site, off-course or other).

According to those interviewed at the Universities of Naples Federico II and University of Bologna, it is difficult to define who is the student generally interested, because new technologies allow them to study anywhere and therefore there is no immediate reference in terms of students typologies. According to the head of the University of Dresden, students are progressively welcoming such methodologies; according to the manager of Queen's University Belfast, it depends heavily on the type of course being delivered.

From the observation of the third question on the types of services provided as synchronous, asynchronous and collaborative, the following results emerged. At University of Dresden and in Naples Federico II, services are delivered asynchronously, while University of Bologna relies mainly on the asynchronous approach.

Finally, University of Belfast adopts both synchronously and asynchronously methods and encourages activities in a collaborative form. This latter type is delivered through forums and discussions also within the University of Bologna, while it is absent in the other two universities, i.e. at the University of Dresden and at the University of Naples Federico II.

(iv) Within the "context" area two issues arise. The first one relates to the main factors affecting the increase/decrease in the use of e-learning teaching methods in universities. From the interview to the managers of the four universities, it emerges an increase in the use of such technologies in each of these universities, whose motivation is attributable to the University of Naples Federico II to the policies of institutional actors, but also the tendency to use different technological methods for students not attending the university. This motivation at the University of Dresden is due to the ease with which students are able to use on-line digital devices anytime, and can share educational materials. This increase, according to the findings of Queen's University Belfast and University of Bologna, is due to the development that the technological factor gained in recent years in the university context. The data obtained from the four universities on the second question of improving or worsening learning through the use of e-learning is partially contradictory. At University of Naples Federico II, learning would not depend on the use of technology, but by the way students use e-learning. In the University of Bologna, on the contrary, it would seem that technology would improve students' learning. According to the University of Belfast, the use of technology could affect learning negatively and, finally, for the University of Dresden there is no data to claim about differences with traditional teaching methods. A further line of reasoning is related to the elements of homogeneity and diversity that emerge from the case studies examined. Within the "Strategy" area, there are two elements shared by the four universities: the presence of blended learning and the absence of cost-benefit analysis. In the other three items referring to "Organization", "Users" and "Context" respectively, there are no similarities in the responses provided. There are also situations in the different parts of the interview, where not all four universities responded in a uniform manner. In the strategy area two interviewees focused on teaching innovation and the other two on delivering a smoother service to the student/user. In the question whether the cloud computing exists or not, it emerges that two universities are planning to implement this and the other two do not, while only one university is unable to use mobile-learning.

Questions related to the students interested in the courses delivered in synchronous, asynchronous and collaborative courses have revealed that in only two universities these three types are present. In the field related to the context there are similar responses related to the increase in the use of technology in learning, although the motivations differ. The overall analysis suggests that, although the four universities adopt some of the common strategies, they differ as pointed out by the organizational and personal-related analysis. There is a total divergence in the context responses, both in the light of the motivations that push the use of technologies, as already mentioned, but above all on the issue of worsening or improving learning.

14.6. Conclusions

From our investigation has emerged that all aforementioned 100 undergraduate universities in Europe provide training not only through classroom lessons, but also with special courses that are held via the web. From the examination of the responses obtained from the qualitative interviews, the attention of the four universities studied (University of Naples Federico II, University of Dresden, Queen's University Belfast and University of Bologna) regards the dynamics related to the design of e-learning courses. The lack of data concerning the real usage of these platforms and the impossibility to know what kind of user adopts the service, directly impacts in estimating the return of investment, in term of people reached and cost decrease. It is not clear if universities consider e-learning as a tool to improve their educational process and to offer people an opportunity to develop their competencies or more as a fashion tool able to attract people to visit websites and to advertise specific activities. In conclusion, it should be emphasized that, based on current data related to the design of e-learning courses, there seems to be some affinity between the four observed experiences.

We are aware that research is not currently concluded, but that there are some limitations. The first criticism is related to the difficulty of having a complete view of the phenomenon examined referring solely to the design of e-learning. The intention is therefore to ask new questions and make further inquiries. The second limitation refers to the number of interviewees and universities contacted. So, future research steps will cope with these activities by involving other actors (teaching staff, governance) and new universities.

References

Adeola, S. O., Adewale, S. O., and Alese, K. B. (2013). Integrated E-learning System (IES) for the Nigeria Universities: An Architectural Overview, in *American Journal of Database Theory and Application*, Vol. 2, No. 1, pp. 1-8.

Al-Qahtani, A. A., and Higgins, S. E. (2013). Effects of Traditional, Blended and E-learning on Students' Achievement in Higher Education, in *Journal of Computer Assisted Learning*, Vol. 29, No. 3, pp. 220-234.

Asfor Glossario (2007). *Le parole dell'e-Learning. Vademecum per la realizzazione di progetti formativi in modalità e-learning nelle pubbliche amministrazioni*, II Ed., Quaderni Cnipa, No. 32, pp. 365-366.

Banerjee, A.V., and Duflo E. (2014). (Dis)Organization and Success in an Economics MOOC, in American Economic Review, Vol. 104, No. 5, pp. 514–518.

Begg, M., Hellaway, R., Dewhurst, D., and Mcleod, H. (2011). Logos and Mythos: The Political Dilemmas of Web 2.0 in an Accreditation-driver Educational Environment, pp. 73-82, in R., Land, and S. Bayne (eds.), *Digital Difference: Perspective on Online Learning*, Rotterdam: Sense Publishers.

Bell, B.S., and Federman, J. E. (2013). E-learning in Postsecondary Education, in *The Future of Children*, Vol. 23, No. 1, pp. 165-185.

Carril, P.C.M., Sanmamed, M.G., and Sellés, N.H. (2013). Pedagogical Roles and Competencies of University Teachers Practicing in the E-learning Environment, in *The International Review of Research in Open and Distributed Learning*, Vol. 14, No. 3, pp. 462-487.

Cochrane, T., and Bateman, R. (2010). Smartphones Give you Wings: Pedagogical Affordances of Mobile Web 2.0, in *Australasian Journal of Educational Technology*, Vol. 26, No. 1, pp. 1-14.

Corbetta, P. (2014), *Metodologia e tecniche della ricerca sociale,* Second edition, Bologna: Il Mulino.

Creswell, J.W. (2014), *Research Design: Qualitative, Quantitative, and Mixed Methods Approaches*, Fourth edition, London: Sage Publication.

Kurilovas, E., Kubilinskiene, S., Dagiene, V. (2014). Web 3.0–Based Personalisation of Learning Objects in Virtual Learning Environments, in *Computers in Human Behavior*, Vol. 30, pp. 654-662.

Kukulska-Hulme, A. and Traxler, J. (2005). *Mobile Learning: A Handbook for Educators and Trainers,* Abingdon: Routledge.

Lin, W.S., and Wang, C.H. (2012). Antecedences to Continued Intentions of Adopting E-learning System in Blended Learning Instruction: A Contingency Framework Based on Models of Information System Success and Task-technology Fit, in *Computers & Education*, Vol. 58, No. 1, pp. 88-99.

Masud, M.A.H., and Huang, X. (2012). An E-learning System Architecture Based on Cloud Computing, in *System,* Vol. 10, No. 11, pp. 74-78.

McAuley, A., Stewart, B., Siemens, G., and Cormier, D. (2010). *The MOOC Model for Digital Practice*, http://www.elearnspace.org/Articles/MOOC_Final.pdf.

Moore, J.L., Dickson-Deane, C., and Galyen, K. (2011). E-Learning, Online Learning, and Distance Learning Environments: Are they the Same?, in *Internet and Higher Education*, 14(2), 129–135.

Oproiu, G.C. (2015), A Study about Using E-learning Platform (Moodle) in University Teaching Process, in *Procedia-Social and Behavioral Sciences*, Vol. 180, pp. 426-432.

Parkes, M., Reading, C., and Stein, S. (2013). The competencies Required for Effective Performance in a University E-learning Environment, in *Australasian Journal of Educational Technology*, Vol. 29, No. 6, pp. 777-791.

Riahi, G. (2015). E-learning Systems Based on Cloud Computing: A Review, in *Procedia Computer Science,* Vol. 62, pp. 352-359.

Roberts J. (2006). *L'impresa Moderna*, Bologna: Il Mulino.

Sangrà, A., Vlachopoulos, D., and Cabrera, N. (2012). Building an Inclusive Definition of E-learning: An Approach to the Conceptual Framework, in *The International Review of Research in Open and Distributed Learning*, Vol. 13, No. 2, pp. 145-159.

Schoop E., Köhler T., Börner C., and Schulz J. (2016). Consolidating eLearning in a Higher Education Institution: An Organisational Issue integrating Didactics, Technology, and People by the Means of an eLearning Strategy, pp. 1545-1557, in Spender J.C., Schiuma G., and Noenning J.R. (ed.), *Towards a New Architecture of Knowledge: Big Data, Culture and Creativity.* Proceedings, IFKAD.

Simkova, M., Tomaskova, H. and Nemcova, Z. (2012). Mobile Education in Tools, in *Procedia - Social and Behavioral Sciences*, vol. 47, pp. 10–13.

Sinclair, J., Boyatt, R., Rocks, C., and Joy, M. (2015). Massive Open Online Courses: A Review of Usage and Evaluation*, in *International Journal of Learning Technology*, Vol. 10, No. 1, pp. 71-93.

Starkey, K., and Tempest, S. (2006). The Business School in Ruins, pp. 101-112, in Gagliardi, P., and Czarniawska, B. (eds), *Management Education and Humanities*, Southampton, MA: Edward Elgar.

Yin R.K. (2014). *Case study research: Design and methods*, fifth edition, London: Sage publications.

Yuan, L. and Powell, S. (2013). MOOCs and Open Education: Implications for Higher Education, JISC CETIS.

Chapter 15

STRATEGIC DECISION-MAKING PROCESS IN RM PRACTICIES: DATA ANALYSIS AS INNOVATIVE TOOL TO PREVENT CORRUPTION

Federico Ceschel-Alessandro Hinna-Alessandro Pastorelli

SUMMARY: 15.1. Introduction. – 15.2. Theoretical background. – 15.3. Research Methodology. – 15.4. Case study background. – 15.4.1. Regulatory background. – 15.4.2. The National Anti-corruption Plan and the standard ISO 31000:2010. – 15.4.3. The state of implementation of anti-corruption strategy. – 15.4.4. The National Institute for insurance against Accident at Work. – 15.5. Empirical evidence of the case study. – 15.5.1. "ARCO processes" e "ARCO risks"– 15.5.2. "ARCO compliance" – 15.5.3. "ARCO operational audit". – 15.5.4. "ARCO transparency". – 15.6. "ARCO Data Analysis". – 15.6.1. Predictive analytics. – 15.7. Conclusion. – References.

15.1. Introduction

The present chapter addresses the topic concerning corruption prevention from an organisational point of view. More specifically, it investigates if and how Information Technologies (IT) investments can lead organizations to generate a value added and meet institutional goals concerning anticorruption.

The chapter analyzes the risk management system (RM) and IT tools as an integral part of the management operating systems in support of decision-making regarding choices for the prevention of corruptive behaviors, whether they are individual or collective. Decisions that are increasingly frequent and relevant in the organisation and management of public and private companies (Auriol, 2006; Auriol and Blanc, 2009; Argandoña, 2003; Lange, 2008). Specifically, the need for greater protection against the risks and the ability to mitigate them has meant that the role of the RM, in recent decades, has become central even in public administrations (McGoun, 1995; Hood et al., 2004; Miller et al., 2008; Bhimani, 2009; Boden et al., 2009). RM systems are seen as the solution suited for managing the complexity and specific needs of public administrations, but their mere introduction is not an exhaustive condition to ensure their real effectiveness. In fact, if not duly managed, RM systems can remain formal tools that help maintain current situations or even favor opportunistic behaviors (Arena et al., 2010; Power, 2007; 2009).

In this framework, the chapter analyzes and describes the complexity of the concrete adoption of a RM system through the INAIL case study below. As mentioned, although RM systems are part of the more general public and private management systems, their application has shown several difficulties in bureaucratic organisational structures (Weber, 1922), certainly not meant to dialogue with dimensions of "uncertainty" typical of the philosophy of RM (Power, 2007). Many of the recent Public Administration Reforms at international level have been characterized by an attempt to increase productivity and improve the quality of services, even in the presence of budget cuts, which have evidently affected the financial and instrumental resources available (Calogero, 2010; Holzer & Callahan, 1998; Islam, 2015). In this context, while many Governments have defined a regulatory framework for the development of internal control systems in public sector organisations, various and relevant institutions – including INAIL – have promoted the adoption of RM systems (methodologies and specific tools to support) that have complemented the "typical" internal control systems (Kolisovas & Škarnulis, 2011).

This chapter aims to help to fill this gap by exploring the implementation of the RM system and IT tools in INAIL, looking at the organisational practices and capabilities adopted to meet anticorruption goals set by the Institute.

In this regard, it has been chosen to go beyond a simple analysis that considers RM systems as merely "formal" processes, investigating the modalities used in the implementation process and its impact on the organisational life of the Institute. By leveraging the provisions of the so-called Anti-Corruption Act (Law 190/2012) and of the so-called Decree on Administrative Transparency (Legislative Decree 33/2013), INAIL not only has built a set of corruption prevention measures to enforce regulatory guidelines, but has considered it essential to define a new global approach to the broad concept of "security" of operating systems.

15.2. Theoretical background

The information system (IS) literature for the last decade has been investigating whether Information Technologies (IT) investments can lead organizations to generate a value added and meet achieve competitive and sustainable goals (Brynjolfsson, 1993, Melville et al., 2004, Kohli & Grover, 2008). Several academic researches confirm a positive correlation between

IT investments e firm performance in term of productivity, profitability and market value (Brynjolfsson and Hitt, 1996, Bharadwaj et al., 1999, Anderson et al., 2006). These results are not applicable to the public sector due to its specific characteristics, such as the absence of profit-seeking motive and competitive environment, plurality and trade-off in value (Molina and Spicer, 2004, Cordella & Bonina, 2012), political or bureaucratic nature of public organizations (Cordella, 2007, Yildiz, 2007). As such, academic literature has not adequately addressed the contribution of IT resources to the creation of public value.

In addition to this research question focusing on the direct implication of IT on firm performance, a second one should be investigated regarding "how" investments in IT contribute to organizational performance (Piccoli & Ives, 2005). Combining the IS and the public administration literature, and according to Pang et al. (2014), we suggest that the relationship between IT resources and organizational performance in the public sector is mediated by organizational capabilities. More specifically, by using a process view approach as theoretical model for our case study, we go beyond a mere relationship input-output to assess how IT resources (input) affect public value (output) through certain organizational capabilities (process).

According to Davis and West (2009), there are two major research streams in the public-value management literature. The first one, the "institutional perspective", aim is to understand what public value is, how it is defined and what it entails. Public value is defined as the value created by government through services, laws, regulation, and other actions (Kelly et al., 2002). However, it is noteworthy to mention that there is no universal definition of public value (Alford and Hughes, 2008, Alford and O'Flynn, 2009) as the needs and desires of the public as well as social and environmental circumstances define what is publicly valued. For Stoker (2006), for instance, public value is more than a total sum of the individual preferences of the users or producers of public services. In the second stream of research, the "generative perspective", researchers suggest normative frameworks for appropriate behaviours of public managers willing to achieve greater public value. In particular, the generative perspective emphasizes how public managers, in an unstable and uncertain environment, play a key role in clarifying value added in the public sector and defining modalities to achieve it.

In line with the objective of our research and in light of the generative perspective, we adopted a public-value management theory as theoretical basis for our study, according to which public officials strive to maximize public value, similarly to business managers who maximize private business value (Moore, 1995). Adopting from the approach of Pang et al. (2014), we selected four key organizational capabilities moderating the relationship between IT resources and public value. With regard to the first key organizational capability, namely (1) public service delivery capability, we refer to the capacity of the public sector to develop its public service delivery capability by improving the quality or increasing the quantity of public services. The public-value management (2) argues that the engagement of a large number of citizens and stakeholders in policy decision and service delivery is crucial as well as (3) the ability to collect resources. Finally, (4) the public-value research underlines the importance of innovation in public management and argues that public managers with deep knowledge and expertise in administration can play a pivotal role in initiating and leading innovation (Borins, 2002).

To complete our theoretical model, we also selected three key IT resources that we define, following Wade and Hulland (2004), as both IT assets (hardware, software, network infrastructure, etc.) and IT capabilities (a firm's ability to mobilize and deploy IT based resources in combination with other resources and capabilities' (Bharadwaj, 2000:171)). In particular, we chose: (a) digitized administrative process; (b) public intelligence analytics and (c) public information dissemination. The first key resource, (a) refers to a set of IS and infrastructures which enable the digitization of administrative tasks and transactional processing (assets) as well as to the ability to develop and implement such systems (capabilities). The second key resource (b) refers to both technological tools (assets) to collect information from the public and the environment and to the ability to analyse and gain knowledge and insights from the information (capabilities). Finally, public information dissemination (c) refers to infrastructures and channels through which the public can access government information repositories (assets) and the ability to publish government information assets in a manner that is easily accessible and comprehensible to the public (capabilities).

15.3. Research Methodology

Since only limited empirical research (Leung & Isaacs, 2008; Woods, 2009) on how public organisations deal with RM has been found, an explorative approach has been chosen. In our study, a single case is used, which is an appropriate way of establishing the field at the early stages of an emerging topic (Eisenhardt, 1989). Moreover, the single case study approach is normally preferred when an inductive approach can be adopted, using theory to explain empirical observations and also to inform refinements and extension of the theory (Berry et al., 1991; Otley & Berry, 1994; Yin, 1994).

The case study presented in this paper aims to explore and to understand the organisational approach used to implement the RM system. In particular, we investigated how the RM system is implemented within the

Italian National Institute for Insurance against Accidents at Work (INAIL) and how organizational capabilities can moderate the relationship between input, in our case IT resources, and output, namely public value obtained thorugh the adoption of an anticorruption strategy.

According to our exploratory approach, we selected INAIL as an exemplar case study (Yin, 1994), with unique circumstances. In line with a normative provision on the need to implement a RM systen, INAIL has been working not only on a narrow defition of corruption risk mitigation but has been also implementing a RM system whose objective is linked to the broader concept of operational security. On the one hand, this security is in favour of the user through the regularity and quality of services received and, on other hand, in favour of internal professionals by enabling them to work in a context of reasonable certainty.

In this framework, the RM immplementation has been supported by the development of extremely innovative IS.Furthermore, the RM process has been applied to organisational risks in order to avoid overlapping with other control systems already in use. All operational activities necessary during the pilot phase and for the final implementation of the RM system have been completed. RM process is now effective, from the analysis of the control environment, to the identification, evaluation and risks treatment.

To improve validity and reliability (Yin, 1994) of our finding and conclusions, we collected data from different sources and a triangulation was carried out between documental information and several meetings. Documents showing processes, organisational structure and RM tools were collected and analysed by the co-authors, within the confidentiality constraints required by the organisation (i.e.: methodological notes, extracts from the risks catalogue, project progress reports; summary reports on the identification and assessment of risks; reports summarising responses to risks, analysis of the types of risks observed; articles and presentations prepared by the members of the RM office).

15.4. Case study background

15.4.1. Regulatory background

The new strategy to prevent and address corruption defined in the Law 190/2012 takes into account several recommendations from international organizations, including those put forward by OECD, the United Nations Convention against Corruption dated 31 October 2013 (the so-called "Merida Convention"), the Criminal Law Convention on Corruption of the Council of Europe dated 27 January 199 (Strasbourg Convention), as well as the GRECO Report which has encouraged Member States to adopt a system of sanctions promoting efficient measures against corruption.

According to the new anticorruption system, each administration plays a critical role in developing a prevention strategy, which includes specific Triennial Plans to Prevent Corruption (TPPC), guided by the National Anti-corruption Authority (ANAC). ANAC is in charge of promoting a coherent strategy at the national level through the development of a National Anti-corruption Plan (NAP). This is a comprehensive system to prevent corruption, which is focused on the formulation and implementation of the anti-corruption strategy at two different levels: the national level (NAP) and the decentralised level (TPPC). Both levels are based on the risk management approach. In particular, article n. 1, provision n. 5 of the Law 190/2012, reads, "plans to prevent corruption shall include an evaluation of the corruption risks for all offices as well as appropriate measures to prevent them. Furthermore, the NAP assumes "the TPPC include specific risks, measures to be implemented to prevent risks, responsible parties and time frame for implementation". The application of the plans above-mentioned is a continuous process in order to ensure a coherent system at the national level and, at the same time, a certain level of autonomy at the decentralised level. National strategies have to be developed and contextualised according to the needs and feedback received from the local administrations.

It is noteworthy that all public administrations are required to appoint a risk manager who is the "Person in Charge of Corruption Prevention" (PCCP) and a risk owner, namely civil servants. While risk managers are required to coordinate the drafting process of the TPPC, to be adopted on an early basis (by 31 January), the PCCP needs to verify the implementation of the plan and suggests possible corrective measures to be taken, where needed. Civil servants, as risk owners, are required to actively participate in the risk management process, for instance through providing suggestions as to risk management measures (disciplinary measures, staff suspension and/or staff rotation) or through monitoring overall adherence to the code of ethics.

In this context, INAIL has been seeking to adapt to new policies right away, enhancing concepts such as ethics, transparency, correctness and highlighting the figure of the "good official" whose role and work within the administration are bound up to these principles. The notion of corruption considered by INAIL, according to the indications of the law, has been considered including all the situations in which the public official is found to abuse, in the exercise of the administrative activity, of the power entrusted to him/her, in order to obtain undue private benefits. Such unlawful behavior, as well as determining ethically controversial attitudes, is a cost to the community, not just direct (as in the case of illegitimate disbursements of public money), but also indirect, when it causes delays in the conclusion of administrative proceedings, in the malfunctioning of the offices and the consequent lack of confidence of citizens in public administration.

15.4.2. The National Anti-corruption Plan and the standard ISO 31000:2010

The key principles for an efficient risk management approach defined by the NAP are based on the UNI ISO 31000:2010 guidelines, which are the national adaptation (in Italian) of the international norm "ISO 31000 (November 2009)" drafted by the Technical Committee ISO/TMB "Risk Management". Furthermore, the main ISO excerpts are included in annex 6 of the NAP 2013 and confirmed in the NAP 2015, which aim to guide all organizations that indent to implement and effective and efficient risk management (Figure 1).

Figure 1. Relationships between the risk management principles, framework and process.

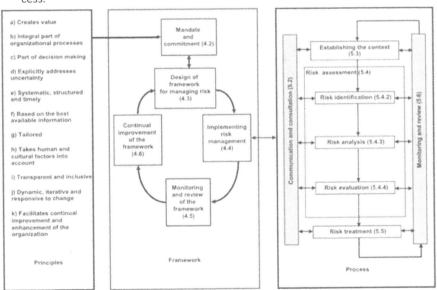

Source: ISO 31000:2009(E).

The ISO standard clearly establishes, as correctly reported by the NAP, a number of principles that need to be satisfied to make risk management effective and recommends that organizations develop, implement and continuously improve a framework whose purpose is to integrate the process for managing risk into the organization's overall governance, strategy and planning, management, reporting processes, policies, values and culture. In particular, the ISO standard underline that the success of risk management will depend on the effectiveness of the management framework providing the foundations and arrangements that will embed it throughout the organization at all levels. In fact, the framework assists in managing risks effectively through the application of the risk management process at varying levels and within specific contexts of the organization. Moreover, the framework ensures that information about risk derived from the risk management process is adequately reported and used as a basis for decision making and accountability at all relevant organizational levels.

In general terms, the framework suggests: a) the internal environment creates a risk culture in the organisation by calling upon the risk awareness of employees b) risk attitudes are aligned with strategies and objectives c) hazards and opportunities are identified in relation to the organisation's objectives d) risks are assessed by the potential likelihood and impact of their harm. Additional management components include: control activities, information and communication and monitoring of risk management processes. The ISO standard is diffusely considered one of the most comprehensive standard in that it offers a systematic, proactive and integrative approach that can be applied in a wide range of organisational contexts. Management of risks is seen as an integral part of good governance. It is an iterative process of continuous improvement that is best embedded into existing practices or business processes (Figure 2)

Figure 2. Risk Management Process.

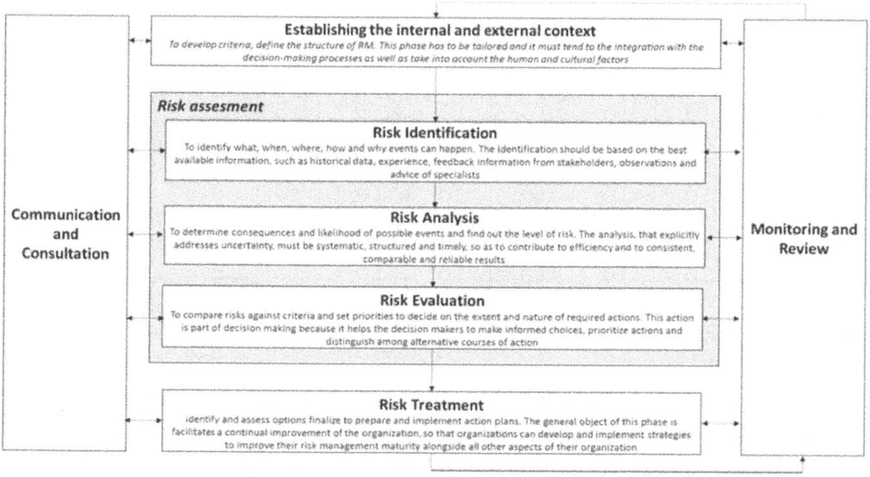

Source: adapted from ISO 31000:2009(E).

The five phases showed in the figure form an iterative process of continuous improvement that is linked by f) communication and consultation, and that is documented as well as integrated in the g) risk monitoring process.

15.4.3. The state of implementation of anti-corruption strategy

Consistent with the ratio of the rule, ANAC has considered a priority examining the quality of the TPPC adopted by public administrations. This strategic choice derives from the need to precede the upgrading of the NAP update (first published in 2013, followed by the 2015 update and the new NAP 2016) and the identification of key guidelines for future supervisory activities, through a rigorous review of the state of implementation of anti-corruption strategy at national level over the three-year period 2015-2017 and the three-year period 2016-2018.

To some extent, both evaluation documents show, on the one hand, a very high TPPC adoption rate (with 96% in the first three years), on the other hand, a general inadequacy (from the qualitative point of view) of the process of risk management implemented by administrations, mainly due to a general non-governmental administration due to the substantial novelty and complexity of the legislation. In particular, it is emphasized that the most critical phase is the analysis of the external environment, insufficient or inadequate in 96.52% of the plans analyzed (even absent in 84.46% of cases) in 2015. In the assessment conducted in 2016, the percentage of administrations carrying out the external context analysis has increased significantly (up to 24%), improving the quality levels of this analysis (19.9% of cases).

Even the adequacy of the macro phase of risk assessment is unsatisfactory in most of the plans analyzed in 2015 (specifically identifying and analyzing risks in 67.07% of cases and risk assessment and risk weighting in 62.39% of cases), demonstrating the concrete difficulty of administrations to identify properly the risks of corruption, to link them adequately to organisational processes and to use an appropriate risk assessment methodology. Consistent with the trend described above, the monitoring performed in 2016 shows significant improvement, with about 50% of the sample identifying the risky events for each process, of which 12% also carried out a timely risk analysis through the identification of their causes, which has never happened before. Also with regard to risk assessment and weighting, it is evident a slight improvement.

Confirming the general level of inadequacy of the risk management process, the monitoring system has also been insufficient in 75.22% of the plans analyzed in 2015. These data have been substantially confirmed in 2016, where the TPPC's implementation monitoring system continues to be a particularly critical variable and an improvement in this aspect is necessary to ensure the effectiveness of the system of prevention of corruption in single administrations. Almost half of the administrations examined do not refer to it (45.2%) and much of the remaining administrations express it, but in general terms. To conclude, both ANAC's evaluations point out that the poor quality of TPPCs seems to be closely related to the governance issues of the corruption prevention system within individual administrations.

15.4.4. The National Institute for insurance against Accident at Work

The *Istituto Nazionale Assicurazione contro gli Infortuni sul Lavoro* – INAIL (National Institute for Insurance against Accidents at Work) is a non-economic public body that manages compulsory insurance against accidents at work and occupational diseases. INAIL's institutional objectives are the following: to reduce the incident phenomenon; to ensure workers who carry out activities at risk; to ensure the reintegration into the work life of the injured at work; to carry out research activities and develop control and verification methodologies in the field of prevention and security.

Recent legislation has expanded INAIL's scope of work, so as to enable the Institute to become an entity capable of providing protection against occupational accidents and global and integrated occupational diseases, including research, preventive, curative interventions, indemnities, rehabilitation and reintegration, in a logic of close integration and collaboration with other entities working in the welfare system. In view of the extension of its institutional mandate, INAIL is therefore reviewing its mission in accordance with the following guidelines:

> – from social unique insurance agency to promoter of a network system managing health and safety issues;
> – from entity provider of economic benefits to guarantor of the integrated protection;
> – from rehabilitation as an "additional burden", to rehabilitation as a strategic asset to activate the virtuous circle of the reintegration of the technopathic or injured worker in the labour market;
> – virtualization of multichannel activity as a boost for the reorganisation of processes and structure.

The integrated and global tutelage is intended to trigger new virtuous sequences that involve lower labour costs and lower social costs. In addition, the Institute, having a wealth of information on accidents and occupational diseases, has in fact assumed a role as an "Authority for Occupational Safety and Health Knowledge" by making public (i.e. open source) this information asset to be used for programming, among others, prevention policies and to target supervisory activities.

15.5. Empirical evidence of the case study

In recent years, INAIL has developed a project aimed at identifying corruption and organisational situations inside an organisation that, in the medium and long term, could lead to mismanagement of the main business activities performed by the Institute. In this framework, the overall strategy of the Institute has focused not only on building a set of specific measures to enforce law requirements, but has considered it essential to define a general "security" framework as a general prevention strategy within which to include, on the one hand, the activities already underway (organisational review, controls and transparency), on the other hand, the implementation of the RM system. The synthesis of this approach is the ARCO Project (Application Risk and Organisational Compliance), developed precisely from the provisions of the so-called Anti-Corruption law and the Decree on Administrative Transparency.

In summary, INAIL has initiated a process aimed at updating its "internal security system", both on the computer side and on controls at the various levels, through the involvement of all Central Departments and Liaison Officers, from senior executives, to individual executives and heads of production. The ARCO Project is articulated in several operational areas closely related to each other (Figure 3).

Below is a description of the different operating areas of the ARCO system.

Figure 3. ARCO System.

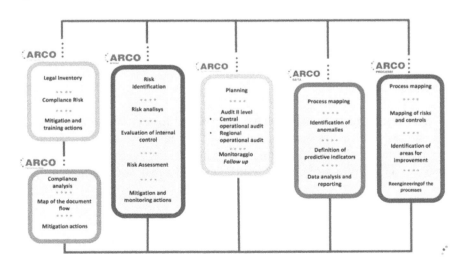

Source: our elaboration.

15.5.1. "ARCO processes" e "ARCO risks"

Consistently with the phases of the risk management process borrowed from the ISO standard described above, ARCO Project's starting point was the areas called "ARCO Processes" and "ARCO Risks" whose scope is represented by mapping of processes and from the management of corruption and operational risks. More particularly:

> the methodology for identifying and assessing the risks of corruption and operation (criteria for assessing the Gross Risk, Effectiveness of Controls and Residual Risk) has been defined and validated) (Figure 4);
>
> the Process Catalog and the Risk Catalog have been developed to identify the risk areas to be assessed together with the relevant departments;
>
> the identification and analysis of the risks that can be detected inside the Institute's processes have been conducted;
>
> the risks related to the prevention of corruption are regularly monitored and updated by the Anti-corruption's Risk owners.

Figure 4. ARCO risks – methodology for the identification and analysis of risks.

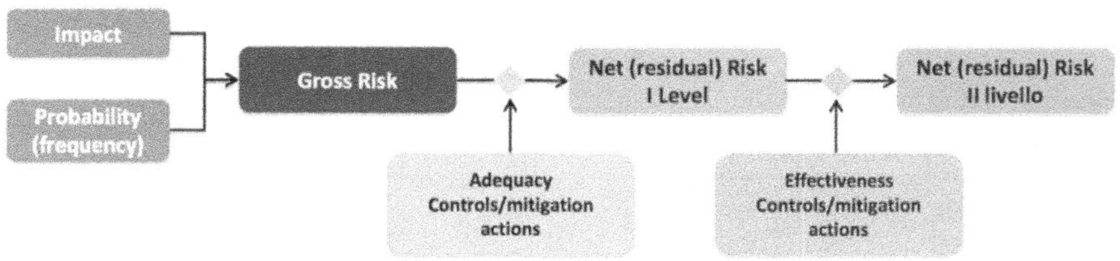

Source: our elaboration.

The results of the analysis have been saved in a database dedicated to the survey and analysis of the processes. In response to the criticalities emerged during the risk mapping, a response strategy was developed which provides a multiplicity of control levels based on a matrix scheme (Figure 5).

Figure 5. ARCO risks – strategy for risks mitigation.

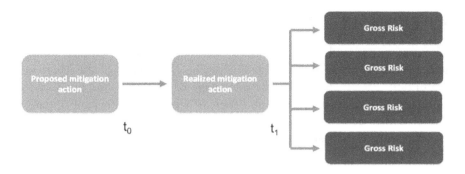

Source: our elaboration.

15.5.2. "ARCO compliance"

Thanks to appropriate audit sessions, the state of efficiency of the control system and the state of implementation of the planned mitigation actions have been verified. In general, the audit examines and documents the effectiveness of the identified risk treatment measures, as well as the compliance with the guidelines set out in the Risk Management Plan. The activities of monitoring and control activities carried out by INAIL are divided into the following areas:

"directional" administrative-accounting audits, also provided by Legislative Decree no. 286/1999 (top-level or line-by-line), which involve, annually, all executives and / or officials responsible for site management or process;
"operational" audits (second level) that are carried out with separate action plans:
in top-down mode by the Inspectorate and Security Service
in bottom-up mode by regional auditors (based on checklists defined at central level);
"professional" audits involving the various business areas of the Institute, using audit's peculiar methods to perform verifications that are able to take into account the specificities of the assigned tasks.

For the management and formalization of audit activities, the "ARCO operational audit" platform has been adopted, which facilitates the operator with specific thematic checklists in carrying out control activities, data collection, reporting and subsequent analysis and tracking of the results. This application has been designed and implemented with Microsoft technology. The system has been implemented by leveraging the potential provided by the Framework 4.5. The back end system has its own relational database created with Microsoft SQL Server 2012. The front-end component has been implemented by leveraging the capabilities of the Microsoft SharePoint 2013 platform to take advantage of the latest functionality for usability and immediacy for the end user. In view of the constant updating of the model, new features are currently being tested for a more precise identification of the perimeters of analysis, data collection and operational planning.

In particular, the application provides for distinct modules (central operational audits, regional operational audits, executive audits) that are continuously updated to simplify the operational management of the same application and, at the same time, provide information feedback for a control of management more oriented towards the objectives of empowerment and self-monitoring of all the operators, from line managers to general level managers, according to uniform detection criteria across the national territory.

15.5.3. "ARCO operational audit"

The operational area called "ARCO Operational Audit" is intended to provide operators with information useful for the proper performance of their assigned tasks, while improving competencies, by making available:

> manuals for operational process controls;
> list of control grids that will be used during the verification;
> practical training paths on operational procedures developed by the Inspectorate and Security Service in collaboration with the Human Resources Management Training Office, the Central Departments and other entities competent in this matter.

In addition, the general planning includes the introduction into the ARCO portal of training material made available by the training bureau, and aimed at enhancing the professional and organisational skills of all employees, both central and regional.

15.5.4. "ARCO transparency"

In this business area, the operations related to transparency have been analyzed and distinguished between general (from the reference standard) and specific (derived from specific measures taken by INAIL). For the first ones, an information system has been developed that automatically finds relevant data within the procedures for their direct publication on the Transparency Portal of the Institute (CAT project). The technical publishing component is assisted by a "legal inventory" function developed in accordance with ongoing regulatory developments that could give rise to objective risks of non-compliance with the procedures in use. The project envisages that the "legal inventory" system communicates to the Institutions' Directions and the IT Department any legislation "change" with a view to managing the necessary adjustments.

In order to make the discipline of transparency organisationally and operationally viable, INAIL has decided to "start" from the de-materialisation of input documents. Thanks to this true "revolution", the Institute can simultaneously handle its proceedings in a totally de-materialised manner and produce exclusively electronic measures. In this sense, the INAIL digitalisation strategy has synergistically addressed the organisational and process aspects as well as aspects related to IT, with the aim of maximizing user support services and the compliance with regulatory requirements, including the regulations in the field of Anti-corruption, Transparency and Privacy.

15.6. "ARCO Data Analysis"

The relevant innovation of the ARCA Project and its utility with regard to the prevention of corruption risks should be viewed within the development of the specific module named "ARCO Data Analysis". Through the use of extremely innovative software for the management of big data, this system allows for both periodical and on-demand analysis of data coming from operational procedures and control systems, as well as their analysis with the aim of predicting possible deviations from the standards of production. The goal is to reduce operational errors and selectively identify possible critical events linked to the operator's illicit conduct to be able to intervene in a "surgical manner" before the damage becomes significant (Figure 6).

Figure 6. ARCO System – analysis and management of data.

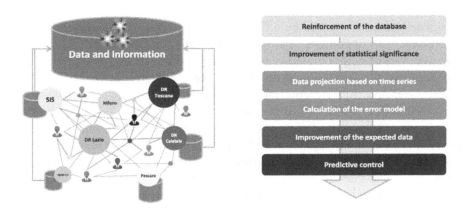

Source: our elaboration.

Concretely, a specific Data analysis function within the inspectorate and security Service develops all the actions needed for the carrying out of the data analysis activity, starting from the identification of objects of control, progressing to the definition of risk indicators, up until finally arriving to the definition of the manner of information diffusion to the various levels of the Institute. The aim of the Data analysis function is to identify three operative areas oriented towards: (1) defining a correct data strategy, (2) creating informative panels; (3) certifying and validating the data used.

Specifically, (1) the single sub-processes that make up the macro-process of "strategy of data" are conceived in a way that allows for a correct and conscious management of information starting from the initial phases of identification of the control objects and their main characteristics. With reference to every risk area, it is then foreseen to: identify the data that is the object of the study during the Data Quality; define the main risk indicators and; define the sentry events for the modelling of a reference data set upon which to base the controls.

The "creation of an informative panel" phase (2) extracts the data set using appropriate criteria from INAIL archives. Within the activities that are taken into account, one that is reconsidered is the one that traces back the phenomena and anomalies observed in the general risk taxonomy and the evaluations of expositions done, with the aim of correcting them. The interaction with the final application users (Directionate-generals and regional directionates) orients the report definition through feedback that then reaches the Operative Committee. The primary reporting flow is destined to foment information – characterized by extreme synthesis or "high specificity" – relative to the different functions of the Institute, whether they are of general governance or of coordination and operational management, allowing for the creation of predefined and ad hoc reports with specific pre-set filters. In any case, it is possible to produce on-demand reports that respond to the requests of unexpected analyses that focus on specific non-recurring phenomena. Within the flow of standard reporting, there is also the design and management of the so called "periodic incident reporting" that is responsible for illustrating, both in the form of stock data as well as periodic trends, the trend of incidents (risk materialization), relative to the main and more sensitive risk cases found and evaluated.

The flow of the data treated, which nurtures the application and successive reporting, is elaborated in function of an appropriate phase (3) of "data certification and validation" through the creation of summary tables that report the main data defined for every activity analysed and that allow for the monitoring of data set variations with each update of the application. The findings of the accesses are summarized in a "finding sheet" which is in turn separated into a section on detection of the "non conformities" found in regard to the Institute's prescriptions for the single subject and into a section of initiatives for continuous improvement of the audited process.

The "non conformities" give rise to both corrective plans of action that, in pre-established time scales, have to be realized by the headquarters) to correct the relevant errors, and to an automatized summary evaluation on the abilities of the headquarters to recover from the crucial issues found. Then, a monitoring of the implementation of the latter follows before a final "follow-up" check. The results of the audit activities generate input for the Institute's central leadership that, according to the respective competences, could evaluate the outcomes also in terms of possible regulation and organization evolutions.

15.6.1. Predictive analytics

The last frontier in the subject of audit activity, still under construction (envisaged for 2018), is formed by the creation of an evolved system which allows for an integrated vision of informations that reside in the different data banks of the Institute through the realization of a single consultation portal that, in the face of the parameters defined by the client and in line with his or her authorization profile, carries out, in parallel, researches on the data banks.

The technology on which the solution is based allows for the identification of corrections through Machine Learning techniques unknown a priori and behavioral profiles able to accelerate the analysis process and explore new hypotheses of audit activity procedures.

The solution consists of technological components able to integrate and mask the access to data banks- implemented with different technologies- both through interface with available native consulting modalities and with a direct modality if the data banks don't foresee an application interview according to the following scheme:

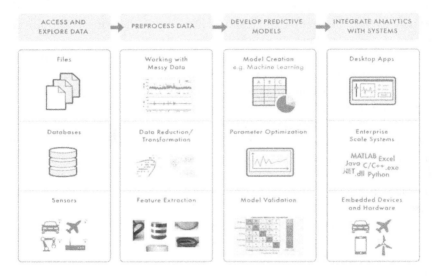

The approach that is being handled will allow for continuous monitoring of the productive flows with alerts generated by activities that differ from ordinary standards and the foreseen logical sequences of the processes that as a whole, can be defined as "process anomalies". The alerts will be communicated to both the operators and the subjects with the responsibility of line control, with the aim of verifying validity. The alert will be annulled by the operator who corrects the anomalies or the superior who validates, with appropriate justification, the deviation from ordinary standards.

As such, this methodology will concretely weld the activity system with the collaborative line controls, becoming a factor of operative standardization on all productive processes of the Institute (Figure 7).

Figure 7. ARCO System – development of predictive approach.

Source: our elaboration

From this approach derives a re-modulation of organizational cyclicality that, starting from context analysis, determines strategic objectives while taking into account the resources and the available times in light of the average cultural data of the operators and the sharing of values. Starting from correct management of control systems derived from construction of the RM system, it's possible to build a system of data analysis that is able to have a function of support for decisional centers, with the aim of elaborating strategies founded on an accurate knowledge of both the internal and external context factors of the organization.

15.7. Conclusion

Public administrations, compared to the private sector, are often accused of using IT potentialities with great delay. Despite a large amount of academic literature and business case studies about the use of IT as a broader topic, the IT value and how it should be implemented in the organizational practices have been hardly investigated. The case study described in this chapter shows how INAIL has defined IT value and, more specifically, the public value and the modalities through which it is developed.

Before defining the characteristics of public value, the case study has highlighted some challenges that the public administrations had to face. The first challenge identified by our methodological framework is about the lack of capacity to manage information, especially as to using a wealth of information to support strategic decision-making. The second challenge is related to the ineffective governance and control on administrative processes and, in particular, on inappropriate employees' behaviours.

In particular, preventing and treating a risk like corruption means, for an organisation, facing an extremely complex issue, since it implies deciding and planning organisational actions that are not guaranteed to be efficient, effective, or even necessary. In other words, seeking to develop a risk prevention strategy, one individual organisation is asked to make rational organisational choices, even though it is aware that this "rationality" is "limited" (Simon, 1947) by the lack of complete information. In fact, in risk management, there is an inherent difference between available and needed information to make the best choice (Thompson, 1967). This evidently undermines some of the basic premises of the bureaucratic organisation of work which, on the other hand, is precisely on the "certainty" and "perfect knowledge" of what must be based on its strength and hypothetical efficiency. What has just been said can not be farther from the philosophy of risk, which instead forces the organisation and its actors to engage in a decision-making process that can not be exhausted by a mating problem between the situation to be faced and the rule to be applied, as the most classic administrative behavior would entail, but which, on the contrary, has the need to decide on the basis of the knowledge gained when analyzing the problem (Perrow, 1967). This is a not trivial passage, and in fact it calls for the support of a "widespread intelligence" organisation (Decastri, 2005), equipped with tools to increase the ability to collect and process information, much closer to a "professional", and no longer "mechanical" bureaucratic configuration (Mintzberg, 1979).

Consistently, the Institute promoted a new strategy based on the principles of the RM that has led to the development of the ARCO System (Application Risk and Organisational Compliance) a project of technological innovation based on the innovative use of information systems which, on the one hand, has led to identification within the organisation of situations exposed to possible risk factors and at the same time sustaining the decision-making process on a continuous basis by collecting and processing the information found throughout the organisational territory.

Identifying a case study about IT investments, even in the private sector, is a challenging task as it is difficult to justify and quantify the return on investments, defined as value added. This assumption is indeed true if we consider that beneficiaries of these investments in the public sector are the citizens whereas the management within public organizations is responsible for the investments.

The work has tried to define the public value in terms of accuracy, transparency, controllability, standardization, compliance, and responsiveness of the public action. It is noteworthy to mention that the majority of these values are intangible as the IT influence on the functioning of the Institute may not be directly reflected on the traditional measures of performance. Decision makers that do not know these potential values may make decisions which are not optimal in terms of IT investments.

The case study has also highlighted the importance of IT-enabled data and process integration as the mechanisms underlying IT value creation. Positive returns are not guaranteed by IT investments. In value creation, the architecture of the overall IT system landscape is the key factor. Our analysis of the development of the ARCO System is not limited to the module called "ARCO Data Analysis" and its developments in terms of predictive analysis. The work shows that an integrated IT architecture is key for IT value creation. While private sector organizations have long noticed the importance of enterprise architecture (Ross, 2003), our case study is among the first to investigate the importance of proper IT architecture in public organizations featured by bureaucracy and rigidity.

References

Alford, J. and Hughes, O. (2008). Public Value Pragmatism as the Next Phase of Public Management, *American Review of Public Management* 38(2): 130–148.

Alford, J. and O'Flynn, J. (2009). Making Sense of Public Value: Concepts, critiques and emergent meanings, *International Journal of Public Administration* 32(3): 171-191.

Anderson, M.C., Banker, R.D. and Ravindran, S. (2006). Value Implications of Investments in Information Technology, *Management Science* 52(9): 1359-1376.

Arena, M., Arnaboldi, M., & Azzone, G. (2010). The organizational dynamics of Enterprise Risk Management. *Accounting, Organizations and Society*, 35(7), 659-675.

Argandoña, A. (2003). Private-to-Private Corruption, *Journal of Business Ethics*. 47, 253-267.

Auriol, E. (2006). Corruption in procurement and public purchase. *International Journal of Industrial Organization*, 24(5), 867-885.

Auriol, E., & Blanc, A. (2009). Capture and corruption in public utilities: The cases of water and electricity in Sub-Saharan Africa. *Utilities Policy*, 17(2), 203-216.

Berry, A., Loughton, E. & Otley, D. (1991). Control in a financial services company (RIF): a case study. *Management Accounting Research*, 2, 109-139.

Bharadwaj, A.S. (2000). A Resource-Based Perspective on Information Technology Capability and Firm Performance: An empirical investigation, *MIS Quarterly* 24(1): 169-196.

Bharadwaj, A.S., Bharadwaj, S.G. and Konsynski, B.R. (1999). Information Technology Effects on Firm Performance as Measured by Tobin's q, *Management Science* 45(7): 1008-1024.

Bhimani A. (2009): Risk management, corporate governance and management accounting: Emerging interdependencies. *Management Accounting Research*, 20,

2-5.

Boden, R., Epstein D., & Latimer J. (2009). Accounting for ethos or programmes for conduct? The brave new world of research ethics committees. *The Sociological Review*, 57, 727-749.

Borins, S. (2002). Leadership and Innovation in the Public Sector, *Leadership & Organization Development Journal* 28(8): 467-476.

Brynjolfsson, E. (1993). The Productivity Paradox of Information Technology, *Communication of the ACM* 36(12): 67-77.

Brynjolfsson, E. and Hitt, L. (1996). Paradox Lost? Firm-level evidence on the returns to information systems spending, *Management Science* 42(4): 541-558.

Calogero M. (2010). The introduction of New Public Management principles in the Italian public sector. *Transylvanian Review of Administrative Sciences*, 30, 30-54

Cordella, A. (2007). E-Government: Towards the e-bureaucratic form? *Journal of Information Technology* 22(3): 265-274.

Cordella, A. and Bonina, C.M. (2012). A Public Value Perspective for ICT Enabled Public Sector Reforms: A theoretical reflection, *Government Information Quarterly* 29(4): 512-520.

Davis, P. and West, K. (2009). What Do Public Values Mean for Public Action? Putting public values in their plural place, *American Review of Public Management* 39(6): 602-618.

Decastri, M. (2005). Amministrazione pubblica e stereotipi. Alla ricerca della burocrazia perduta. In M. Decastri, L. Hinna, M. Meneguzzo, & R. Mussari, (Eds) *Economia delle aziende pubbliche* (pp. 331-380). Milano: McGraw-Hill,

Eisenhardt, K.M. (1989). Building theories from case study research. *Academy of Management Review*, 14, 532-50.

Holzer, M. & Callahan K., (1998). Government at Work: Best Practices and Model Programs. Thousand Oaks, CA: *Sage Publications*.

Hood C., James O., Peters B.G. & Scott C. (2004). Controlling Modern Government. *Edward Elgar*, Cheltenham.

Islam, F. (2015). New Public Management (NPM): A dominating paradigm in public sectors. *African Journal of Political Science and International Relations*, 9, 141-15.

Kelly, G., Mulgan, G. and Muers, S. (2002). Creating Public Value: An Analytic Framework for Public Service Reform, Strategy Unit, UK Cabinet Office, http://webarchive.nationalarchives.gov.uk/20100416132449/http://www.cabinetoffice.gov.uk/strategy/seminars/public_value.aspx.

Kohli, R. and Grover, V. (2008). Business Value of IT: An essay on expanding research directions to keep up with the times, *Journal of the Association for Information Systems* 9(2): 23–39.

Kolisovas, D. & Škarnulis, A. (2011). Risk management in Lithuania's public sector: starting point, current situation and future perspectives. *Intellectual Economics*, 5, 547-559.

Lange, D. (2008). A multidimensional conceptualization of organizational corruption control. *Academy of Management Review*, 33(3), 710-729.

Leung, F. & Isaacs, F. (2008). Risk management in public sector research: approach and lessons learned at a national research organization. *R&D Management*, 38, 510-519.

McGoun, E. G. (1995). The History of Risk "Measurement." *Critical Perspectives on Accounting*, 6(6), 511-532.

Melville, N., Kraemer, K.L. and Gurbaxani, V. (2004). Review: Information Technology and Organizational Performance: An integrative model of it business value, *MIS Quarterly* 28(2): 283-322.

Miller, P., Kurunmaki, L. & O'Leary, T. (2008). Accounting, hybrids and the management of risk. *Accounting. Organizations and Society*, 33, 942-967.

Molina, A.D. and Spicer, M.W. (2004). Aristotelian Rhetoric, Pluralism, and Public Administration, *Administration & Society* 36(3): 282-305.

Moore, M.H. (1995). Creating Public Value: Strategic Management in Government, Cambridge, MA: *Harvard University Press*.

Otley, D. T. & Berry, A.J. (1994). Case Study Research in Management Accounting and Control. *Management Accounting Research*, 5, 45-65.

Pang, M.S., Lee, G., & Delone, W.H. (2014). In public sector organisations: A public-value management perspective. *Journal of Information Technology*, 29(3), 187-205.

Piccoli, G. and Ives, B. (2005). Review: IT-dependent strategic initiatives and sustained competitive advantage: A review and synthesis of the literature, *MIS Quarterly* 29(4): 747-776.

Power, M. (2009). The risk management of nothing. *Accounting. Organizations and Society*, 34(6-7), 849-855.

Power, M. (2007). Organized Uncertainty: Designing a World of Risk Management. *Oxford University Press*, Oxford.

Ross, J. (2003). Creating a strategic IT architecture competency: Learning in stage. *MIS Quarterly Executive*, 2, 31-43.

Simon, H. A. (1947). Administrative behavior: A Study of Decision-making Processes. *Administrative Organization*, 1st ed., New York: The Macmillan Company.

Stoker, G. (2006). Public Value Management: A new narrative for networked governance? *American Review of Public Administration* 36(1): 47-51.

Wade, M. and Hulland, J. (2004). Review: The resource-based view and information systems research: Review, extension, and suggests for future research, *MIS Quarterly* 28(1): 107-142.

Weber, M. (1922/1968b). Economy and society: An outline of interpretive sociology (G. Roth & C. Wittich, Eds.) (E. Fischoff, Trans.) New York: Bedminster Press.

Woods, M. (2009). A contingency theory perspective on the risk management control system within Birmingham City Council. *Management Accounting Research*, 20, 69-81.

Yildiz, M. (2007). E-Government Research: Reviewing the literature, limitations, and ways forward, *Government Information Quarterly* 24(3): 646-665.

Yin, R.K. (1994). Case Study Research–Design and Methods. Thousand Oaks: *Sage*

AUTHORS

Roberto Albano, Ph.D. in Sociology from Università Statale di Milano, is Associate Professor at the Department of Cultures, Politics and Society of the Università degli Studi di Torino, where he teaches Sociology and Methodology of Social Research. His recent research interests include: cultural change in European countries, with a special focus on work values; the epistemological background of organizational analysis and research; smart working and coworking. He is member of the Scientific Committee of MU.S.I.C. – Observatory on social change and cultural innovation

Roberto Bernazzani is an almost 20 years experienced professional in the ICT research and innovation field. Since 2000 he is research coordinator at the Center for Research on the Applications of Telematics to Organizations and Society (CRATOS), Università Cattolica del Sacro Cuore, and lecturer of "Information Systems" at the Faculty of Economics and Law of the same University. He is Partner and ICT Specialist at Univillage Consulting, focusing on information systems design and development, SEO/SEM, Web Analytics, and web applications development. Since 2005 he is member of the Program Committee for several international conferences in the fields of e-learning and information systems, like IADIS Mobile Learning Conference, European Conference on Information Systems (ECIS), and Mediterranean Conference on Information Systems (MCIS).

Rita Bissola, PhD in Management Information Systems from LUISS Guido Carli, is Associate Professor of Organization Design and Organizational Behavior at the Department of Economic and Business Management Sciences, Università Cattolica del Sacro Cuore, Milan, Italy. She has published several articles and contributions on innovation in HRM and organizational creativity both in international as well as national journals and books. She is coordinator of the International HRM Master Program at the Università Cattolica.

Davide Bizjak, Ph.D. in Management at the University of Naples Federico II, Department of Economics, Management, Institutions, and Research Trainee at the University of Essex. His main research interests are in the area of Diversity Management, Organizational Identity, Arts Organization. He actively serves as reviewer for several international Journals and Conferences. He is author of several papers and book chapters published with international publishers.

Alessandro Bottazzi is Competitive Intelligence Manager at Cisco Systems. Currently leading a project on Artificial Intelligence for Natural Language Process Engines applied to Market Analytics. He is a seasoned business analyst specialized in designing, building and optimizing reporting frameworks in a fast-paced cutting edge technology environment. He got his latest Master in Business Administration in 2008, at the Università Cattolica del Sacro Cuore, Piacenza, majoring in Planning and Control: "Multinational Companies: Control Processes and Information Asymmetries", then attended a professional course at the San Diego State University, CA, USA.

Paola Briganti, Ph.D. in Economics and Business Management from University Parthenope of Naples, is associate professor of Organizational and Human resource Management at the University of Naples "Parthenope" (Italy). Research interests: communication, stress, conflict management and learning process in any organizational settings, especially among healthcare units and professionals. Visiting Researcher at Columbia University, Teachers College, New York, NY, USA (2015). Membership at ASSIOA and Counseling Community.

Diego Campagnolo, Ph.D. in in Economics and Management from University of Padova, is Associate professor of Business Organization and Strategy at the University of Padova, affiliate ICRIOS (The Invernizzi Center for Research on Innovation, Organization, Strategy and Entrepreneurship) of Bocconi University and fellow of the National Center for Middle Market at the Fisher College of Business (Ohio State University). He is the Scientific Director of the MBA for entrepreneurs of CUOA Business School. He has been adjunct professor at Bocconi University and visiting scholar at Ohio State University, Guangzhou University, and Boston University. His research interests include the study of organizational design, business model and internationalization of SMEs, organizational modularity and the study of innovation in knowledge intensive business services.

Paolo Canonico, Ph.D. in Business Administration from University of Naples Federico II, is Associate Professor of Organization Studies at University of Napoli Federico II, Italy, where he currently teaches organization and information systems topics. He holds a Master of Science in Analysis, Design and Management of Information Systems from the London School of Economics and a Doctorate from University of Naples Federico II. His research interests are broadly related to the study of knowledge and human resources in project oriented organizational forms.

Franca Cantoni, Ph.D. Associate Professor in Business Organization and HRM at the Faculty of Economics and Law at the University Cattolica "Sacro Cuore", of Piacenza. Graduated in Economics at the Università Cattolica del Sacro Cuore, she holds a Ph.D. in Information Systems at LUISS Guido Carli (Rome). The main topics of research are related to the development and consolidation of soft skills, micro and macro impacts organizational change and outsourcing. She teaches the courses of Business Organization, Human Resource Management and International Human Resource Management both at the graduate and undergraduate level.

Andrea Carugati, MSc in Engineering from Chalmers University of Technology and PhD in Manufacturing Engineering from the Technical University of Denmark is Professor of Information Systems and Innovation at Aarhus School of Business and Social Sciences (Aarhus University). His research focuses on the strategic impact of technology, on IT driven organizational change, and on the deployment of information technology in organizations. Andrea Carugati has published, among others, on Management Information Systems Quarterly, the European Journal of Information Systems, Information Systems Journal, Database for Advances in Information Systems, European Management Review, and European Management Journal.

Federico Ceschel, is Ph.D. candidate in Public Management & Governance at the University of Rome Tor Vergata. He holds a Master's Degree in Law and Economics from the International University of Social Sciences LUISS Guido Carli, Rome (Italy).
He is a lecturer at the Italian National School of Public Administration. His areas of expertise include anti-corruption strategies, risk management, public management, law and economics. As a member of several scientific committees and working groups, he has been providing advisory services and strategic analysis on anti-corruption and risk management to several national and international organizations, including the World Bank, the Organization for Security and Co-operation in Europe, the United Nations Economic Commission for Europe, as well as academic institutions.

Ylenia Curzi, Ph.D. in Management Sciences from the University of Udine, is tenure-track researcher at the Marco Biagi Department of Economics of the University of Modena and Reggio Emilia, where she teaches Business Organization and International HRM. She has been visiting scholar at Cardiff Business School (Wales, UK). Her research interests include the relationships between organizational and technological changes, work organization and wellbeing at work.

Stefano Denicolai, is Associate Professor of 'Innovation Management' at the University of Pavia (Italy), where he is also Head of the Master degree (Laurea Magistralis) in 'International Business and Entrepreneurship' (MIBE). His research interests include the strategic management of intangible assets and technology, the change management, the international entrepreneurship. He has been visiting scholar at Harvard Business School (US) and at SPRU-University of Sussex (UK). He is author of books and articles in the field, including in journals such as R&D Management, Technological Forecast and Social Change, Journal of World Business, International Business Review, and Tourism Management.

Ernesto De Nito, Ph.D. in Business Administration from University of Naples Federico II, is Associate Professor of Organization Studies at University of Catanzaro "Magna Græcia", Italy, where he currently teaches organization theory. He was visiting researcher at the Gothenburg University, Viktoria Institute. His research focuses on knowledge management and knowledge integration in organizations. He has several publications on international journals.

Francesca Di Virgilio, Ph.D. in Organization, Technology and HR Development from University of Molise where she is Associate Professor of Organization Theory and Human Resources Management in the Department of Economics, at University of Molise (Italy). She was Visiting professor at Facultade De Ciencias Sociais e da Comunicacion, University of Vigo (Spain). She was Visiting scholar at Research Center of Industrial relations & Organizational behavior (IROB), Warwick Business School, Warwick (UK). She is member of the Association of Italian Organization Studies Academics (ASSIOA). Her current research focuses on the relationship between knowledge management and social media, conflict and trust, human resources management and innovation in modern organization.

Tommaso Fabbri, Ph.D. in Management from the University of Venice, is Full Professor of Organization and Human Resource Management and Vice Director of the Doctoral School "E4E" / Industry 4.0 at the University of Modena and Reggio Emilia. He is Scientific Coordinator at Marco Biagi Foundation, where he leads Mode2, an interdisciplinary open laboratory dedicated to the digital transformation of organizations and society. He has been visiting professor at the Smeal College of Business Administration, Pennsylvania State University.

Paolino Fierro Ph.D in Management of Public companies and Administrations from University of Salerno (Italy). He is Research Fellow at University of Naples Parthenope, Italy. He graduated at Federico II University of NAPLES. His research interests are: change management in public and private sectors and learning process in any organizational settings. He also is involved in consulting activities and various professional functions related to human resource management area and technology issues.

Stefano Forte is senior project manager at Telecommunication company TIM. He works in the end-to-end management of payment technical services projects for consumer customers, in particular on requirements, support processes (privacy, security, legal, regulatory, customer care, marketing, sales) for roll outing them on different channels (shop, web, ivr, customer care, app).

Teresa Anna Rita Gentile, Ph.D. in Teoria del Diritto ed Ordine Giuridico ed Economico Europeo curriculum "Economia e Management" at University of Catanzaro "Magna Græcia", Italy. Her research interests are focused on the knowledge management and e-learning in higher education and universities. She is a member of ASSIOA, ADI and AIDP.

Cristiano Ghiringhelli, Ph.D. in Quality of life in the Information society (QUASI) from Università degli Studi di Milano Bicocca, whre he is associate professor of

Organizational Theory. He has researched mainly Change Management sub-jects related to the ICT development (with a special focus on IoT), Organizational Innovation and Human Resource Management topics. He had several conference papers in national and international venues. He has also an extensive experience in designing and carrying out Change Management projects. He's member of the Cranfield Network on International Human Resource Management (Cranet) – www.cranet.org.

Martina Gianecchini, Ph.D. in Business Management from the University of Udine, is Associate Professor at the Department of Economics and Management at the University of Padova. She is Scientific Director of the Executive Master in HRM at CUOA Business School. Her main research interests regard career management and labour market dynamics. She is member of the international research group 5C (Cross-Cultural Collaboration on Contemporary Careers) which aims at understanding meanings, determinants and outcomes of careers around the world.

Luca Giustiniano, Ph.D. in Management Information Systems from LUISS Guido Carli, is Full Professor of Organization Studies at the LUISS Guido Carli University (Rome, Italy) and Director of the Centre for Research inLeadership, Innovation, and Organisation (CLIO). During his career, he has been visiting scholar at the Viktoria Institute (Sweden, 1999), the Sauder School of Business, University of British Columbia (Canada, 2011), the Interdisciplinary Centre for Organizational Architecture (ICOA, Aarhus University, Denmark) and the Nova SBE, Lisbon (Portugal). He is a member of ASSIOA, EGOS, and AOM. His papers have appeared in the British Journal of Management, Management Learning, European Management Review, European Management Journal, Journal of Knowledge Management, Journal of Organizational Change Management.

Alessandro Hinna, Ph.D. in Public Administration from Tor Vergata University, where is Associate Professor of Organization Studies and currently teaches Organization Theory and People Management. Alessandro Hinna is Professor of Public Management at the Italian National School of Public Administration. His main teaching areas are organizational design, organizational behavior; organization and change management in public administration. He is editor of Studies in Public and Non-Profit Governance (Book Series), for Emerald Group Publishing Limited.

Aurélie Leclercq-Vandelannoitte, Ph.D. in Management Sciences from University of Paris Dauphine (France) is CNRS (Centre National de la Recherche Scientifique) Researcher at LEM UMR CNRS, Lille, France.

Barbara Imperatori, Ph.D. in Management and Business Administration from Bocconi University, is Associate Professor of Organization Design and Human Resource Management , Department of Economic and Business Management Sciences, Università Cattolica del Sacro Cuore, Milan, Italy. She received her. Her contributions on e-HRM, creativity, employee engagement and hybrid organizations have been published in international and national journals and books. She is coordinator of the International HRM Master Program and of many post-graduate and executive education initiatives, focusing on People management, Project management and HRM practices.

Alba López Bolás, Ph.D. in Citizen participation in media, television and social media from the University of Vigo, Spain. She is marketing online manager in agency of Communication Atlántica in Vigo. She has collaborated in the journalism research department at Facultad de Ciencias Sociales y de la Comunicación, University of Vigo. Her research interests and publications focus on health communication, social audience on television, inbound marketing and social networks.

Federico Moretti is a Ph.D. student in Economics and Management of Technology at the University of Pavia, and a visiting research fellow at Tufts University. He has a MS in International Business and Economics and a BS in Management from the University of Pavia. His research interests include innovation management, open innovation, strategic management and project management.

Caterina Muzzi, Ph.D. in Ph.D. on Information Systems Management from Luiss Guido Carli, is Assistant Professor of Organization and Human Resource Management at the University of Brescia, Italy, Department of Economics and Management. She is interested in organizational networks, competence management in highly complex environment and on entrepreneurial training and dynamics. She has published in R&D Management and International Journal of Entrepreneurship and Innovation. She co-authored documents included in Scopus.

Alessio Paris, Ph.D. in International Private Law from University of Perugia, is Security Manager at GE Aviation. Alongside his 14-years distinguished career in the Carabinieri corps (retired as Captain), he attended a 7-months exchange program at the Beijing University of Technology (2013) to deepen his doctoral dissertation on the relationship between privacy and social networks/web 2.0, from both sociological and legal standpoints. Becoming an MBA graduate (2016), he has started his personal and professional interest on organizational studies, with specific regards to leadership in the ever-growing digital industry.

Alessandro Pastorelli, holds a Master's Degree in Auditing and Internal Control Systems from the University of Pisa (Italy) and a University Degree in Law from the University of Siena (Italy). He is the director of the Inspection and Security Office at Inail (National Institute for Insurance against Accidents at Work) since 2001. In addition, he has been serving as the anti-corruption officer. During his tenure at INAIL, he has been working on performance evaluation systems, risk management procedures, compliance audit techniques. From 1991 to 2001, he worked as a civil servant at the Italian Ministry of Labour. His contributions have been presented in several national seminars.

Mariacristina Piva, Ph.D. in Economics, is full professor in Economic Policy at the Faculty of Economics and Law of the Università Cattolica del Sacro Cuore. In 2002 and 2003 she served as Research Economist at the International Labour Office (ILO) in Geneva. In 2008 she was Visiting Fellow at SPRU (Science and Technology Policy Research Unit), University of Sussex. Her research interests are in the fields of industrial organization, labour economics and economics of innovation. Her papers have been published in numerous refereed international journals, including *Cambridge Journal of Economics, Contemporary Economic Policy, Economics Letters, Regional Studies, Research Policy, Small Business Economics*. She serves as referee of many international journals.

Pietro Previtali is Rector's Delegate for Human Resources management and an Associate Professor of Business Organization at the Department of Economics and Management Sciences, University of Pavia. He got his PhD in Management and Business Administration at Bocconi University. He teaches and conducts research on public organization and management, and on the managerial issues surrounding compliance and the introduction of information technologies in public agencies and private companies.

Aurelio Ravarini holds a Master degree in Management Engineering from Politecnico di Milano (Italy) and a PhD at the School of Computer and Security at ECU (Australia). He is Senior Assistant Professor of Information Systems at the School of Engineering at the Università C. Cattaneo – LIUC (Italy), where he has been director for ten years of the CETIC, Research Center on Information Systems. His research expertise is in Strategic Information Systems, Knowledge Management systems, and Information Systems development, the latter of which is focused on small and medium-sized companies. He has been visiting professor in several universities in Europe and USA, and he is invited researcher at CEROS at Nanterre University, Paris. He served as Associate Editor for the EJIS for ten years and he has been in the editorial committee of several international conferences.

Anna Chiara Scapolan, Ph.D in Management from University of Venice, is Assistant Professor of Organization at the University of Modena and Reggio Emilia, where she is also Researcher at OPERA - a Research Unit specialized in the study of creative industries and innovation, and member of Mode2, an interdisciplinary open laboratory dedicated to the digital transformation. Her main research interests regard organizational solutions and human resource management for creativity and innovation.

Danila Scarozza, Ph.D. in Public Management and Governance from University of

Rome "Tor Vergata", is a Research Fellow in Organisational Studies at the University of Pavia. She teaches Business Organization both at the International Tellematic University UNINETTUNO and at University of Rome "Tor Vergata". She has published and done research activity on topics related to organization and change management in public organizations, behavioural dimensions in public governance, performance management and human resource management.

Mónica Valderrama Santomé, Ph.D in Advertising and Public Relations from the University of Vigo (Spain), is Coordinator Master of Art Direction in Advertising at the Faculty of Social Sciences and Communication and University Lecturer and Researcher. She received an BA in Comunication Sciences: Advertising and Public Relations and in Information Sciences: Journalist. University of Santiago de Compostela (Spain). Lines of research: creative trends in emerging audiovisual media, evolution of television advertising production, new audiovisual advertising formats, television identities, and new technologies applied to organizational communication.

Luisa Varriale, Ph.D in Economics and Business Management from Parthenope University (Italy), is associate professor of Organization and Human Resource Management at the University of Naples Parthenope, Italy. Her research interests range from mentoring relationships, knowledge sharing and creation, learning and e-learning process. She has been Visiting Professor at Arizona State University, W.P. Carey Business School, Tempe, AZ, USA, Columbia University, Teachers College, New York, NY, USA, Salem State University, Salem, MA, University of Porto, FEUP, Porto, Portugal. She holds the membership at ASSIOA, IAME and HMN (Humanistic Management Network). She published her research in several significant outlets.

João Vieira da Cunha, Ph.D. in Management from the Massachusetts Institute of Technolog, is Associate Professor and Head of Research at IÉSEG School of Management in France. His research looks at the impact on leadership of information and communication technologies. His work has been published in journals such as the Academy of Management Review, Information and Organizations, Human Relations, and Journal of Management Studies.

Francesco Virili, Ph.D. in Management Information Systems (MIS) from University of Siegen (Germany), is associate professor of Organization and MIS at the University of Sassari, Italy. He published in peer reviewed international journals on themes connected to the enabling effects of ICTs. He had several conference papers in national and international venues. He serves as reviewer in several journals, and he is currently serving on the editorial board of the Journal of Information Systems and e-Business Management, and in the International Journal of IT Standards and Standardization Research.

Roberta Virtuani, Ph.D. in Management and Business Administration from Bocconi University, is lecturer and senior research fellow of the Department of Economics and Social Sciences at the Faculty of Economics and Law at the Università Cattolica del Sacro Cuore in Piacenza where she teaches the "Communication Skills" courses. Her main interest areas are Organization Theory and Human Resources Management with a special focus on talent development regarding soft and digital skills. She has been a visiting scholar at the University of Amsterdam. She published on the topic of Outsourcing of Information Systems and on Individual Creativity Management to foster innovation.